The Soul Grows in Darkness

The Soul Grows in Darkness

Loren E. Pedersen

The Soul Grows in Darkness

Copyright © 2005 by Loren E. Pedersen

All rights reserved. No part of this book may be used or reproduced by any means, graphic, electronic, or mechanical, including photocopying, recording, taping or by any information storage retrieval system without the written permission of the publisher except in the case of brief quotations embodied in critical articles and reviews.

For my daughters, Sheryl, Stephanie, and Laura

The Sea of Faith
Was once, too, at the full, and round earth's shore
Lay like the folds of a bright girdle furl'd.
But now I only hear
Its melancholy, long, withdrawing roar,
Retreating, to the breath
Of the night-wind, down the vast edges drear
And naked shingles of the world.
Ah, love, let us be true
To one another! for the world, which seems
To lie before us like a land of dreams,
So various, so beautiful, so new,
Hath really neither joy, nor love, nor light,
Nor certitude, nor peace, nor help for pain,
And we are here as on a darkling plain
Swept with confused alarms of struggle and flight,
Where ignorant armies clash by night.

—Dover Beach
Matthew Arnold

Contents

Apologia xiii
Chapter 1 There Ain't No Such Address 1
Chapter 2 Casper the Ghost and Other Firsts 10
Chapter 3 My First Arrest 21
Chapter 4 The Rumble 28
Chapter 5 High School 39
Chapter 6 The Black Iris 48
Chapter 7 Johnny Mathis 58
Chapter 8 Lincoln Avenue 63
Chapter 9 Detention Camp 72
Chapter 10 The End of High School 84
Chapter 11 Starting Over 89
Chapter 12 Jean 99
Chapter 13 Leaving Chicago 109
Chapter 14 Marquette 118
Chapter 15 Back on Rush Street 125
Chapter 16 St. Joseph's Hospital 137
Chapter 17 Blood Money 145
Chapter 18 Separation 155

CHAPTER 19	Chicago, '68 166
CHAPTER 20	Pork Department 180
CHAPTER 21	El Intermedio 196
CHAPTER 22	Turning Inward 206
CHAPTER 23	Starting Psychoanalysis 220
CHAPTER 24	In the Belly of the Whale 235
CHAPTER 25	Reasons of the Heart 247
CHAPTER 26	The Truth Breeds Hatred 260
CHAPTER 27	My Truth 272

Acknowledgments

I am deeply grateful to the many friends and colleagues whose interest, effort, encouragement, and expertise helped shape this book and brought it to life. My writing mentor, Mark Spencer, a great novelist and short-story writer, was immensely helpful for more than a year and a half. Over that time, he read, edited, made suggestions, and encouraged me. His wisdom and skill have not only contributed to this book, but have taught me to be a better writer.

For their reading, help, and zeal for the budding manuscript, I owe a great debt of thanks to: Dr. Richard Carlson, Karen Diane, Dr. Lynne Ehlers, Lynn Garnica, Linda Schiller-Hanna, Tracy Johnston, Miranda Kentfield, my best friend, Robert G. Lange, Susan Miller, Dr. Alexander Nemeth, Marianne Nemeth, Ruth Pierce, Carol Jean Todd, and especially Trina Swerdlow. Trina's many and diverse talents in publishing, artwork, and marketing were an enormous benefit to me. Her optimism, commitment, enthusiasm, and energy have nurtured me throughout the writing of this book.

I would also like to thank my Publishing Assistant, Ron Amack, my editor, Mark Newton, and the other staff of iUniverse for their encouragement, editing assistance, and many insightful suggestions.

Apologia

It is fairly well-known in psychological circles that if six people witness the same automobile accident, there will be six variations on the facts of what happened. Maureen Murdock titled her delightful little book on memoirs, *Unreliable Truth*. That title was also how she described memory. As a psychoanalyst, I know just how capricious memory can sometimes be. I also had a mother who, for as long as she lived, always doubted my memories—especially if they were true. In fact, I could glean some measure of the memory's truth from the intensity of her protest. One of her effects on me was that I often came to doubt what I believed. It seems as if what is "true" is only what we believe is true—and yet, that itself may not be *The* Truth.

I say this by way of apologizing in advance for any bending of events, dates, or facts that might be found here. Nothing here is meant to befuddle, deceive, or accuse. I have changed the names of everyone but my own. Since I am writing about how I *experienced* my life, the facts are less important. Were my experience to be yours, undoubtedly you would write an entirely different book, even if the facts were the same. That's not only human nature and what makes our personal stories interesting; it's our interpretations of our experience that make us who we are.

As William Zinsser says in *Inventing the Truth: The Art and Craft of Memoir*, "Memoir writers must manufacture a text, imposing narrative order on a jumble of half-remembered events. With that feat of manipulation they arrive at a truth that is theirs alone, not quite like that of anybody else who was present at the same events."

So my story is not my history, it's about the insights I discovered in my experiences and the psychological and spiritual truth and meaning I drew from them.

1

There Ain't No Such Address

"Oh, what an imagination you have!" That was my mother's predictable refrain for my stories about childhood. Her remedy for distress over the past was simple enough: "Do what I do: Whenever I think of anything unpleasant, I just reach up, pull the shade down, and it goes away." That attitude had at least part of its intended effect because most of my life I asked myself if much of what I had felt and experienced as a child was unreal. Having heard her rejoinder so many times, coupled with having told my share of white lies in childhood, even I doubted whether some things I said were true—especially since I typically lived more in my imagination and dreams than anywhere else. Being born nearly deaf didn't help either. Nearly lacking that sense made me feel as if even what I heard wasn't right and, much of the time, it wasn't.

But I always wanted my first memory to be true because it held so much meaning for the remainder of my life; so much so that I guarded it from my mother most of her life. Many years later, I decided to take a chance. I was warily relating it to my daughter, Lynn, at a Thanksgiving gathering. Despite my uncertainty about it, my first memory was always vivid. Even as I told it, I wasn't sure it was true. Leaning on her walker like a hawk on a perch, my mother was eavesdropping from across the room. I was sure that just a moment before the end of the story, if not sooner, she would try to stop me. But for some reason, she didn't; she listened.

It happened late at night in our Morton Grove house, I told Lynn. My mother and father were having a noisy and bitter fight. I woke to loud swearing and sounds of falling pots and pans and breaking dishes in the kitchen. My father ran out of the house with his suit jacket flung over his shoulder, jumped in his 1938 black Dodge, and gunned it. As he was backing out of the gravel driveway, my mother, still in her old faded blue housecoat, came rushing out after him. She jumped on the running board and grabbed the side aerial, but slipped and fell. Her right leg was trapped under the car. I don't know if my father saw this, but he continued speeding out of the driveway. A soft thud interrupted the sound of crunching gravel as he ran over her bare leg. He never stopped—and I never saw him again.

The clearest part of this memory was standing beside my sobbing mother who was half-sitting, half-lying in the gravel driveway. One of her eyes was red and swollen. Her leg was twisted, dusty, and bleeding, with small pieces of gravel imbedded in it. With my arm around her, I was trying to comfort her saying, "Don't worry, Mommy. I'll take care of you."

I was stunned when my mother yelled from across the room, "Oh my God, how did you ever remember that? You were only three years old!"

I looked at my daughter in amazement, "It really *did* happen!" My mother's shocked confirmation was especially gratifying because not only was she one of the most repressive people I have ever known, she was the only person who could verify it.

In any case, my recollection of that ghastly night is all the more remarkable since memories like that are too easily forgotten—especially by small children. I've also experienced something I once read about—a brain mechanism that sometimes kicks in to block unbearable memories. If a brain or mother doesn't block them, they're often just dismissed. They're just too painful for anyone to want to remember.

◆　　◆　　◆

Nearly fifty years after that memory I decided to revisit Chicago; the place I spent most of my childhood and adolescence. Against my better judgment, I hoped that returning would catapult me back to my childhood. Before leaving California, I had imagined returning and finding that at least some of the scenes, people, and flavor of the place would still be as they once were. The thought of meeting with someone in the neighborhood who knew me those many years ago made me smile. I also wanted the chance to reexperience what I had felt then. My more logical mind knew it might not be the same. It was all too long ago. Maybe little to nothing of what I once knew of this place remained. It was a little silly to say so, but I said it to myself anyway, as I had many times since I left, "If you hadn't lived there you wouldn't even know it existed." And if it didn't, I knew I would feel like a solitary remaining witness. But witness to what? I guess the *what* was the emotional part that still haunted me for so many years. I wondered if the old demons I left behind so many years ago would still be there, as if awaiting my return. After all these years, those feelings and a deep sense of foreboding were hard to forget. It was difficult to imagine being back there without them.

That seemed part of why I came back now—to prove that the feelings were real. I doubted anyone else, anywhere, really cared. But to me it mattered a lot. I had to make a decision, maybe the most important one of my life. I was seriously considering giving up all that I had and becoming a monk—cloistering myself in a monastery somewhere and spending the rest of my life in prayer and meditation. The idea of spending my last years in peace and solitude had enormous appeal for many years. I imagined a life as simple as daily meditation and prayer, taking care of a garden, or being of service to others.

But being sure of what to do with whatever remaining years I had left was critically important. Becoming a monk was hardly an abstraction; it meant rarely seeing my family and friends and giving up my practice and beautiful home. It meant sacrificing everything for which I had worked. Most importantly, I needed to know if this was my truth, the final goal of my spiritual journey. My entire life was about trying to understand who I was and what I was supposed to be doing. So I hoped that this last look back would help reveal my life's final direction, pull my life together, and make some ultimate sense of it. With luck, it might also answer any remaining questions I had about its meaning. And, to do that, it seemed as if I also needed to review my life in detail—again. I say again because even after years of telling my stories in psychoanalysis, I felt I still needed to retrace my life as deeply and accurately as I could. That meant trying to recount the problems, blessings, friends, and, most importantly, the mysterious lifelong prodding of my unconscious. Actually returning there felt like a vital part of being able to do that. So I desperately wanted it to be the same as my memory said it was, if only for this last time.

◆　　◆　　◆

"There ain't no such address." Over the roar of a jet, I was trying to hear this semitoothless cabby sitting in line at the O'Hare airport taxi stand. He was talking around an unfiltered Camel, the dry end dangling from his mouth. I was trying to read his lips.

"I'll take ya there, but believe me, pal, I know Chicago."

Even with the noise, his cigarette, and my hearing loss, I could make out that he said "Chicago" like only a true Chicagoan could. He reminded me of Mickey, my oldest brother. Before he died, Mickey drove a red, white, and blue Vet's cab, too.

"You *sure* you got the right address?" He looked me up and down through his open window. "Ya know that's a hellhole you're talkin' about?"

"The address is right," I said and eagerly opened the door.

The inside of the cab reeked of stale smoke and old pizza, but at least it was partly air-conditioned. I cracked the window a bit. During the half hour or so ride from the airport, I was eager to see my old neighborhood. I hoped the cabby was wrong. I could hear him talking, but the only words I could make out were "restoration project." Since I couldn't read his lips, I did what I usually do, let him talk, occasionally nodding my head. I hoped I wasn't agreeing to go somewhere else. Over the years, I've discovered that I could ignore most of what cabbies say, and they rarely seem to notice. More often than not, they seemed more interested in talking than what they had to say. I admit that may be the rationalization of a person well over half-deaf.

Well, there was one exception. The time a cabby pulled over to the side of the road just as we were approaching an airport. He had been talking intently, and I could only see his expectant eyes and furry eyebrows in the rear view mirror, but I couldn't read his lips, so I just kept nodding in agreement. Then he suddenly pulled over to the side of the road and turned around with an exasperated look. In a loud voice cabbies use on people they think don't understand English, he said, "I'm going to try this *one* more time, pal. Which *airline* are you taking?"

Anyway, in the Chicago cab, my mind raced back and forth, occasionally interrupted by a familiar landmark. Entering the city via Edens Expressway was a fitting prelude to its ashen soul. Whoever painted Chicago was not a colorist. In the distance, the pointy black spires of Sears Tower were rising to meet the sooty gray skyline. I could feel pressure mounting in my head. The tension in my head matched the excitement in my stomach. Sporadic views of red brick apartment buildings offered a little relief from the city's overpowering grayness; they reminded me of my old neighborhood.

My old neighborhood was part of the Near North Side. After the annihilation of the Great Chicago Fire, a new Near North sprang up. Concrete sidewalks, red brick, or stone-faced buildings replaced the wooden sidewalks and buildings of the late 1800s. Lake Michigan marked the East End, a halcyon shoreline of beautiful architecture and Lincoln Park—not surprisingly called the Gold Coast.

That magnificent perimeter shielded a bleak interior from the eyes of tourists and even many Chicagoans. It wasn't long before the core of the Near North became ghettos settled mostly by poor Italian, German, and Polish immigrants. It was slated as a slum clearance project ten years before we arrived there; yet the slums survived because the locals protested the loss of affordable housing. Even before World War II, the Near North was already notorious thanks to personalities, such as Al Capone and John Dillinger, and events such as the St. Valentine's Day massacre. After my father left toward the end of the war, my mother, my brothers, Mickey and Dino, and I moved to 555 Blackhawk Street—a $25-a-month walk-up flat.

I especially wanted to see our old apartment building just as it was when we lived there. Some part of me knew better than to expect it to be the same; yet I wished it would be exactly as it was.

The abrupt screech of the cab jarred me back.

The cabby turned around with a proud smile and said, "See. If it was here, it'd be right over there," pointing to an empty lot next to an alley and a boarded-up wooden house. "That deserted house is 553 that lot is 555." He was tapping another Camel on his Zippo lighter. "So where to now?"

"I'll get out here."

"You sure?" With raised, sweaty eyebrows, and a new Camel in place, he said, "It's up to you."

"I'm sure." I slid across the slightly sticky patched vinyl seat and got out. At his window, I paid him and mumbled, "Thanks."

Even more than at the airport, it was sizzling outside the cab. The brilliance of the afternoon sunlight was intense. It reminded me of living here in July of '55 when Chicago's worst heat wave hit, killing hundreds of people. Today was July 13, 1995 and the temperature was 106; the beginning of Chicago's second worst heat wave. It seemed a bit uncanny to have another such heat wave the day I returned.

The cabby was right. There was no 555 Blackhawk Street. As I stood there staring across the street, he yelled a parting warning. "Get outta here before dark, pal." His last words sounded something like, "The only thing to do here after dark is get mugged!" Then he sped off, his laugh fading in the distance.

I stood there in the glaring heat and unusual quiet, unwilling to move. Except for an occasional black passerby, the street was largely deserted. Since the summer weather hadn't changed, it felt much like the many summers I lived here. The thick humidity of the late afternoon was inescapable. Its mugginess clung to my clothes, stuck to my skin, and couldn't be shaken off. A familiar musty smell rose from the dusty, hot pavement. It was an oppressive combination to be standing there for long, but I couldn't shake my fixed stare. It was as if what I was looking at was more compelling than it should have been. To anyone else, the scene was at best inconsequential, or even mildly repelling. 555 Blackhawk Street was now nothing more than a large dirty vacant lot. It was strewn with some old red bricks, a few empty beer bottles, rusty cans, smelly pieces of garbage, and a scattering of ragged newspaper. An old, tired, and heat-worn dog with matted black fur rifled hungrily through some bits of debris.

The heat made me look for the corner fire hydrant. On a day like this in the past, the owner of the grocery store that used to be on that corner would come out with a wrench and open the hydrant. For just a moment, the quiet, empty street filled with all my childhood friends, laughing and wildly playing in the gushing water flooding the gutters and cooling us off.

Maybe the slum clearance project slated sixty years earlier had finally begun. I wondered exactly when 555 was knocked down, regretting that I hadn't been there to witness its demolition. An imaginary invitation would have both excited and saddened me. Seeing it destroyed might have brought some closure for the lifelong feelings I held about the place.

An abysmal feeling of disappointment and loss crept over me as if somehow my childhood and adolescence here might never have happened. Or maybe just not the way I remembered it. Staring at the emptiness was as if trying to remember a distant dream. This vacant lot was no different from a number of others that randomly ruptured the area. Now it looked even worse. What began as an inner-city ghetto now resembled a bombed city. The only timeless quality of the old neighborhood was the late afternoon's sweltering heat.

In the past, many white folks used to say, "Before the blacks started moving in, it was a nice neighborhood." That was generous. It was a terrible neighborhood even before the blacks started moving in. But the whites still blamed the blacks for causing things to get bad. Blacks had lived in the lower end of the Near North a long time. But new migrations from the South during the war increased their numbers dramatically in the Near North's upper end. They needed more housing and the only place for them to go was farther into the Near North. People said the blacks were leaving the South Side because the Near North was "better." That surprised me because it was hard to imagine a worse place to live. Many years later, I discovered that sociologists gave this ghetto a fitting distinction by dubbing it "Little Hell," "Hell's Kitchen," and the "Black Belt."

In the old days, men would sit outside on hot summer nights, dressed in their faded cotton slacks and dingy undershirts. They sat on stoops or sagging orange crates, their faces shiny with sweat as they drank beer and talked well into the night. Most of the women stayed inside. When the blacks started moving closer to the old neighborhood, there was less of that. People stayed inside more, sat in open windows beside tied and knotted curtains, hoping for a soft, cool evening breeze to lighten the heaviness of the summer night's heat.

The movement of blacks into the Near North created vicious racial tension that eventually erupted into race wars. In time, just being outside after dark was dangerous, especially when there was a race war. It seemed as if there were lots of race wars in those days. Folks in the neighborhood seemed to know when one was going to happen just before it did. They just knew in their bones that something bad was about to happen. Most of the time they broke out just as the streets darkened and an eerie stillness crept over the neighborhood. People hurried inside.

One in particular I remembered: it was the first time I saw someone killed. My friend Mike Alene and I were sitting on wooden crates in front of Sam's grocery store at the corner of Larrabee and Blackhawk when a bare-chested, muscular black guy suddenly emerged from around the corner across the street. He had a thin red bandana tied around his forehead; his eyes darted up and down the street. When he saw us he suddenly stopped, his shiny black chest heaving and covered with sweat. In his right hand, he held an old baseball bat with nails sticking from its top. He scared me, but I thought there was something beautiful about him. Seeing we were only kids, he took off south down Larrabee toward the fight. A few minutes later, as we expected, white guys began streaming from out of alleys and gangways from all directions, filling the streets. Mike and I ran down Larrabee Street to get to the roof of the church next to Evergreen Park. Calling it a park was a joke; it was only a very large treeless dirt lot with a couple of broken swings.

Going those two blocks was dangerous. The trip meant risking being overrun by swarms of blacks streaming up from the Cabrini-Green housing project, or even caught in the middle of the horde of whites from the north running to clash with them. We got to the church safely and, from the roof, we looked out over the park; it was like having a front-row seat.

This war was a big one. There must have been hundreds of guys on each side. When they all got there, there was a moment of silence as the black and white gangs faced off. It started with the pops of zip guns. Then bricks began flying through the air as masses of young men clashed together. That's when the same black guy with the bandana got hit in the face with a baseball bat. His tall body just crumpled to the ground like a piece of paper. In just minutes, it was over. Squad car sirens came screaming from several directions, and the fighters quickly scurried away, leaving a few unmoving bodies and pools of blood—one around the head of a black guy. The next day I heard that someone was killed in the fight. I think it was the one with the red bandana.

My thoughts returned to the barren lot. The once loathsome red brick tenement at 555 Blackhawk Street was now just another uncertain memory. As if it contained the evidence for so much of what I once felt there, its absence dissolving what I believed was my childhood. My mother, stepfather, and brothers were all dead, and my sister remembered little to nothing of it. I felt alone, empty, and deeply sad.

I tried to fill the emptiness by recreating the vividness that building had when I started high school. That was 1955; the year *Blackboard Jungle* came out, and a year hard to forget. I recalled the immense facade of the red brick three-story apartment building with its enormous black-iron fire escape—so huge and heavy that I often wondered why it didn't just pull the building face down into the street. The front of it was the neighborhood chalkboard scribbled with all kinds of crap like Kilroys, "Jessie sucks," and "Fuck you!" I used to scrub off the dirty words so my little sister Christie wouldn't see them. Doing that reminded me of Holden in *The Catcher in the Rye*. She was nine years younger than I was and the neighborhood was no place for little girls.

The ground floor had a small "candy store" owned by the Vet's Club; everyone knew it was really the neighborhood bookie joint. The heavy dark gray front door that led up to the apartment was pockmarked and topped by an always-dirty glass transom. At the right side of the door dangled two wires. Holding their ends together rang the upstairs bell. If it worked and anyone was home, he or she would drop the key from the upstairs window. If that didn't work, kicking the door became the doorbell.

Entering the hallway often caused a loud bang as the door slammed against a large, smelly, oil barrel garbage can behind it. The crash also scared a rat or two, making them jump around in it. A dark, moldy-smelling, and cool hallway led up to our flat. It was lined with a handrail that, in certain places, pulled away from the wall. Above and below the shaky banister were scattered spots of broken plaster exposing slats of wood. A blackened string threaded through metal eyelets lined one wall; pulling the string turned on a bare light bulb at the top of the stairs—sometimes.

Imagining that apartment reminded me of a dream that I had when I was about seven. It was the first dream I ever remembered. I dreamt I was coming down the stairs to leave the apartment. Suddenly, large roots began forcefully growing through the holes in the plaster walls on the sides of the stairs, crisscrossing the hallway. They grew thick and fast. In only moments, they surrounded me, lifted me up and formed a dense, black, suffocating tangle around my suspended body. As I struggled in terror to get free of their grip, I woke up, sweating and breathing heavily.

That dream and my first memory stayed with me all my life. Over the years, I came to think of the dream as a remarkably wise voice forewarning me of the need to break away from that place. Not only escape from that place—that was only the external meaning of it—but also the need to understand the emotional, psychological, and spiritual impact of all that I would experience there. In retrospect, the dream also seemed to suggest that my life and its difficulties would require a great effort to overcome.

Yet, the source of its insistent wisdom was mysterious, like a natal imprint not directly available to my conscious mind. Throughout my life that voice intermittently revealed itself in dreams, imaginings, and confusing life experiences—as if trying not only to persuade me to learn about myself, but about all the things in life I felt compelled to understand.

Maybe I put too much stock in what my mother thought of my memories. Mothers, just because they're mothers, have inordinate power—whether they want it or not. Moreover, at some point I had to stop being her child and listen to my own voice. I know my mother also had an inner voice, but she couldn't listen to it. Hearing her inner voice would have been an ominous crack in the dam of her memories; a threat to her reasons *not* to remember—reasons undoubtedly so painful and difficult to bring into awareness that her life remained an enigma, not only unknown to me, but to herself. After all, imagined or not, our memories are who we are.

So perhaps revisiting my life is ultimately about whether my effort to understand myself had been effective—and it would be—only if I had learned what I was supposed to.

2

Casper the Ghost and Other Firsts

Catholicism was my first religion. When I was six years old, I remember going to St. Michael's Church and School in the old neighborhood. It was 1947, the year Al Capone died. Father Alberti was the head priest. He had a gray wrinkled face that always looked mad, like someone caught in the rain without an umbrella.

Sister Elizabeth was my first teacher. She had wire glasses and wore a long black dress and veil with white on the inside. The white stuff was wrapped really tight all around her face. I guess only her face was supposed to show. I wondered if she was bald.

In Catechism class one day, she was talking about the Holy Ghost. "Now tell me, children, who knows about the Holy Ghost?"

I raised my hand, excited to have the answer.

"Yes, Larry. Tell us what you know about the Holy Ghost."

"The Holy Ghost is called Casper."

She gave me a mean look. "Come to the front of the room, Larry."

I was happy because I thought I was going to get a prize for giving the right answer.

She pulled me closer to the side of her big oak desk. "Hold out your hand." She opened her drawer, where there was a rosary and a ruler. I thought she was going to give me the rosary. Instead, she took out a really long wooden ruler, raised it above her shoulder, and slapped the palm of my hand so hard it made a thwack sound. The rest of the kids jumped in their seats. My hand hurt like hell. It surprised me that a nun would do something so mean; I heard nuns liked kids.

"Now go stand in front of that window and be quiet until the class is over." Then she turned back to the class. "Boys and girls, making fun of the Holy Ghost was a venial sin. If any of you do what Larry just did, you'll be punished."

I didn't know what venial meant, but I knew it wasn't good. As I stood by the window, the heat of the sun on my back and my throbbing hand made me feel sick to my stomach. I didn't say anything because I was afraid of making another venial sin. Then I threw up and the class laughed. I had to get some paper towels from the bathroom and clean it up.

After class, Sister Elizabeth said she wanted to talk to me. "You know, Larry, every time you sin you get a black spot on your soul." She handed me a piece of paper. "Now read this for me."

I took it with my left hand and began reading it. "Now I lay me down to sleep, I pray the Lord my soul to keep, if I should die before I wake, I pray the Lord my soul to take." I wasn't sure why she thought I was going to die.

"Now go home and ask for God's forgiveness by saying this prayer every night before you go to sleep."

After school, I went home and sat on the landing at the top of the stairs. I didn't know if my mom was home yet, and I was scared to tell her what happened at school. So I waited out there. I could tell if someone was home or not if I felt the wooden floor with my back against the icebox that was across from the front door. Since my ears weren't as good as other kids, I could still feel if someone was home or not. I didn't feel anything, so I went into the kitchen and looked around. It was always filthy and stunk of oil from the stove next to the front door. It was cold and dark, so I turned on the heater. That made the cockroaches behind it start racing up the wall.

I jumped when my mom came in the front door. "You home from school already?"

"Yeah." I don't know why she always asked me that.

"It's dark in here," she said and reached for the chain of the bare light bulb over the kitchen table. She knocked the dirty pink and black plastic dishes on the dinette table aside and slammed her purse down. Then she went to her room to take off her dress. I knew she wasn't feeling good, so I decided to wait to tell her about school.

She came running back to the kitchen and turned her ear to the floor. "Goddamn rats!" She pulled back the curtain under the sink, got some lids of #10 tin cans, and started nailing them to the floor where the rats were chewing the wood under it. Then she went to the kitchen window, opened it, and yelled, "Shut up, Tony!" across the alley. Tony had a tin shop over there, and I guess he was making noise. Or maybe he yelled at her first. I don't know. They both yelled a lot.

That night I decided to show the prayer to my mom anyway. I handed her the piece of paper. "Sister Elizabeth said I should read this every night."

"Why's that? You do something wrong at school?"

"Uh, no. Not really." I lied about my venial sin.

"Well, memorize it and say it when you go to bed."

As I said the prayer that night, it was the first time I thought I was going to die. I thought my soul was probably about as big as a baseball, and I guessed it was somewhere in my chest. Then I started counting all the things I did that were probably venial sins. I decided that all those venial sins already filled up my soul, and I was probably going to die that very night. Only, I didn't think God would take my soul because it was so black from all the sins on it. After awhile it got really hard to breathe, and I was sure I was dying.

"Mom," I called.

"What?" she yelled from her room.

"I can't breathe 'cause I'm going to die."

"Go back to sleep."

"How can I go to sleep if I'm dying?"

"You're not dying. Go to sleep."

"I'm sure I'm dying, mom. I can't breathe." I didn't want to tell her about all my venial sins.

In a few minutes, she stormed into my room, grabbed me by the arm, and dragged me into the kitchen. She put a pot of water on the stove and got a piece of newspaper. "When the water boils, put the newspaper over your head, and breathe the steam. When the steam is all gone, turn off the stove, and go to bed."

Then she went back to her room. I breathed the steam until it was gone and went back to bed. I could breathe better, and I didn't die that night. That was the first time I thought about my soul, the first time I thought I was going to die, and the first time I breathed steam. It was also the first time I saw the mask. As I was going off to sleep, hanging in the air about three feet above my head, looking down at me, face to face, was a mask. It was gray, not smiling, and made a low buzzing sound. I thought that maybe it was God looking down at me.

After that, I tried not to make any venial sins or trouble for my mom. Since we moved here, she had to take a job as a maid at the Y down the street and was always tired. When she came home, she took off her gray uniform and her shoes and didn't get dressed again until the next day. I don't think she even took a bath very often because her feet were always dirty. I wished she still looked as she did in the picture I found in the bottom of the hallway closet. It must have been a really old picture because she was dressed in a clean white uniform, had a pretty face, and was skinny. I don't know how she got so fat. I felt sorry for her.

After my first year at the Catholic school, I had to go to a special school on the West Side. It was only for kids who were really hard of hearing or deaf. At first, my mom didn't believe Sister Elizabeth. She said I could hear; I just didn't pay attention. But they did some hearing tests that proved I had a really bad hearing problem.

After they found out I really couldn't hear, I had to take the North Avenue bus to a school for deaf and hard-of-hearing kids because it was more than five miles from where I lived. It was a long ride, but I liked watching how the neighborhoods got cleaner as I got farther away from where I lived. I never once saw any garbage or rats in the alleys around there. The school was in a really neat neighborhood that had newer wooden houses instead of brick ones. Some of them even had fences and grass. That was the first place I ever saw a lawn mower. I liked the smell when those people cut their grass.

I didn't miss Sister Elizabeth. My new teacher, Mrs. Carmella, was kind of old, but pretty. Her hair was bright silver, and she put a new flower in it every day. She also had fancy clothes, pretty purses, and always smelled good. One of her purses was bright red, like her lips, and always looked new and shiny. When I asked once where she got the flowers, she said she had a garden where she grew her own flowers. I thought that was amazing.

At my new school there were only about five or six kids in each class. The other kids always seemed to have money on them. They had new clothes, not stuff from the Salvation Army. It took a long time to figure out why the other kids kept asking me if I had a horse—it was my pants with the puffy legs.

We learned regular school stuff but we also learned how to speak correctly by using headphones to help us pronounce words like hearing people did. I didn't know I spoke weird before I came to this school. Mrs. Carmella said I sounded as if I came from another country. She said it was like an accent, except it was a speech impediment. I thought a lot of kids in my neighborhood had speech impediments, like my Puerto Rican friend, José. One day he said, "I'm going to brush my teet."

I said, "No, you're going to brush your tee*th*."

"OK," he said, "I gonna brush my teets."

I gave up on him.

They taught us how to tell how words sounded by looking them up in the dictionary and making the sounds like the little signs said to. I liked the dictionary. Every day we also learned lip reading and American Sign Language. I thought sign language was pretty cool because I secretly could talk to other deaf kids without hearing kids knowing what we were saying. I even learned to sign some swear words the other kids taught me.

One of the greatest things about my new school was the smell that came up the stairs to our room from the cafeteria. It was always the same—French fries and peanut butter cookies. And I never, ever heard of free food, so I usually took an extra cookie for the bus ride back home.

But back in my neighborhood, kids started calling me "deaf and dumb." And to them, dumb meant stupid. They would talk at me really loud and then ask if I could hear them. If anything was stupid, that was. They didn't know that, and because we knew lip reading and signing, we didn't even need to hear. Anyway, it still made me feel bad because I didn't like being different. It seemed like I was different no matter where I went. I didn't understand why, but if you're different, it's bad. Period. That always seemed strange to me. So when I was in my neighborhood, I did what our teachers always told us *never* to do: I pretended I could hear.

I found out that there were other ways being different was bad. I had a friend named David Steuben. His father came from Germany and owned the Beer Garden on Larrabee Street. David knew all the waiters there and used to take me to the kitchen and get us free cold cuts and pretzels. One day, another friend, Bennie Golden, asked David if he could come with us to the kitchen.

"No, my dad wouldn't like it."

When we were in the kitchen, I asked David, "Why wouldn't your dad like it if Bennie came with us?"

"'Cause Bennie is a kike."

I never heard that word before. "What's a kike?" I asked.

"What are you? Stupid? You never heard of a kike before?"

"Nope, never did."

"Well, kikes are bad people; they cut their kid's dicks."

"What? They cut their kid's dicks off? Why do they do that?"

"Not all the way off, stupid. I don't know; I guess they're just mean. My dad told me to stay away from them 'cause they cheat you out of your money."

I guess that if kikes cut their kid's dicks and stole your money they must be bad. Kike sounds like spike, maybe they cut their kid's dicks with spikes? I later found out there were not only kikes, but also niggers, dagos, wops, spics, hillbillies, and some others. Everyone seemed to have a bad name for anyone who was different.

One day I found out what people like me are called. I was walking down the street close to my house, and this black kid yelled at me, "Hey, honkie muthafucka, you got some change?" I guessed that was the name blacks had for whites, "honkies."

Later I asked my mom, "Why do black people call us honkies?"

"I don't know; I guess because we call them niggers. We all hate each other."

"Why do we hate each other?"

"I don't know. Ask your teacher. You ask too many questions."

Sometimes she would walk away in the middle of my questions. I wanted to ask her why kikes cut their kid's dicks, but I didn't. We weren't supposed to talk about dicks, so until my sister Christie was born, I didn't even know that girls *didn't* have them.

Sometimes I felt like mom hated me. I don't know why, I just felt like it.

It was kind of like the time the weird guy who owned the candy store on Larrabee Street kicked me in the stomach. He was really tall and skinny and had an eye that kind of moved around. His little store was always dark and dirty. He didn't even clean the glass case where the candy bars were. I tried to buy a candy bar with a nickel slug. Somebody gave me the slug and said I could use it just like a nickel. It didn't have an Indian head on it, but it was the same size as a nickel.

I went into that guy's store that day and told him I wanted a Babe Ruth bar. He gave me one, and I reached up and put the slug on the counter. He took a long look at the slug. Then he grabbed the candy bar back. His face looked really mean. He grabbed me by the back of my shirt, pulled me outside the store, and said, "You think I'm stupid? You think you can cheat me you little punk?" Then he kicked me in the stomach. I felt like I was going to throw up, and I couldn't breathe for a long time. Somebody across the street at the Y saw him kick me and called the police. I was still lying on the sidewalk trying to get my breath when they got there. The police came and put handcuffs on the guy and took him away. The policeman who took me home told my mom the story I told him. She got mad and said I shouldn't have tried to fool the guy. It was stuff like that.

◆ ◆ ◆

When I was about nine my mom met a guy at a Halloween party at one of the neighborhood bars. His name was Bud, and he had just come back from the war. He must have gotten pretty drunk at the party because the next morning when I got up, he was sleeping on our couch. He was snoring and drooling and still had a Lone Ranger mask twisted on the side of his head. He smelled like Old Spice aftershave and whiskey. Mom thought he looked pretty cute. I thought he looked pretty stupid.

He looked even more stupid when he got up and stumbled down the hall to the bathroom. He tripped on the step up trying to get into it. I'd be damned if I could ever figure out why the bathroom was a step up from the rest of the floor. Then he left the door open when he peed and used the chain that was used to flush the toilet to hold himself up. The chain broke, and he fell out of the bathroom with the long chain in his hand. He looked like one of the Three Stooges.

Anyway, I guess Bud and mom liked each other because after they went out on some dates they decided to get married. I don't remember a wedding, but they did get married somewhere. Maybe it was downtown.

I wish I could say I was nicer to him when he first married mom. I guess I didn't trust him. It wasn't long before I called him a son of a bitch and suggested he go back to wherever he came from. He slapped me across the nose so hard that blood splattered all over my face. Mom was really pissed at him, and so I wiped the blood over more of my face so it looked even worse than it was. He never hit me again.

◆   ◆   ◆

It wasn't long after they got married that old Father Alberti from St. Michael's came by our apartment. Bud wasn't back from work yet, and I could hear Father Alberti almost yelling at mom in the front room. "Because your first husband is still alive. You can't come back to church, and you can't take the sacraments."

The old goat didn't even say sacraments right. He pronounced it something like *sacaraments*.

"But Father, I got kids. I got divorced. I haven't seen him since he left us. He doesn't even support my kids."

"That doesn't matter. You broke your faith. You'll go to Hell."

That made her cry. I guess it was because she married Bud. When he left, I went to the window and could see him going down the street.

"Hey, Father Alberti!" I called. When he turned around I yelled, *"Va' a farti foterre!"* I heard people say that a lot in the neighborhood. I don't know what kind of sin *that* was, and I probably would go to Hell for saying it, but I didn't care. Mom's eyes were still red from crying when Bud came home.

"Father Alberti said I couldn't go to church anymore because I married you. Then Larry tells him to fuck off in Italian."

Bud looked at me and tried not to laugh. "You shouldn't talk to priests like that. It's not respectful."

"Well, he shouldn't talk to my mom like he did either."

That's when Bud decided we would all go to the Methodist church in his old neighborhood. It was a really small church in a nicer neighborhood. Reverend George was the minister there and, for some reason, it was OK for him to be married. His wife taught Sunday school and was always smiling, especially when she told stories about Jesus. Reverend George wore a tie instead of a priest's collar. It wasn't like St. Michael's. Bud's church was a lot smaller, and it didn't have as many people. Reverend George talked about a lot of boring stuff from the Bible that put me to sleep. They had an organ, and people sang church songs so loud even I could hear the words. The windows weren't as pretty as St. Michael's; there were no bells or statues, no incense or communion. And people didn't have to genuflect in the aisle before they sat down. I did it once by mistake, and some people just looked at me and smiled. At the end of the service, Reverend George always managed to get to the door outside before anyone got out of the church so he could shake hands with people as they left. He must have run really fast around the back of the church or something.

We didn't last too long in Bud's church. None of us liked it. And Bud got tired of waking us up during the sermon.

When I was nine years old, my sister Christie was born. Mom and Bud brought her home from the hospital covered in a pink blanket that smelled like baby powder. Her thin blonde hair was one big curl on top of her head, and she had amazing blue eyes. When she looked at me, she jumped a bit, and then burst into a huge wet smile. She was the most beautiful little thing I ever saw.

Mom stayed home with Christie for a few months but then started going to a cooking school downtown. She was tired of being a maid at the Y and wanted to learn cooking to get a better job. She met some friends at the cooking school who were called Theosophists. So we became Theosophists. Instead of going to Bud's church, we started going to Theosophy school on Sundays.

Theosophy school was even more boring than Bud's church. It was downtown and the church was more like an office building. There weren't any stained glass windows. The teacher was an older, bald-headed guy called Mr. Frommer. He was always smiling. Mr. Frommer didn't have a black gown; instead, he always wore a bow tie and a suit. There was no crucifix, no statues, or even an altar. The only things behind Mr. Frommer were two pictures, one of a lady called Madame Blavatsky and another of a guy named William Q. Judge. They both looked pretty serious. Madame Blavatsky wore a black dress that was tight around her neck and went all the way up to her chin. She had weird dark eyes that made her look like she was staring right through me.

Anyway, I guess Madame Blavatsky started the whole thing with her partner, Mr. Judge. Instead of missals or a Bible, we had a book called the Bhagavad-Gita. This was a very old story; it happened even before the Jesus story. It was about two men, one is a prince named Arjuna and the other is Krishna. Krishna drove the prince's chariot and did most of the talking. It was supposed to be about learning how to live. The story was complicated, and Mr. Frommer tried to make it easier to understand, but it was still confusing to me. It was different from being Christian. Christians only got one chance to be good or bad at life. When they died, they went to heaven if they were good and went to Hell if they were bad. Some people went to purgatory where they had to wait until God made up his mind about them.

Theosophists believed in reincarnation. We lived many lifetimes, so we learned how to be enlightened. I wasn't sure what enlightenment meant. It was interesting but confusing at the same time. The most confusing part was about sins. Mr. Frommer said we don't have sins but we have karma. I didn't really understand karma either. But it was sort of as if what we do follows us around.

The best and worst part of Theosophy school was my friend, Clay. Clay was very different from me, but we became good friends anyway. One way he was unlike me was he never wanted to talk about Theosophy. I did because it was so different from being Catholic or Methodist. I hoped Clay would help me understand it because he was a Theosophist all his life. He was really smart, but most of his answers were like "I don't know" or "I don't care."

Clay also was different because his family was polite. I think from all the fancy stuff he had, they were rich. Clay never came to my house, but after Theosophy school I often went to his. I would have been ashamed to have him see where I lived. Besides that, there wasn't much to play with at my house. His house was in a nice part of Chicago. It was always clean, had pretty curtains on the windows, and smelled like Lysol or something like that. Clay had a huge white room all to himself and lots of toys—more than I ever saw in any kid's house. But all his toys were from another time. Sometimes I got the feeling that he lived in another time. He had this big plywood board in his room covered with gray rocket ships and different colors of plastic spacemen with helmets and a lot of other stuff I hardly ever saw before. It was full of strange buildings, people in spacesuits, and lots of different space cars. There were no plants or animals, and people couldn't live outside without their space helmets.

"What's that?" I asked him.

"It's Quastar. A model of a city on another planet."

"Where is it?"

"It's on another planet far from Earth."

"But it's not real, right?"

"It's real, but people just don't know how to get there."

"I'm gonna invent a rocket fuel for a spaceship that will take me there. I don't like planet Earth."

"What's wrong with Earth?"

"Earthlings."

"Earthlings? You mean Earth people?"

"Yeah, I hate them. Earth people are nasty and evil. All they care about are themselves. People on Quastar are nicer to each other. They're more advanced than Earth people, and they live in peace. They don't kill each other like earthlings. They have stuff earthlings never thought of."

I liked listening to the stories he told about the people on Quastar. I think he really believed Quastar was already somewhere in the universe.

One day Clay didn't come to Theosophy school. Everyone was very serious and looked like Blavatsky and Judge.

Mr. Frommer spoke, "I need to tell you that Clay is no longer with us."

"Is he leaving Theosophy school?" I asked.

"Well, Clay committed suicide. So he is no longer with us in any way." Then, with a weird smile, he said, "Clay is on his way to his next incarnation. Someday his soul will be born again and return in a different body."

I was completely shocked. I didn't understand at all. "Why did he kill himself?"

"I can't tell you his reasons; just that it was his karma."

"How did he kill himself?"

"I'm sorry to tell you this, but Clay chose to hang himself."

When I got home after Theosophy school that day I went to bed. I couldn't stop crying. It was still daytime, but it seemed dark outside. I felt sick, like someone with a strangled heart. I imagined Clay hanging in his bathroom. The image of his dead face scared me. His face was gray, and his head was twisted to the side. One moment I imagined him smiling, telling his stories, and the next moment I saw his dead face. They went back and forth, back and forth. I stayed in bed past supper. Finally, Bud came in. "Larry, you want something to eat?"

"No! I want to know why? *Why, why, why?*" I screamed. "Why is Clay dead? Where is he? Why did he do that?"

"I don't know, Larry. I'm sorry, but I can't explain it."

"Well, who knows? Who can tell me?" I was crying and yelling at the same time. "Does Father Alberti know? Does Reverend George know? Does Mr.

Frommer know? None of those *bastards* knows, do they? Mr. Frommer says he's coming back again. Bullshit; it's all bullshit."

"I'm sorry, Larry. I don't know what the answer is either." He patted my back and left. I cried for a long time. I think I cried myself to sleep, but just before I did, I saw Clay's bent neck and gray dead face. Then I saw the mask again. It was making that same humming sound.

3

My First Arrest

I was waiting for Bud to come and get me from the Chicago Avenue Police Station. Still handcuffed, I sat in a windowless interrogation room with nothing but a table and three chairs. On the table was a yellow writing pad and an aluminum ashtray with some crumpled butts. A somber black-and-white picture of the mayor, "Big Boss" Richard J. Daley, hung on the wall. He was elected in 1955, a couple of years before this.

The detective brought Bud into the room. He was still in his gray, oily work clothes that smelled like the metal factory—and pissed. He stood over me quietly, looking at me up and down as if he was seeing me for the first time and said, "I thought when the sergeant called he meant he was holdin' Dino. 'No, not Larry,' I told him, 'you're talkin' about Dino, right?' The sergeant tells me, 'No, we're holding Larry.' But I can't believe it." His eyes returned to the blood stained bandages on my hands as they had five times already.

"What the fuck did you do to your hands?" Bud asked.

"That fuckin' cashier in the subway…" I said, beginning to make my case.

"Don't swear. You're in a police station."

Even though my hands were hurting bad, I almost laughed. Not because he just said "fuck" himself, but because I'd been sitting in the station for the last three hours and heard the cops say fuck about as much as they said anything else.

"I asked what happened to your hands…" Bud started again.

"Mr. Pedersen," the detective began, "we are holding Larry for assault on a city employee, damaging city property, possibly robbery and resisting arrest. We need to check with the subway cashier on some things, though."

"Assault!" Bud yelled. "Who the fuck did you assault, Larry? Who? Jesus Christ, who did you assault?"

"I didn't assault her…" I started.

"*Her*? A woman? Don't lie, Larry," he said looking at the bloody bandages on my hands.

"Anyway," the detective stepped in again, "do you have an attorney, or do you want a public defender?"

"I can't afford a fucking attorney."

"Well, have a seat then, Mr. Pedersen; I need to make a phone call."

The detective made this all seem so routine, as if it was no big deal.

Not like the red-faced, uniformed cop who arrested me. After he handcuffed my hands behind my back and put me in the paddy wagon, he punched me in the stomach with his billy club, saying, "So you like to assault old ladies, tough guy?" The resisting arrest was bullshit and so was the assault. I never touched the lady. Besides, there were so many cops on top of me in the subway I couldn't even get up.

Now Bud was sitting across from me, lighting up one of his Camels and still staring at me. He was muttering to himself through the smoke of his cigarette.

"Assault, goddamn, Larry, I thought it was Dino. That woulda made more sense." As he exhaled, the smoke came out of his nose like an angry bull. "Wait till I get your ass home. *If* I get your ass home. You may have to stay here."

As it turned out, we didn't have to stay. I was released and given a court date.

What really happened was my friend Sal and I were trying to use the same bus pass in the Chicago Avenue subway. The cashier knew Sal used my pass and dropped it, so I could pick it up and use it again. She asked to see my pass and when I handed it to her, she said she was keeping it because we used it illegally. I didn't really mean to, but I broke her cage window in on her by pounding on it hard. I was so mad that she could just take my pass. Once I broke it, I knew I was really in trouble, so I reached inside and tried to grab my pass so I wouldn't be identified later. The lady kind of flipped out, picked up a piece of glass, and started stabbing my hand. I don't know why, but then she opened the door of her cage and ran out. I figured as long as the door was open I might as well go in and get my pass. As soon as I was in the cage, the police were all over me. I guess they thought I was in there trying to steal the money. I really wasn't; I just wanted my pass back.

In court, they dropped the attempted robbery and assault charges because the cashier admitted she stabbed my hand with the glass. She even admitted the whole thing was about my pass. Anyway, I was only sixteen, with no priors, and Bud said I was really a good kid—just had a bad temper. So they gave me two years' probation.

A few weeks later, I met Joe Casellti, my probation officer. Some of the guys in the neighborhood said he was a pretty cool head. He was Bruce Orlando's P.O. and the P.O. for almost everybody in the old neighborhood. Tony Spinata told me some stuff about him once. He said Joe was from Sicily, and was banging Bruce Orlando's mom.

"Banging Bruce's mom?"

"Well, it's not like he's *just* bangin' her," Tony said. "He stays over there sometimes. I think he really likes her. She's kinda pretty for a mom."

"What does Bruce say?"

"He don't. He just shrugs."

I figured it must be hard to get out of line with your P.O. banging your mom.

"He must like making house calls," I said. Tony thought that was pretty funny.

Anyway, when I finally met him in his office downtown, he seemed cool. He looked as if he didn't get ruffled easily. I could see he didn't want to come off as being too hard-assed, or too nice.

"So what? You gonna follow in Dino's footsteps now?" It surprised me that that was the first thing he said to me. He wasn't smiling or angry; kind of hard to figure at first. He wore a rumpled brown suit jacket and a tie loosened so it was almost halfway down his shirtfront.

"So you think your brother's a hot shot?" he started up again.

I asked myself, "Why is he talking about Dino?"

"Dino is very smooth. I guess you could like that about him. He's a good-looking kid, too. Yeah, he's tough, and he talks a good line. He could sell your mother her toilet seat for more than she paid for it and make her think she got a bargain."

I didn't know what to say. Why was he talking about Dino?

"You know I've been Dino's P.O. since he was twelve? Little bastard stole a car before he could see above the steering wheel." He smiled slightly.

I couldn't figure if he liked Dino or not. I remember when Dino stole the car; someone left it running in the alley right across the street from our house. Dino just jumped in and drove off. I didn't even know Dino knew how to drive.

But then he got more serious. "You know, Larry, that was four years ago. Now he's sixteen and no better off than when I met him. You understand me?" I did, sort of. For as well as he knew Dino, he forgot he was seventeen.

"Dino's on the wrong path. He actually likes the shit he does. He's no mentor, you know?"

I nodded as if I knew what a mentor was. I looked it up in my dictionary later.

"I just have this gut feeling that you are no Dino, *capisce*? I think this start of yours is a big mistake, so I'm going to try and knock your little ass off this path right now. Understand?"

"Well, maybe if you had to live where we live, you would know what it's like for us." I thought what I was saying was partly true and partly stupid. I don't know why I always felt I had to protect Dino.

Joe laughed out loud. He was grinning now when he looked at me. "Larry, I grew up there. I was born there, and my mother stills lives down on Mohawk Street. You think I don't know what it's like to live there. I grew up there. I was even a member of the old Aces.

"No way!" I blurted.

"Oh yeah, right, the original Aces. I even led them for a while."

I didn't know whether to believe him or not. The old Aces were a legend on the Near North Side, one of the meanest, hard-ass gangs in their day. They were on the North Side what the Black Rangers were on the South side. Now they were Dino's gang. The *new* Aces, that is.

"Larry, you know where the Aces are today? I don't mean Dino's Aces, I mean the *old* Aces." Before I could answer, he went on. "Those who are not *dead*, are either in Pontiac or lying somewhere on Halsted Street so strung out on heroin that they don't even know who the fuck they are anymore."

I knew this wasn't right; he was sitting in front of me, and he was one of the Aces. Him and Sam Bargio. "What about…"

"I know what you're going to say, except me and Crazy Sam."

I'd heard about Crazy Sam in the neighborhood. He's a made guy in the Outfit.

I thought of Joe banging Bruce's mom. "So you two are like the angel and the devil?" It was a weak joke, and I knew it.

"Don't try to break my balls, Larry." He wasn't smiling. "I can sleep at night."

"You ever meet up with him again?"

"I've seen him around. He still comes back to the neighborhood. His mother used to live there till he moved her to Park Forest. A lotta people say, 'Oh, he's not so bad. Look at all the money he gives to the church.' It's bullshit if you want the truth. He gives part of what he *steals* to the church. I think the first guy he whacked was some poor sucker who stole money taped to the Virgin Mary in a street *Festa*. Your brother's hero is a world class fuckin' hypocrite—if you didn't already know that."

I never imagined Dino having a hero. He never talked much about Sam Bargio that I knew about. Dino made it seem as if he looked up to nobody. But if he did look up to Sam Bargio, he picked a real killer. I already had heard the story of how Crazy Sam killed a guy for stealing money off the Virgin. The Sicilians imported their *Festa*, the feast of the Virgin Mary, directly from the old country—and took it very seriously.

I realized Joe was still talking to me. "You need a new role model, Larry. I know what it's like in the neighborhood. You don't have much to feel good about, so you join a gang, you do crazy things, you fight, you feel tough, you get some respect and, finally, a feeling of power. And you start thinking that this is what life is all about. But it's all a dead end. Once you're too deep into it, it's hard to get out, it's like quicksand."

"I don't plan on staying in the neighborhood too long."

"Oh? Well how do you plan on getting out?"

"I'll get a job, make some money, and move out."

"You think it's that easy? You need an education, not just a job. Without an education, all the jobs you can get are crap. Are you even interested in school?"

"Not particularly."

"Well, 'not particularly' isn't good enough. You have to want an education bad enough to work at it. You're not really listening to me are you?"

"I'm trying."

"OK, that's enough, you get out of here. You know the terms of probation, stick to them. See me when you're supposed to and stay out of trouble."

"End of lecture?"

"Yeah, Larry, end of lecture."

"See you around."

I found out later that Joe Casellti really was one of the original Aces along with Crazy Sam Bargio. I guess they went in opposite directions. The Aces and Deuces were old gangs, going back to Joe's days in the neighborhood. It was Joe that kept them alive—not to promote what they used to be, but to try and straighten them out by making them more of a club than a gang. I guess it was his way of keeping track of all his probationers. It obviously wasn't going the way he expected, or at least he didn't know it wasn't. So all the Aces and Deuces were guys on probation with Joe. The ages of the Aces were sixteen to eighteen; the Deuces were from thirteen to fifteen. Dino and Mickey were members of the Aces. Dino was their leader. When I went on probation, I automatically became a member of the Deuces even though I just turned sixteen that summer. Besides, Joe didn't want Dino, Mickey, and me all in the Aces. The Deuces elected me to be their leader shortly after I joined them. Joe also didn't know that anyone elected leader of the Deuces had to be initiated by the Aces before he could actually take on the role of leader.

Chicago was always known as Gang City; every poor neighborhood had at least one gang, and some gangs were almost as old as the city itself. Some had only a few members; others had hundreds. Kids were often members by the time they were twelve. Most gangs were about turf and race, so in those days your race and where you lived said a lot about your gang. There also was a pecking order among gangs. In the fifties, whites were at the top, then blacks, then Puerto Ricans. I always wanted to be a gang member like Dino and Mickey. Gangs had turf, power, and got respect. It was almost like a family. If you belonged to a gang you were protected by it, loyal to it, fought to protect its turf, and always hung out with its members.

Not long after I was elected, the Aces told me on a certain night I had to hang out with them—without my guys. It was my initiation night. I met with all the Aces on the corner of Larrabee and Blackhawk. The mass of all twenty of them in their light and dark blue jackets was really quite a sight. Each one of them looked more than six feet tall, but that was probably because I was so much shorter. I asked what the initiation was going to be, but they wouldn't tell me. We walked up to Halsted Street and got on a bus that was almost empty. We almost filled it up. We didn't pay, and the driver knew it was best just to let us go. Once we got on, no other people dared get on that bus. The Aces were all eagerly looking out the windows. Finally, Vern, who looked like a Viking with red hair, called to Dino at the back of the bus to come forward. He was pointing to this greaser walking down the street in a black motorcycle jacket who was at least six feet tall and made me look like a midget. Dino said, "He'll do." Then Dino signaled for all of us to get off the bus.

He turned to me and quickly said, "Here's the story. You take that guy down with your bare hands till he's out cold. We're here only to watch you do it. You don't do it, it's your ass. Got that?"

"Look at the size of that fucker. What if he doesn't go down?"

"That's your problem. Gimme your stiletto."

"I haven't got it," I lied.

"You've always got it. Hand it over."

"What if he's carrying? He could have a knife, or a piece."

"I don't give a shit. Gimme the stiletto."

I slapped it in his hand.

My mouth became so dry my tongue stuck, and my heart was beating like a racehorse. I'd been in lots of fights on the street, a lightweight for the CYA—and never lost a fight. But this was like the David and Goliath thing. One wrong move and I was dead meat. All I knew for sure was that every knockout punch I ever threw was aimed to land about three inches *behind* the guy's head. I don't know why it worked, but it always did.

The guy was still walking on the other side of the street. So I ran back down the street a bit before I crossed over so I would be behind him. I was very quiet, practically on my tiptoes, and fortunately he didn't know I was moving up on him. I prayed he had a glass jaw. When I was just behind him, I tapped him on the left shoulder, ducked, and crouched down. He turned his head to the left but didn't see me because I moved to his right side. When he turned around to look on his right side, I sprung up and hit him on the chin with all my might. I hit him so hard, he just toppled like a tree. To my amazement, he not only crumpled to the sidewalk, he didn't get up; he was out cold. The Aces were across the street, everyone but Dino was clapping and yelling, "Yayyyyy, Larry!" They came over and lifted me up on their shoulders. When they put me back down, someone poured a can of beer on my head. We drank some beer. Then everyone split up.

I was glad I was able to knock the guy out, but I felt guilty for doing it. He didn't have a chance to fight back, but if he did, I might have been on the ground. The only way I could feel OK about what happened was to think that they could have asked me to do something even worse to the guy. If they had, I really don't know what I would have done.

On the way home, I asked Dino and Mickey, "If that guy didn't go down, you guys really wouldn't have helped me?"

"Nope," Dino said, "and you wouldn't be the new leader of the Deuces either."

"Gimme my fucking stiletto."

4

The Rumble

Sitting on my concrete stoop on Blackhawk Street, I watched old man Carone down at the end of the block getting ready to close his grocery store. He was a huge mustachioed man with a belly that stretched his dirty, blood-flecked apron, which covered him chest to ankles. He yawned massively, like the walrus at the Lincoln Park Zoo. I once told Harvey, the hunchback who rented a room in the flat above us, that Mr. Carone reminded me of the walrus. He laughed, which was very unusual for him. Harvey was the keeper of Judy, the elephant at the Lincoln Park Zoo. Mr. Carone finished what he did every night of the week in the springtime. He rolled up his awning, and lifted a huge wooden barrel of pickles from the sidewalk onto the sawdust-covered floor inside. Then he put out the coals he used for cooking Italian sausage, green peppers, and onions at the side of the store; their faint smells still drifting in the breeze coming down the block.

I was waiting for Mike Batter to show up. He called earlier to say he had bad news and needed to talk to me. Mike was one of my guys in the Deuces. Mike's dad owned Batter's Tavern on Larrabee Street.

Mike came around the corner, panting. He had asthma or something that made him out of breath when he ran or got excited.

"They knocked the shit outta him." Mike was giving me the word that Tiny got banged up by the Warlords because he wandered into their territory.

"Did they ever give him a warning?" I asked.

"Tiny says no, says he never even went into their territory before."

"You sure?"

"Larry, all I'm telling ya is what Tiny said. Besides, I thought we and them had an agreement."

"We did, and they just broke it. OK, call a meeting; I want to see all the guys as soon as possible. Tell them we meet tomorrow at 5 in the empty lot next to the brewery."

"Why there?"

"Just do it, Mike."

"You got it." Mike said excitedly, "'Bout time we kicked some of their asses. They need a lesson, a big lesson. Jesus. Tiny even, why Tiny?"

"He was in the wrong place at the wrong time."

"But he's so small. Why not one of us?"

"Mike, none of us were *there*. Tiny was *there*. That's why."

"What about the Aces?"

"I'll get Dino to meet with us tomorrow."

When I was eleven, a gang of blacks from the Cabrini-Green projects caught me. Even though I was on my own turf, I still got a hell of a beating, and they threw my bike over a cyclone fence. By the time they finished with me, my face was not only black and blue like Tiny's, but also the inside of my mouth was hamburger meat. It was the first time I got my nose broken.

The next evening all the Aces and Deuces met in the empty lot next to Steuben's Bier Stube. Before they burned down years ago, there were a couple of wooden houses on it. The lot was set below the sidewalk and, in the early evening, it was darker than up on the street. A narrow concrete runway sloped from the sidewalk to the bottom of the lot. On the one long side of the lot was Steuben's brewery with no windows, and on the other side was a long two-story wooden building—Pat Foley's pissy-smelling house. At the back of the lot was a cyclone fence with a hole big enough to escape into the alley. It was a perfect spot for my surprise. The evening air was cool but sour from the smell of malt from the brewery. Rumor had it that during Prohibition Al Capone owned Steuben's, or at least part of it. I didn't know which was worse, the smell of the brewery or the bloody smell of the Stockyards. At least we didn't live close to the Chicago Stockyards.

Dino was there with the rest of his guys. Leaning against the wall, clipping his nails, he spoke first. "So what's up?"

"We're going to get the Warlords. They caught Tiny on Evergreen and messed him up pretty bad," I said.

"Give it a pass," said Dino. "We'll need them against the niggers before long."

"No way. If we give them a pass, they'll just walk all over us. We need respect. And I need you guys there for backup."

"And revenge!" piped up Tiny out of his crooked little mouth. "Look at my fuckin' face, man."

"Dino glanced sidelong at Tiny's mostly black-and-blue face.

"OK, okay. What kinda plan you lookin' at?" Dino was impatient.

"I'm going to use Tiny as a decoy…" Before I could finish, Tiny was jumping up and down.

"What the fuck! No way I'm going back there without you guys!"

"Hold on, Tiny. Nothing's going to happen to you. Listen to my plan. You and Mike go over to their territory on Saturday night. Go over past Evergreen into the park next to the church. That's where they hang out on Saturday nights. You stay out of sight until it's 7 o'clock. Just before dark, the rest of us will meet down here in the lot at quarter of seven. It'll be hard to see us since the lot is below street level. Most of the Aces will be hiding in the two alleyways coming into the lot at the end of the brewery. Dino, you have six or so of your guys hiding in the gangway next to the tin shop out front." I liked the feeling I got giving the plan.

Dino looked at his guys and pointed to me with his thumb. "Little General fuckin' MacArthur here," he said, laughing and running his hand over his long dark hair. Except that he didn't like animals, he treated his hair like a pet. Without that little droop of his left eyelid, you could say he was handsome. He had no trouble getting girls.

"Yep," I smiled at him. It was a rare Dino-kind of compliment—I think.

"At seven sharp, Tiny and Mike, you let the Warlords see you. As soon as they do, you haul ass back here to the lot and run down to the end. We'll be waiting in the back. When all the Warlords are in the lot, the Aces by the tin shop come in behind them to block their exit. Then the rest of the Aces in the alley come in. Then they're all ours. And," I continued, "I want none of them standing. Tiny you can sit it out if you want."

"No way I'm going to sit it out. I want my revenge," Tiny squeaked. "I'm bringin' my Zippo!"

"You got a gun, Tiny?" I asked.

"I got a Zippo, just made it."

"You test it?"

"No, it's cool though."

"Tiny, I don't want you getting hurt again."

"Not with me and my Zippo, man. Don't worry."

"What about cops?" asked George. George was as big as any of the Aces. If he hadn't been fifteen, he would have been an Ace, not a Deuce.

"Same as usual, when you hear sirens, we go out the back of the lot to Ogden, ditch your weapons in the alley, and go home. We'll meet Sunday afternoon at the fire escape behind the Y for a victory party. Bring some beer."

Dino and I walked home. As usual, he was quiet. I wondered what he was thinking. It was pointless to ask, because his response would be, "Nothin'." We each smoked a Lucky. The streetlights came on just as we got home. We put our cigarettes in their hiding place behind the heavy downstairs door before walking up to the flat. In the kitchen, the bare light bulb was slowly swinging back and forth. I hated that light bulb. Mom was standing in the kitchen, barefoot in her slip, washing dishes in her white pan. Bud, my stepdad, was in the living room drinking a beer and watching television. From the cans on the floor, this wasn't his first beer.

"Where you guys been?" ma asked.

"Out," we both said it at the same time. As usual, there was nothing to do, and the last thing either of us wanted to do was be around Bud when he was drinking. We both went to bed. I don't know if he had anything to eat for supper, but I didn't. I was hungry. I went to the icebox out on the landing by the front door. Along with some cans of beer and a carton of milk, there were some cold cuts in new crumpled butcher paper. I took two pieces of bologna and went back to my room.

My room was down the narrow hallway at the back of the apartment. There was a closet, and then a bedroom on each side of it. Mickey and I shared a small dark room on the right side that smelled of urine. We had a green bunk bed Mom got from the Army surplus store. I had the top bunk because Mickey still peed the bed, and I didn't want to be underneath him when he did. The only light came from a small narrow window that Bud had nailed shut because I used to climb through it and sit on the small ledge over the alley.

As I lay in bed, I put my hand on the cool wall. I could feel the scratching and chewing of the rats inside of it. I hoped they didn't smell the bologna. Rats scared me. I imagined at any time they would break through the wall or the floor. I had reasons to be scared because they bit some little kids in our neighborhood. I also saw them under the sidewalk of our house—hundreds of beady eyes, just sitting in the dark, waiting.

That gray mask was above my head as it always was when I tried to sleep. A long time ago, I grew tired of turning on the light to see if it was really there. It was always just there, above my face, with its steady low hum. I thought about Tiny. Poor little bastard, he really got fucked up for no real reason. He was no fighter. He was on probation like the rest of us, but only for small stuff, petty theft maybe. I imagined him in his oversized Deuces jacket with his messed up face in the top of it. The light and dark blue of his jacket matched his face. He couldn't have been more than ninety pounds. I fell asleep.

◆ ◆ ◆

The next day I paced back and forth in the apartment rehearsing my plan for the rumble. It was the first one I called and I wanted it to come off without any of my guys getting hurt. I also knew Dino and the Aces were wondering if I could pull it off. I wanted their respect. The Warlords were older and bigger than the Deuces, but I was relying a lot on tricking and surprising them. This way they wouldn't likely have weapons since they wouldn't be expecting a rumble. They'd just be thinking that they were going to kick Tiny's ass again. I was a little smaller than most of my guys, and I learned by fighting Dino and Mickey to rely on surprise and an attitude. I never lost a fair fight, but Dino and Mickey were another story. Mickey wasn't as tall as Dino, but he was built like a small bull. He was always telling me, "I'm gonna throw your little ass in a garbage can." He said that because he liked putting guys he beat up headfirst in garbage cans. Dino was more than six feet tall and his fist was so big that it covered the whole side of my head. I couldn't come close to beating either of them but, by relying on surprise, I could at least bloody their noses once in a while. Even that wasn't a great victory because whenever I got to Dino's nose, he would hold me down and let his nose bleed on my face until it stopped.

That night everyone was in his jacket in the lot. There were probably fifteen Aces and about twenty of us. It was a pretty dramatic sight. We had baseball bats, chains, and whatever else in our pockets. I had my stiletto. I wouldn't use it unless I had to. Funny, I thought, the only person I had to use it on was Dino. I just fucked up his hand, but at least that convinced him I would use it. And that finally stopped him and Mickey from beating on me—among other things I don't care to talk about.

Tiny and Mike had already gone to Evergreen. Almost everybody was smoking. We were all a little jittery and excited. I could feel my heart pounding against my T-shirt inside my jacket. It was an unusually quiet night. No one talked about being afraid or nervous. I never did. It was bad for a leader to even look scared.

"George, go up to the street, look out, and signal me when you see Tiny or Mike coming." I saw the Aces were in place, barely visible in the back alleyways and by the tin shop. The rest of my guys stood around darkened edges of the lot.

The minutes dragged out. Finally, George made a thumbs-up sign to me. I motioned my guys to the back of the lot. In seconds, Tiny came running like a scared rat into the lot. Mike was just behind him. I counted the Warlords as they came running around the corner of the lot. There were fifteen, maybe sixteen of them. That was good. As I planned, they brought no weapons that I could see. That was even better. I don't think they knew what was happening until they were all already well into the lot. Then the Aces by Alene's tin shop came in behind them; their leader looked over his shoulder at them. I could read his lips making the word "Fuck!" In just seconds the Warlords knew they were surrounded. The other Aces came out of the alleyways. For a moment, it was quiet. The Warlords just stood there looking at each other. Tiny came running up from the back with his zip gun aimed at the Warlords' leader. There was a pop sound as Tiny fired, the leader ducked, but Tiny went down, screaming and holding his face. For a second we all looked at Tiny. Blood ran between his fingers, covering his face. Then we all went at the Warlords with everything we had. We were crushing them down so fast that they were hardly able to fight back. A few of them got hit in the head with baseball bats. One guy's head just seemed to lop over; he went down like a sack of potatoes. I landed some well-placed punches on a couple of guys without weapons. My blows felt solid. I felt a nose crack under one of them and ripped a knuckle on another guy's front teeth. Mickey hit the Warlords' leader in the face with a chain; he was the last to go down. When it was over, a couple of Warlords looked knocked out or dead; I couldn't tell. All of them went down quickly and were scattered across the lot. Then the sirens started.

"Get out of here! Get out of here!" I yelled at my guys. All of them were scrambling to the end of the lot, going through the alleyways. Tiny lay in a heap not far from the pile of Warlords. I ran over to him and picked him up by the back of his jacket. Then I dragged him, half running, half stumbling through the alleyway toward Ogden Avenue. He was crying and couldn't see where he was going. My guys were gone. I took Tiny behind the garment factory on Ogden. Streaks of blood and black spots of gunpowder covered his face.

"Oh Jesus, Tiny, Jesus!" I started to cry. "I've got to take you to a hospital, man. I don't know how bad it is."

"I can't see! I can't see!" he screamed.

"I know, man. I know. I gotta take you to a hospital."

Tiny kept crying and mumbling as we headed to the hospital, but I couldn't understand him. One lady we saw on the way looked like she was going to faint when she saw Tiny's face. An old guy called after us when we passed him, "Goddamn punks!" Other people occasionally stopped to gape as we struggled down the streets to get there, but no one offered to help. It seemed as if it took us forever to get to Alexian Brothers Hospital over by Sedgwick and Fullerton.

When we got to the emergency room, they wouldn't touch Tiny. I didn't think of it but, because he was a minor, they had to call his mom.

"They're gonna call your mom, Tiny."

"No, man, don't let them do that. She'll kill me." He started crying again.

"She won't kill you. She'll just be upset. I'll talk to her."

"OK, okay," he finally agreed.

They called his mom and she got there in about an hour—she had to walk. They were already prepared to take him to surgery. When she came out of the emergency room after talking to the doctors, she started yelling at me. Like Tiny, she was a small person but loud. She was still dressed in her wrinkled gray work uniform. She worked with my mom at the Y, except her job was in the laundry.

"What did you do to Timmy? You know he's gonna lose his eye, huh? You listenin' to me, Larry? The doctor says there was a piece of lead in his eye. Whose gonna pay? I got no money." She started crying.

"I...I didn't do anything. It...it was an accident," I said. I looked at the floor. She had welcomed me into her home, fed me, and thought I was her son's best friend. Now I was worse than a bum. "I feel sick," I said, wanting to escape. "I need to go home."

"Yeah, you go home, you bum. Stay away from my Timmy. You and your gang are nothin' but trouble."

On the way home I felt like I was going to throw up. I started seeing stars and got a headache that felt like someone was beating my right temple with a ball peen hammer. I hid my jacket behind the garbage barrel in the downstairs hallway. There was blood all over the light blue Deuces emblem and the right sleeve. I thought I'd take it to the Laundromat on upper Ogden in a few days.

Upstairs, my mom asked, "Where's your jacket?"

"I left it at Mike's."

"You eat?"

"Yeah, at Mike's," I lied.

That night images of Tiny's bloody face kept coming into my head. I couldn't shake them. I felt bad about Tiny's eye. He couldn't see all the way to the hospital. I felt guilty about it, but I was glad he didn't see me cry. I wondered what Dino thought of the fight. He hadn't said anything. It was unusually warm for this early in the spring. I wanted to open the window but remembered that Bud nailed it shut a long time ago. Then the mask was there again. My head pounded mercilessly until I fell asleep.

◆ ◆ ◆

On Sunday we all met at the fire escape behind the Y. There was beer, but it wasn't much of a victory party. By then everyone knew Tiny had lost an eye. Dino was there and, as usual, he spoke first. He was looking at me disapprovingly. My guys were quiet, watching closely.

"You didn't really need us. We could have watched." He was brushing his hair back again.

"I didn't know how many there'd be." I kicked the dirt with my boot.

"And Tiny?" Dino chided.

"It's too bad about Tiny." I knew I should have made him test his gun.

"What was with the gun?" someone asked.

"Dumb fuck doesn't know the difference between steel and lead. He used a lead barrel." Dino was smiling.

"Jesus!" several guys moaned together.

"I asked if he tested it!" I felt defensive, and Dino knew he was getting to me.

"How do you test a zip?" George asked.

I thought everyone knew. "You put the barrel in a vice..."

"Right," interrupted Dino, "and the vice crushes the barrel." He was laughing again.

"Fuck you, Dino. It's one way, and it works."

"Whatever," he replied, "he didn't test it, and it blew up in his face."

"I'm saving to get me a Saturday night special. Fuck zips." Frankie said.

"We don't use zips and neither should you dumb fucks," Dino said.

We all drank some beer and went home. It was an empty victory. I was tired of Dino's disapproval and superiority. I lay in my bed thinking about Tiny. Then the gray mask appeared again, humming.

◆ ◆ ◆

The hospital reported the incident as "gang-related," and my P.O. was notified. So Monday morning I had to skip school to go downtown and see Joe Casellti.

I walked into the probation department and saw Joe through his office door, sitting in his chair, feet on his desk, talking to another kid, and puffing on his pipe. He looked up and motioned me to sit down outside the door. There was a constant clacking of typewriters around the room and the sweet smell of Amphora tobacco coming from Joe's office. I bought him some last Christmas.

A few minutes later, the other kid left. Joe pointed with his pipe to the chair in front of his desk. "Take a seat, Larry. He tapped the tobacco in the top of his pipe, lit it, and blew out some smoke at me. He was shaking his head. "You're in deep shit, my friend. You disappoint me. I don't expect this kind of shit from you. You've got more brains than your whole gang and you sit on them. Your brains are nothing more than a soft cushion for your ass."

I knew this was coming. "I didn't..."

"I'm not finished. Shut your mouth until I ask you to speak. Understood?"

"Yes, sir."

"Your job as a leader is to be an example to your guys. They look up to you."

"I know."

"Quiet!" he yelled from around his pipe. "What I want to know is how you feel about this. You and your guys not only messed up quite a few of the Warlords, one of them might have a broken neck, but you also got Tiny walking around for the rest of his life with one eye. You've got a hearing problem; you know what it's like having a handicap. Tiny has about as much a chance as a snowball in hell with two eyes; what's he going to do with one? You know I could send you to Saint Charles for quite some time for this? Is that what you want?"

"No, sir, that's not what I want. And I feel bad about Tiny."

"Well, tell me what you want to do. Where are you headed? Just what the fuck do you want out of life? You want to follow in Dino's footsteps? You want to be a big shot? Well, Dino's a big shot going to hell in a hand basket, my friend. And I don't think there's any saving him. Maybe you just want to follow him. Is that it?"

"I guess I'm not sure what I want."

"Well, you better start thinking about it. What's happening at school?"

"Not much. It's boring."

"If you think school is boring, your whole life's going to be boring unless you get some education. You're wasting yourself, my friend. And if you're not careful, there is a point of no return."

"What do you mean?"

"I mean if you don't straighten out, one day the course you're on is going to turn into a tar pit. You'll be stuck in a rut you can't get out of."

"I was only trying to help Tiny." Before I finished my sentence, I knew it was stupid.

"Help Tiny? Are you joking? A lot of fucking good you did Tiny. Go home and think about it. Get outta here and don't be back until your next visit."

"You letting me go?"

"Get out of here before I change my mind."

I took the noisy downtown El train back to the neighborhood. I was relieved that Joe let me off, but I was ashamed and embarrassed. He could talk, I thought. He has a good life, or I think he does. He's got a nice house somewhere, plenty to eat, and no rats in his walls. Besides, he's dating one of my guy's moms. That couldn't be right.

I decided to take the rest of the day off to go and see Tiny at the hospital.

When I got to his hospital room, he was sitting up in bed with a lunch tray in front of him. The room had that disinfectant hospital smell.

"Hey man, how's the service here?" It didn't make sense, but I was hoping he wasn't mad at me.

"Hey, Larry!" he looked up with his good eye, surprised. "What's happenin' man?"

"Not much. I had to go downtown to see Joe."

"Was he pissed?"

"You bet he was. He read me the riot act and told me how fucked my life was."

"Shit, my mom says I have to go see him when I get outta here. I fuckin' dread it."

"Just be cool, don't interrupt him, and always say, 'Sir.'"

"He didn't send you to Juvie?"

"Actually, no. Surprised the shit out of me. But he's worried about you."

"About me? Why's that?"

"Well, you know your eye and all. I think he thinks I'm responsible."

"Fuck, man, it wasn't your fault. You asked me if I tested the gun. And I didn't. I didn't even use steel. I used a lead pipe that exploded like shrapner, or whatever they call it."

"Shrapnel. Your mom still pissed at me?"

"Well, some, you know. Don't sweat it. I told her it was my fault. She'll get over it; she likes you. Besides, she knows you brought me to the hospital. If you hadn't, I'd be running the streets like a blind man."

"That's cool. Well, at least the Warlords won't be fucking with us. I think we taught them a lesson."

"Thanks for that, man."

"Well, listen, I gotta cut out. You take care, my man."

"Larry, thanks for comin' by. Ask the other guys to come see me."

"The leader always comes first. Respect, you know." I winked. "I will. You take care." I stopped at the door and turned around. "Know what, Tiny?"

"What?"

"You look like a pirate now." We both laughed.

I walked home from the hospital and avoided the Warlords' territory. I still felt bad about Tiny. I hoped Joe was wrong. I didn't want to fuck up Tiny's life any more than it already was. He was a good kid, tiny or not, and I liked him. Even before now, he was kind of an embarrassment to the other Deuces. They didn't think he was bad enough or big enough. They wanted to vote him out, but I said no. Shit, Tiny wasn't *that* much smaller than me.

5

High School

The next day I had to go back to school. I had missed so many classes I was in danger of failing everything I was taking. Besides, I wanted to run into that cute chick with the reddish hair. God, she was gorgeous, and she dressed like a model. She was from the Gold Coast and probably Jewish. She'd probably puke her guts out at the thought of dating someone like me. But I wanted to see her anyway. I just liked looking at her. Besides she did look at me sometimes. Maybe the way I dressed amused her. I sure didn't dress like a preppy. If it weren't for the Deaf-Oral department, I'd be at a high school closer to my neighborhood like Waller or Washburne. In those schools everybody dressed like me. Either of them could have been the scene of the *Blackboard Jungle*. Before they dropped out their sophomore year, that's where Dino and Mickey went.

Today I was lucky. I saw the chick I liked in the cafeteria. She smiled at me from across the room. She was sitting with her other Lake Shore Drive friends. Like her, they all looked rich. She wore a violet sweater and snug purple skirt. I would never dare talk to her, especially with her friends around. It would be bad enough what *she* might think, much less all her friends thinking the same thing at the same time. If we ever talked, it would have to be her talking to me. At the end of lunch, her friends left and she was sitting alone. I couldn't get up the courage to talk to her. To my amazement, she came walking toward my table carrying her lunch tray. When she was almost past me she hesitated a second, turned around, and said, "Hi." She had that smile.

"Uh, Hi." I didn't know what to say next.

Fortunately, she said, "So are you Lake View's bad boy?" Her eyes sparkled with an intense aqua blue I don't think I had ever seen.

"Uh, I guess so. Why? You like bad boys?" I felt awkward and hoped this conversation didn't go stupid on me.

"Yes. I like bad boys, and I like Johnny Mathis." She was smiling. Then the bell rang. "Sorry, I have to go."

"Wait," I stammered. "What's your name?" I was glad I got that out.

"Frankie," she said.

"Frankie?"

"Yes, Frankie, like the boy's name. And yours?"

"Larry." My mouth felt dry and sticky.

"Well, see you around, Larry." God, I loved the way she said my name—it was like the way some people talk to their pets. I went to my afternoon classes, but all I could think about was her. I must have looked really dopey sitting there mentally repeating a thousand times how she smiled and said my name.

I was still thinking about Frankie when I came back home later that afternoon. Dino was home by himself, sitting on the fire escape smoking a cigarette. He had the best room. He could usually get what he wanted by the way that he treated Mom when he wanted something; like the time when he was twelve and tried to get her to buy him a bike.

"How's my mom today?" he asked mom.

"Your mom is damn tired. It's been a long day for me."

"Well, you look good, even if you're tired."

"Oh, c'mon," she'd say, smiling.

Then, stroking her hair, he'd say, "You know how pretty you are Mom?"

"Well, your stepfather doesn't think so anymore."

"What does he know? He should look in the mirror sometime." Then they would both laugh.

"You know that Schwinn *Phantom* my friend Eddie just got for his birthday?"

"You keep tellin' me."

"Do you think I could get one for my birthday?"

"You know we can't afford a bike like that. I don't know where his mom got the money for it."

"Oh, please, Mom. I'll even pay you back one day," he pleaded.

"You'll never have money like that."

"One day I'm gonna be rich. I'll pay you back every penny I ever got."

"Sure, you will. Well, I'm not promising, but I'll talk to your stepdad. Maybe we can find a way."

"Aww, Mom. You're the greatest Mom anyone could have!"

"We'll see. We'll see."

Dino never did get the Phantom. Bud thought it was ridiculous to spend that kind of money on a bike. "A week's pay, a god-damned week's pay," he said. If Mom could have gotten that bike herself, she would have. But that was two week's pay for her.

Anyway, Dino's room was on the street side of the building and a lot lighter than mine was because it had a large window that opened onto the fire escape. Sometimes on hot summer nights, if Dino was in a good mood, he'd let Mickey and I sit out there and drink Cokes with him.

Old Crazy Joe and his wife lived in a flat directly across the street in an even bigger red brick building. From Dino's room I could see straight into their kitchen.

From where we sat, we could see a wooden table covered by a dirty red oilcloth. Strewn over it were plates of old spoiling food and encrusted tableware. Behind the table were ivory-yellow, finger-smudged cabinets. They often screamed and cussed at each other across that table. I hated Crazy Joe because he used to beat his wife and lock her out of their apartment. Then she would sit out on their concrete stoop and piss down her hairy, yellow legs that had many little brown sores. It should have been Joe pissing down his leg, at least one was wooden. If Crazy Joe were out on the street, we would swear at him from the fire escape. Some of the kids in the neighborhood used to throw darts at his wooden leg. He couldn't run fast enough to catch them.

I would die if Frankie knew where I lived.

◆ ◆ ◆

That night I had to work for Dino as a car hiker at Mario's restaurant on Rush Street. I don't remember how Dino got his job there, but it was a big step up from working in the neighborhood Laundromat. He once told me a story about the Laundromat that he thought was pretty funny. An older lady who always came to his Laundromat saved her money and finally bought a washing machine of her own. She told him that but continued to use the Laundromat. When he asked her why, she said she was afraid to wear out the new machine. I guess it was funny, but I understood exactly why she thought that way. Poor people think like that sometimes.

Anyway, during high school, I worked a lot of clubs and restaurants on Rush Street, but most often it was Mario's. Mario's supposedly belonged to the Outfit and they often met there on Friday nights. Somewhere around nine in the evening, a procession of glinting black Cadillacs, Lincolns, and Buicks signaled their arrival. Cadillacs were the most popular. Since the Outfit guys didn't get claim checks, they never waited for us; they just left their cars double-parked and still running. We knew who they were and what cars they drove. The Outfit guys rarely came with their wives; most of the time they came either with girlfriends or alone. Occasionally, one would show up with a girl on each arm. Dino usually introduced me to them and later told me their rank so I would remember where to put their cars. Frank Gianni was the boss, or the *capo di capo*. When he came in, his car was always in what we called "first place." That was at the curb just to the left of the front door in a loading zone. If another car was there when he arrived, we replaced it with his. Sam Bargio, Gianni's *consigliere*, had his car parked just behind his. Most of the Outfit guys had places pretty close to the front door, or at least somewhere in sight on Erie Street. A lot of them didn't like their cars being out of sight of the front door. Even when Hugh Hefner from *Playboy* came in, he was put behind the Outfit lineup.

Other regulars of Rush Street were drawn from various ranks of the dispossessed—gamblers, burglars, pickpockets, drug pushers, prostitutes, pimps, and an odd and sundry assortment of waiters, waitresses, wise guys, and wannabes. There also were children, many of them gypsies, whose parents sent them there looking purposely pathetic to beg for spare change. Women were particularly easy pickings for kids with dirty torn clothes and snotty noses. They usually got more than small change since just the looks of them could easily break the hearts of tourists already spending a bundle on food and entertainment. Since it had such a remarkable cast of characters, Rush Street was like a movie set where, while going about your business, you might look behind yourself and see lights and cameras ready to roll. The din of its traffic, sidewalks full of noisy people, marquees, neon lights, and billboards caused me to dub it "Tinsel Town." I often thought it existed only to the tops of the buildings. On Rush Street everyone seemed to feel important, at least until the night was over. Night usually ended at four or five in the morning when the last of the stragglers set out to find breakfast in an all-night diner or White Castle.

◆ ◆ ◆

I went to school again the next day. Staying away from Frankie proved to be difficult because we kept running into each other, and I really didn't mind. I just didn't want her ever to see where I lived. That day I saw her talking with some of her friends in the hallway as I walked to class. I had to pass by her, and I could feel a sense of excitement mounting in my stomach as I got closer. I swear I could almost smell her. I wondered if she would speak. She did.

"Hi, Larry." Her smile made me feel warm.

"Hi. How's it going?"

"Great, and you?"

"I'm good. What's new?" I didn't know if I should stop or just keep walking. I hesitated.

"Oh, we're just talking about Delta's dance Tuesday. You going?"

"Delta?" Her question stupefied me. I never went to a high school dance.

"Yeah, Delta's dance at the Lincoln Avenue Y. Are you going?"

"Er, I wasn't invited."

"Well, consider this an invitation then." Her friends looked surprised.

"Besides, I think I have to work Tuesday."

"Oh, well, too bad," she pouted slightly," maybe another time."

"Yeah, another time. See ya." I walked toward my class.

"See you around, Larry."

I started frantically talking to myself. "Jesus, I can't believe that. I just blew her off. I'm not working Tuesday. I never work Tuesdays! Why did I say that? I guess she caught me off guard. What the fuck was I so nervous about anyway? She's just a girl, man. Just a girl." I yelled at myself all the way to class.

In class I tried to figure out a way to go to the dance. I don't know much about what went on in class but, by the time it was over, I figured out how to go to the dance. It was simple; just show up and tell her I got the night off.

That's just what I did. I showed up at the Lincoln Avenue Y awhile after the social started. I didn't want to look too eager to be there. It was a lot nicer and cleaner than the North Avenue Y where I lived. I was nervous not knowing what I'd say to Frankie if I saw her. I could hear Bill Haley's "Rock Around the Clock" blaring from the entrance of the room where the social was. I walked in trying to be cool and disinterested. The room was warm and so dark it was hard to see. The dance floor crowded with kids doing the jitterbug; other kids stood in a circle around them clapping. Gray and pink crepe paper streamers looped from the ceiling. I scanned the room looking for Frankie, trying to be inconspicuous. I didn't see anyone I knew; most of them were preppies. Then there was a tap on my shoulder. I turned to see Frankie, smiling.

"Hi, Larry. Get the night off?"

"Uh. Yeah, I did. Lucky I guess." Now "Ain't That a Shame" was playing.

"Well, I'm glad you did. Come to many socials?" It was hard to hear her over the music.

"Not many," I lied. I could feel myself beginning to perspire and hoped it wouldn't show.

"I haven't seen you at any."

"So what's Delta?" I wanted to change the subject.

"Delta's my sorority. Just a girls' social club."

Social club. Shit. I didn't know what that was.

"We have dances, sponsor parties, stuff like that."

"You're in that?" Jesus, what a dumb question.

"Yep. It's no biggie."

The Platter's song, "Only You" came on.

"Want to dance, Larry?" She was smiling that beautiful smile.

"Sure." I was hoping my hands weren't too sweaty. When we started to dance, I held her lightly; she felt like a flower. She pulled me in closer, placing her head on my shoulder, her lips close to my ear, and our bodies in full contact. I was being careful not to step on her toes. I enjoyed holding her hand and touching her back.

"When you hold my hand I understand." Frankie seemed to saying something.

"What?" I asked like a numbskull. I could barely hear her.

"I'm just singing to myself."

"My one and only you." She finished singing the song as it ended. From what of it I could hear her voice was sweet and soft. We stopped dancing. "You dance well," Frankie said.

"Thanks, you do too."

Another song came on. "This reminds me of you," she said.

"What is it?"

"'Black Denim Trousers.' You know, black leather jacket, boots, bad boy clothes." We stood in silence until the song ended. Then a fast Elvis Presley song came on. "Wanna dance again?" Frankie asked.

"Uh, I'm kinda warm." I knew my hands were really sweating now. I could feel beads of moisture on my palms.

"Wanna go outside?"

"Sure. Let's go outside." I was relieved. We went outside and stood by an open window with the ending sounds of "Blue Suede Shoes" coming from inside.

We stood there silently. My half-smile must have looked stupid. I didn't know what to say.

"What are you thinking?"

"About Fats Domino." I was and wasn't. I must have heard a bit of his song from inside.

"That's his song playing now, 'I'm in Love Again.'"

"Yeah, I know." I could hardly make it out.

"Larry, you don't always hear very well do you?" She was touching my arm.

I blushed and felt ashamed. "Not always. I read lips."

"I'm sorry, I didn't mean..."

"It's OK." I wanted to get away from the subject. "You sure know a lot of music. So you said you like Johnny Mathis?"

"I *love* Johnny Mathis!"

"Ever see him?"

"Only on album covers. I really want to see him some day."

"I could take you."

"You *could*?"

"Sure, he's coming to the Black Iris in a few weeks."

"But night clubs are so expensive. My sister Tori goes there a lot with her fiancé." I was surprised she thought anything about money.

"Won't cost me anything." I was smiling widely. This was a moment of glory. "I know the owners; I can get us in free."

"Really? That's great, let's go!"

"OK, I'll take care of it and let you know when he's here. I could even get you his autograph."

"I'd die for his autograph!"

"Would you die to meet him?" I laughed.

"Doubly! Is that possible?"

"Could be arranged if you know the right people."

"Are you kidding me?"

"Nope, consider it done." I hoped I could pull off this promise.

"How do you know the owners?"

"I work for them. Sometimes I hike cars there. I hike cars for lots of places on Rush Street."

"Oh, you're one of those crazy drivers my dad complains about when he and my mom go down there?"

"We're good drivers, the best actually. We can drive cars faster in reverse than most people can forward. It just looks reckless. We know what we're doing. Besides, if we didn't drive like that, your dad would be waiting all night to get his car back." What I was saying was true, and I was enjoying bragging. "Well, just don't tell your dad."

"He'd give you a lecture. He thinks the police should crack down on you guys."

"If we didn't pay them off they would."

"You pay them off?" she asked incredulously.

"Of course. We pay off the whole Chicago Avenue Station."

"C'mon!"

"It's true. Take my word for it. Another thing not to tell your dad." I wasn't sure I should be telling her this. "Well, anyway, we'll see Johnny Mathis. I didn't hear him played tonight."

"They played 'Chances Are' before you got here. It's my favorite."

"Sorry I missed it."

"Me too, we could have danced to it."

We stood close, silently looking at each other. It made me nervous. I broke the silence. "We'll, I guess I should take off."

"You ever offer little girls a ride home?"

"Uh, yeah, I do. I mean, sure." I laughed. Stupid me.

"Let me tell my friends I'm going. OK?"

"Sure, I'll get my car and meet you in front."

As I was getting in my car, I realized I didn't offer her a ride because I didn't want her to see my car. I had just gotten it a few weeks ago for three hundred bucks. It was a '53 Ford coupe, an ex-telephone company car, dark olive green, with the bell-shaped emblems on the doors painted over, and the driver's side window missing. It didn't have a radio, but I had a little red plastic transistor I taped to the dashboard. As I came around the corner, I could see her smiling. She had put on her gray and pink Delta jacket, brushed her hair, and freshened her lipstick. I was glad she wasn't throwing up; she didn't even look disgusted at the sight of my pea green ride.

She had a big smile when she jumped in. "OK," she said. "Show me your reckless driving."

"This car won't go reckless. It's good if it just goes. Which way?"

"Take Ashland to Irving Park, right on Irving and down to…"

Before she got it out, I said, "Lake Shore Drive."

"How'd you know I lived on Lake Shore?"

"I figured."

"Do you mind?"

"No. Not at all, should I?"

"Nope."

When we turned onto Lake Shore Drive there was a huge, nearly all-glass apartment building on the right with a semicircular driveway. The building faced Lake Michigan and the Yacht Club Harbor across Lake Shore Drive.

"That's it," she pointed. "Just pull up into the drive but not all the way to the front door."

I wondered if she was ashamed to be seen with me. There was a doorman in a dark green uniform waiting at the front door. I stopped about twenty feet before we got to him.

"This OK?"

"Yep, I just didn't want Clifford to open the door right away." She scooted across her seat next to me and put her head on my shoulder. I could smell the delicate fragrance of perfume I hadn't noticed at the social. I wondered what kind it was. "Larry," she lifted her head and looked at me with those amazing blue eyes, "I had a great time."

"I did, too. It sounds like we had a date."

"Why don't we?" She was smiling again.

"You mean to see Johnny Mathis?"

"Yes, but why not before that?" I loved her forwardness and confidence.

"Another date?"

She burst out laughing; it was a delightful melodious laugh. "Well, it's not like I want to wear you out or anything. Would a movie be too taxing?" She enjoyed teasing me.

"No, not at all. I'd like that. Where do you go to the movies?" I knew that sounded stupid as soon as the words left my mouth.

"Well, movie theaters are nice." Now she was laughing almost uncontrollably. "You are so funny!"

Then there was a light tap on her window. The doorman was standing there. "Everything all right, Miss Feldman?" he asked.

"Just fine, Clifford. Thanks. I'll be up in a minute." He slowly walked back to the front door.

"Clifford your bodyguard?"

"At the moment. Why? Want the job?"

"It's a possibility. Does it pay well?"

She leaned toward me and kissed me on the cheek. She was smiling sweetly. "Night, Larry. Thanks for the ride. Sleep tight."

Before she was out the door, I asked, "What about the movie?"

"Call me."

I drove home listening to my little red radio, hoping it would play a song we heard together tonight. It didn't. I wondered how long I could go without washing my face before it fell off. I wanted to keep her kiss forever. I think my little green Ford just floated me back home. When I got there, I remembered I didn't have her phone number.

6

The Black Iris

Some weekends I worked the nightclubs instead of Mario's. The Black Iris was one of them and, fortunately, this particular weekend I was working for their doorman, Big John. I was glad because Johnny Mathis was going to be playing there in a couple of weeks, and Big John was the first person to talk to about getting in.

Big John earned his name partly by his size and partly by the way he ran his door. You could say he ran it mostly by his presence and his looks. I don't know how tall he was, but I knew he had to take off his doorman's hat to get through the door of the club. His face was very badly scarred but, strangely, rather than making him look disfigured, it made his face more interesting. Somehow, it made him more like himself. The other way he ran the door was with a tire iron that he always seemed to be able to come up with when the occasion required it. The tire iron wasn't just a threat. Anyone who knew him knew he didn't hesitate to use it. Cabbies, for example, knew they had to form their wait line a certain distance from his door. If they didn't, out came the tire iron and he used it to wave them back to their place. I only saw a smart-ass cabby defy him once. When he did, Big John walked over to the cabby and very calmly said, "I'm going to count to three. If you don't move back to that line by the time I finish, I'm going to start putting dents in your front fender." He was almost nice about it. The cabbie moved back.

Big John was a veteran of the Korean War but, like Bud, he never talked about it. I tried asking him about it once, and he just mumbled he didn't want to talk about it. For some reason, Big John took a liking to me. He was always especially nice to me and probably saved my life once.

That night I was standing at the curb by the Black Iris door and, the next thing I knew, he tackled me and had thrown me into the street almost under a car. His massive frame covered everything but my face. Only then did I hear gunshots coming from all directions. When I looked up, police cars were coming from every street, and the cops were all shooting at a single car coming down

Ohio Street the wrong way. When the car got almost to our intersection, it came to a screeching halt, tried to turn around by slamming into reverse, but instead backed through the showroom window of the Cadillac dealership across the street. It was pretty wild. From on top of me I could hear Big John mumbling something like, "Fuckin' Korea."

When we got up, I said to Big John, "Wow, did you see that?"

"Yeah, you little shit, but you missed the beginning. It looked like you were going to take one of those bullets."

"I didn't even hear it till they were almost on top of us."

"I figured you didn't."

It took awhile to clean up the mess in the street and board up the Cadillac showroom. Even with all the rounds the police fired, they didn't hit either of the two guys in the stolen car, even though I counted twenty or so bullets in the windshield. Later that night when things quieted down, John and I were having a cup of coffee and talking.

I asked Big John, "Why do you think the cops shot at those guys so much? It was just a stolen car for Christ's sake."

"That's cops for ya."

"Want to see something interesting?" he asked.

"Yeah."

"Come over here." Big John put his heavy arm around me and walked me over to the jewelry store just next to the front door of the Black Iris.

"See that?" he said pointing to an almost clean bullet hole about five feet high in the window.

"Jesus, I was standing right there!"

"I know. That's why I tackled you. You were almost a better target than the car thieves."

"Thanks, John. You saved my life."

"Well, I don't know about that. But you really should get a hearing aid."

"I know. My mom would get a kick out of that."

"Out of what?"

"Tell her I need a hearing aid so I can hear gunshots."

Big John laughed so hard his whole body shook. He took out his handkerchief to dry his eyes. "You're a kick Larry, a real kick."

"John, I've been meaning to ask you something."

"Something you thought of while we were under the car?" He started laughing again.

I smiled, "No, actually before that, like for a week."

"Ask away."

"You know Johnny Mathis is coming to play here in a couple of weeks…"

"Stop. Let me guess, you've got a girlfriend you'd like to impress?"

"Well, I just met her, really, and she really loves Johnny Mathis, and I said I might be able to get us in. No, I said I *would* be able to get us in. I guess I really stuck my neck out."

"Give me a couple of minutes. Watch the door. What's your girl's name?"

"Frankie."

He went inside the club. A few minutes later, he came back smiling. "Well, even though the show's sold out, Larry and Frankie are down for Friday, May 16, first show, eight PM."

"Oh God, John, thank you, thank you, thank you!"

"And, Larry," he added, "front-row seats."

"No way! Really? God, she is gonna be so happy. She won't believe it!"

"Compliments of the Black Iris."

"And you, John. You didn't have to grease any palms, did you?"

"Nope, I just told Gino that Larry and his girl Frankie want to see Johnny Mathis. That was it."

"Thanks, John."

"You already thanked me. Thank the bosses."

◆ ◆ ◆

On Monday I went to school and I could hardly wait to see Frankie. I wanted to tell her the big news. At lunch I saw her in the cafeteria with her friends. I waved from across the room and motioned her over to my table. I watched her closely as she came over to where I was. I liked watching how confidently she moved. As usual, she looked stunning, even in everyday clothes.

"Hi, Hot Shot. What are you up to?" Her bright blue eyes shining just as they always did.

"Looking for you."

"Oh, I'm flattered. I was kind of hoping to see you, too. How was your weekend?"

"Except for almost getting shot, it was good. I worked the Black Iris."

"Really? You drive someone's car a little too crazy?" she laughed.

"No, it wasn't a customer. There was a shootout on the street."

"You like living dangerously, don't you?"

"Hey, I didn't ask for the shootout. I was just standing there when it happened."

"What I meant was that you like that kind of excitement."

"Yeah, I guess I do. Breaks the monotony."

"Somehow I don't imagine much about your life is monotonous."

"Well, anyway, guess what?"

"We're going to the movies this weekend?"

"Well, I was going to call you this last weekend, but you didn't give me your number."

"Shame. Well, I'll give it to you now, if you promise to call and ask me to go to the movies."

"OK, shoot." I got out a pencil.

"LA5-2416."

"Listen, thanks for your number, but why don't I ask you now."

"I'm waiting."

"Frankie, do you want to go to the movies this weekend?"

"Yes, Larry, let's go to the movies this weekend."

"What day?"

"You pick."

"Friday."

"Friday's not the weekend."

"I know, but I have to work the weekend."

"OK, I'll take Friday. What time?"

"What do you want to see?"

"*The Four Hundred Blows*. It's a new French film by Truffaut."

"I don't know French or anything about it, but sure." I wondered how to spell Truefoe.

"You don't have to know French. It has subtitles, silly"

It was almost the end of lunch, and I knew the bell was about to ring.

"Frankie, before you go, I have some good news."

"Oh?" She smiled expectantly.

"We're going to see Johnny Mathis."

"You're kidding."

"Nope, serious."

Frankie started jumping up and down and screaming so loud everyone in the cafeteria turned around.

Then she shouted so loud that everyone could hear, "We're going to see Johnny Mathis!" It seemed like everyone in the cafeteria broke out laughing.

Then the bell rang. Frankie gave me a huge hug and said, "I can't wait!"

I was so happy. I loved that she was happy. She was radiant.

When she was halfway across the cafeteria, she turned, blew me a kiss, and said, "Call me about Friday."

◆ ◆ ◆

I waited until Thursday to call her. I'm not sure why, but each time I picked up the phone I got serious butterflies and put it back down. I guess I wondered if she really liked me. We were so different, and I would never want her to know where I lived. I finally called, and she seemed happy that I did. I agreed to pick her up at seven Friday night.

On Friday, I got even more serious butterflies. I felt almost a little sick to my stomach and prayed that I wouldn't get another pounding headache. I wasn't looking forward to meeting her parents, even though I bought a new shirt and slacks. I worried about not being able to hear them well and making a fool of myself.

When I arrived at her building, I drove up the driveway to where the doorman stood. It was the same guy I saw there the first time. I got out of my car, said "Hi" to the doorman, and started walking toward the lobby door.

"Er, excuse me, sir," called the doorman. "On whom are you calling?"

"On whom?" I asked.

"Yes, sir, whom are you visiting in the building?"

I wondered about all this "whom" shit. "I'm going to see Frankie Feldman. Why?"

"I need to call you up, sir."

"Why do you need to call me up? You mean call upstairs?"

He had a patronizing little smile. "Yes, sir, I need to inform the Feldmans."

"She knows I'm coming."

"Sir, it's a policy of the building to announce new guests."

I think this guy was enjoying this crap.

"Who shall I say is here?"

I thought it was whom. I forgot the rule. Is it I am here, or me? I wondered. Shit, it didn't matter. "You may say, *sir*, that Larry Pedersen is here," I said sarcastically.

"One moment, sir."

He went to his desk phone. "Good evening, Mr. Feldman. It's Clifford at the door. A young gentleman, Larry Pedersen, is here for Miss Feldman. Yes, sir. Thank you."

"You may go up, sir."

"Thank you, Clifford." I started toward the elevators.

"Er, sir? Your car?"

"The keys are in it."

"Would you mind parking it down at the end of the drive?"

He said it like my car was a piece of shit. Well, I guess it was. "You're the doorman, right?"

"Of course, but we don't park the guests cars unless they are going to the building garage."

"Whatever." Clifford was watching while I parked my car at the bottom of the drive. When I got out of my car I made sure he saw me walk across the grass on my way back to the door.

He had a disapproving look when he opened the door. I thought, "At least he opens the fucking door."

"It's the 18th floor," he said.

I tried to seem casual as I walked to the elevators. The lobby was done up entirely in beige marble. It was so shiny you could see your face in it.

At the elevator, I called back to Clifford, "Which apartment number?"

"It's the 18th *floor*. That *is* the apartment, sir."

"Oh." I thought I had them in check, but my butterflies came back in full force. I felt queasy.

When the elevator got to the 18th floor, the doors opened onto a foyer of light blue marble. There was a thick light and dark blue oriental carpet in front of two large doors with brass handles; one door was partly open. The colors of the carpet reminded me of my Deuces jacket. Then the door opened completely.

"Hello, you must be Larry. I'm Frankie's father, John Feldman."

"Hi, Mr. Feldman. Nice to meet you." We shook hands. My hands were sweaty.

"Please come in and sit down, Larry. Frankie is almost ready." He had an accent I didn't recognize. But fortunately, he spoke loudly enough, and I could read his lips pretty well. I still couldn't relax, but hearing him helped a little.

As we walked into the living room, the place looked like something out of a magazine. Everything was of some shade of blue; even the carpet was light blue. Large windows spanned the entire living room, looking out across Lake Michigan.

"Have a seat, Larry." Mr. Feldman motioned with an opened hand to a couch next to his chair. I assumed it was his chair because it was a large dark blue leather armchair with a folded newspaper on it. Next to it was a tall brass lamp with a black lampshade. It looked like a throne.

I sat down nervously and crossed my left leg so it rested on my right knee.

Mr. Feldman moved his newspaper and sat down in his chair. "So, tell me Larry, where are you from? You have an interesting accent." As he asked me that I got of whiff of what smelled like dog shit.

"Uh, it's not really an accent. Er, I live, not close by, I live farther south, near Old Town." That was as close as I could say without giving away my neighborhood.

"That's not what...? Oh, the Near North, is it?"

"Yes, sir, the Near North." Just after I said that, I looked down and noticed that there was dog shit on the bottom of my left shoe. *Oh, Jesus Christ.*

Fortunately, Frankie popped into the room. She was dressed casually in white jeans and a black sweater. She looked lovely.

"Hi, Larry, so you met my dad? You need to meet my mom, too."

All I wanted to do was get out of there as quickly as possible.

"Oh, uh, sure," I mumbled. All I could think of was the dog shit. Frankie called her mom who was in the kitchen. She came in wearing a crisp white apron over a white silky blouse and black slacks.

"Mom, this is Larry. Larry, my mom."

I got up to greet her, but held my left foot slightly up from the carpet.

"Hi, Mrs. Feldman. Nice to meet you."

"Would you two like some hors d'oeuvres before you go?" she asked.

I thought hors d'oeuvres were only served in restaurants.

Luckily, Frankie chimed in, "No, mom we have to get going. The movie is at eight."

"Nice to meet you both," I said.

"It's our pleasure, Larry," her dad said.

Frankie and I walked out the front door to the elevator. Actually, I sort of hobbled.

"Have a nice evening," her mother called out to us.

In the elevator, I prayed the scent of the dog shit stayed away.

Then Frankie asked, "What's wrong with your foot?"

"Er, nothing. I stepped in some dog shit." I blushed.

"Oh, my gosh. Why didn't you say something upstairs? We could have cleaned it off."

"I was too embarrassed."

"Larry, I'm so sorry. That must have been terrible for you."

"Yeah, great first impression, huh?" We both laughed.

In the lobby it looked like Clifford was just finishing cleaning up some spots of dog shit from the beige marble floor. He looked up. "Evening, Miss Feldman."

"Hi, Clifford. This is my friend Larry."

"Yes, ma'am. We met."

"Night, Clifford," I said smiling.

Clifford called to Frankie as we went out the front door. "Miss Feldman, be sure to avoid the grass." Frankie and I both laughed to ourselves.

When I got to the car, I cleaned my shoe with some rags from the trunk, but by then most of the dog shit was gone. Then I stopped at a gas station to wash my hands.

At the theater, which was fancier than I was used to, I asked Frankie if she wanted some popcorn. I hoped she didn't so I wouldn't have to put my hands in it after all they had been through. I'm sure it passed her mind, too.

"No, thanks. I'm fine."

The movie was a story about a poor, neglected French boy named Antoine. He was always getting into trouble for no good reason. In one scene when he was in his bed at night, I started to feel the mask above my head. It was the first time I had ever felt it when I was not in bed. It made me feel nervous. I got an uncomfortable feeling in my chest; it felt a little hard to breathe and I started to get a pounding headache. Frankie must have noticed because she put her hand lightly on top of mine. At first I enjoyed the feeling, her touch was warm, soft, and comforting. But the discomfort in my chest didn't stop, and I began to feel restless.

"I'll be right back," I said. I went outside. Standing outside the theater in the cool night air made it feel easier to breathe, but the pain in my temple throbbed each time my heart beat. I don't know how long I stood there but, before long, Frankie appeared beside me. She put her hand on my arm, "Are you all right?"

"I'm fine. I guess I just needed some fresh air. It was stuffy in there."

"We don't have to go back. Do you want to take a walk?"

"Sure, that'd be good."

We walked down Michigan Avenue in silence, holding hands. I noticed its bright streetlights, the fancy clothing stores like Bonwit Teller and Saks Fifth Avenue, and the famous Water Tower that was always illuminated at night. This was Chicago's fashionable "Magnificent Mile." Frankie broke my thoughts with a question, "Larry, was there something in the movie that bothered you?"

"Hmm, I think so, but I'm not sure what it was."

"Antoine reminded me of you."

"How so?"

"Well, maybe his vulnerability, his always getting into trouble, his parent's neglect."

"I'm not vulnerable; I can take care of myself." I knew I sounded a bit defensive.

"I don't mean on the outside. I know you're strong in a lot of ways. I admire that, but what I really mean is on the inside."

"Well, doctor, what's on the inside?"

"I'm sorry. I'm not trying to be Freud. I don't mean to pry or analyze you. I just think you're a lot different on the inside from what you appear to be on the outside."

Froyed? I didn't know who she was talking about. I promised myself I'd look him up later.

"You like what's on the inside?"

"Yes, very much. I think you're intelligent, sensitive, and have a good heart."

"Are you going to be a psychologist?"

Frankie smiled beautifully and said, "No, I'm going to study English literature at the University of Wisconsin, I hope."

"You're going away to school? You already have a school picked out?"

"Of course, you have to get ready early. I already took my entrance exams."

"Hmmm." I didn't even know about entrance exams. I didn't know that much about colleges either; no one in my family ever went to college.

"And you, what are your plans?" she asked.

"I don't have any. I guess I'll just get a job and try to move out of my neighborhood."

"Why do you want to get out of your neighborhood?"

"I just do. It's not really important."

We went back to the car, and I drove back to Frankie's place. We parked in the same place we did the first time. We were quiet; Frankie was sitting right next to me. I could smell her hair and perfume. I put my arm around her and pulled her closer, burying my face in her hair. Then she turned her face directly to mine, our lips touched lightly at first, our bodies pressed closer together, and I could feel the warmth of her leg against mine. I felt her lips open slightly, her warm tongue gently parting my lips. When our tongues touched, it was electrifying, something I never felt before. Then we stopped. I wanted to keep kissing her, but the pain in my head started up again.

"I better let you go," I said.

"Night, Larry. Thanks for the movie and the evening."

"Thanks for talking to me."

Frankie got out of the car and walked toward the lobby doors. I opened my door and called to her, "Tell Clifford I'm sorry about the dog shit." She laughed hard, then waved goodbye.

7

Johnny Mathis

As I drove home from Frankie's I wondered if this was what it felt like to be in love. I had never been in love before. I'm not even sure I loved my mother. I loved my sister, Christie, but that was different. I tried saying to myself, "I love Frankie." It felt right. Frankie was very smart, confident, insightful, aware of herself, knew what she wanted, sensitive, and gentle. She seemed genuinely happy. I didn't think I had ever been genuinely happy. Sometimes I was happy about something that happened, or about something I got. But that feeling always passed, leaving me as I usually felt. I decided that most of the time I felt genuinely unhappy.

When I got home I looked for Froyed in my dictionary. It took me awhile to figure out it was Freud. It said: "Freud, Sigmund. 1859–1939. Austrian founder of psychoanalysis." There was a small picture of him; he looked liked William Q. Judge. I didn't know where Austria was or what psychoanalysis was. I liked my dictionary. It was one of my few books. Another book I had was *The Catcher in the Rye*. I read it only because one of my teachers said it was banned in some places. I figured if it was banned, there had to be something good in it. I liked the character Holden and his little sister, Phoebe. As I said before, Holden used to try to wipe off the "Fuck you" scribbles so his little sister wouldn't see it. I liked them both so much I started calling Christie Phoebe. She liked that, too. Anyway, I decided I would find out more about Freud. Maybe reading his book could help me figure out why I was always unhappy.

The next time I worked the Black Iris I took my dinner break and went around the corner to the bookstore on Michigan Avenue. I had never been inside a bookstore before. This one looked like it was for rich people because it had nice carpets and dark wooden bookcases. The clerk was a middle-aged guy with only a little graying hair left on the sides that he combed from one side straight over his bald top and down the other side. He wore a tweed suit and bow tie and had wire-rimmed half-glasses set halfway down his nose. He looked like a librarian, except he was twirling a pencil around his fingers like a girl with a baton.

"Do you have Freud's book?" I asked.

"Which one?" he asked smiling. "There are quite a few."

I took a chance and said, "The one about why everyone is unhappy." He looked at my hiker's uniform. I hoped he wasn't going to ask me if I was unhappy.

"Do you mean *Civilization and Its Discontents*?"

"Yeah, that's it." I didn't know if that was it or not, but it was a start.

"You'll find that in the psychology section on the back wall. Authors are listed alphabetically. Would you like me to go with you?"

"No, thanks. I'll find it."

He smiled at me again, looking me up and down. "Let me know if you need more help."

The back wall had a lot of psychology books, and from the number of books by Freud, it looked as if he wrote most of them. *Civilization and Its Discontents* was there, and it was kind of small compared to the rest of his books. There was a much bigger one called *The Interpretation of Dreams* that I thought might be interesting since I had such weird dreams, but I thought I would wait until I finished this one. I brought my book to the clerk.

"So you found it?" He was smiling again, still twirling his pencil.

"Yep, just the one I was looking for."

He took my money, pushed the change into my palm, and said, "Well, do come by again."

He was friendly; maybe a little too friendly.

I read the whole book that night in bed. For a small book, it sure had lots of words I had to look up in my dictionary. It didn't give any real answers to unhappiness except that I got the idea that Freud thought unhappiness is just part of being alive. He seemed to be saying that religion was just something people made up to keep themselves from going even more nuts than they already were. And civilization was just a way to keep our anger under control. I thought his idea about the "death instinct" was interesting but pretty scary—and Freud didn't make any promises about how the whole civilization thing was going to end up. He sounded a bit sour about it. Even though I think I was unhappier after I read it, it opened my eyes to some things I never thought about before. I thought next time I would get his dream book.

◆ ◆ ◆

The next week was our date to see Johnny Mathis. I went to Frankie's place to pick her up and avoided the grass when I parked my car. Clifford was tolerating me and even said, "Good evening, Larry." He turned and glanced at my shoes as I walked by.

Frankie looked stunning in her slightly low-cut, long black gown. It must have cost a fortune. She had black patent leather shoes and a simple string of pearls around her slender neck. She also smelled great.

"You look beautiful," I said.

"Thank you. I dressed to please you, and Johnny too."

"He'll be impressed, I'm sure. Tonight you have a bad boy *and* Johnny Mathis."

"That's a first. What more could a girl ask for? It's perfect."

"Maybe a nicer car."

"Want to take mine?"

"Your dad's?"

"No, mine. I have my own car."

"Sure, why not. I'm sure it's nicer than mine."

"Yours has more character, but let's take mine."

"Give me a second. I'll be right back." She walked back to Clifford, said a few words, and handed him her keys.

A few minutes later Clifford came driving out of the building garage in a gorgeous, new, perfectly clean, white Ford convertible. He got out and handed Frankie the keys.

Frankie nudged me with the keys. "You mind driving?"

"I'd love to. I only get the chance to drive cars like this when I'm hiking them."

"Well, tonight, it's all yours."

When we got to the Black Iris and Big John saw us pull up to the door, he had a huge smile when he opened Frankie's door.

"You got the wheels to go with the evening. I hope you didn't rent this," he said.

"Nope, it's Frankie's."

"Frankie, this is Big John. John, Frankie." They shook hands.

One of those huge airplane lights sat on the corner; its beacon slowly swept back and forth across the night sky.

"Did you put that there so we wouldn't get lost?" I joked.

"Yeah, we figured you'd know to follow the big light in the sky. Well, you kids better go on in. Gino's got your table waiting."

Inside the club, it took a moment for my eyes to adjust to the dark, but then I saw Gino in his black tux. He was at the *maitre d's* stand with its small brass lamp looking over the reservations book. He looked up and called, "Larry!" and motioned us toward him. We walked over to him. "And this beautiful young lady must be Frankie," he said, taking her hand and kissing the back of it. "Come right this way." He led us to our table, right smack in front of the darkened stage with long black velvet curtains at the back of it. Gino pulled out a chair for Frankie. "Enjoy the show."

Frankie was wide eyed. She reached over, took my hand, and said, "Larry, this has got to be the best table in the house!"

"Only the best for you." Actually, *I* was impressed.

In a few minutes Nicola, our waiter, came by. "*Buona sera, come va*, Larry?"

"*Buona sera*, Nicola."

"Nicola, meet Frankie."

"A pleasure, Frankie."

"Larry, I didn't know you spoke Italian," Frankie said.

"I don't. Nicola's trying to teach me. That's about all I know so far."

"So what you gonna have?" Nicola asked. "*Lista?*"

"Frankie, you want something to eat?"

"I'm too nervous to eat. Maybe a Coke?"

"Nicola, a Coke and a 7 & 7."

"Larry, you gonna get me in trouble."

"Ok, two Cokes."

Nicola returned in a minute with a Coke and a 7 & 7. "*Buon divertimento!*"

"*Grazie*, Nicola."

"Everyone seems to really like you here…" Frankie started but Gino started to announce Johnny Mathis. The bottom of the microphone stand was right in front of us.

A moment later, there was a long applause as Johnny Mathis walked into the spotlight. He stood right in front of us and began his first song, "Chances Are." As he sang, he looked right down on Frankie. Tears welled up in her eyes. I put my hand on hers to stop the rattling of the ice cubes in her Coke.

The show was great; he sang all of our favorite songs. Fortunately, Frankie didn't cry through most of the performance. I was a little afraid people were looking at us, but I loved seeing her so happy. When the show was over, we said goodnight to Nicola and Gino.

"*Grazie, grazie*, Nicola. We had a wonderful time." I pushed some bills toward Nicola's hand, but he pushed them back.

"*Prego*, Larry."

Nicola took Frankie's hand and kissed it, "*Piacere*, Frankie."

Outside the club our car was in the Number One spot. All we had to do was walk five feet to it. Big John was holding the door for Frankie and had a flat paper bag under his arm. After she was in, he came around to my side and quietly said, "Give this to her later." I tried to give him some money, but he refused, "It's on the house."

On the way home, Frankie was quiet but beaming. I parked in the apartment building garage.

"Larry, tonight was the best time of my life." I noticed her tears had smeared her mascara. She still looked beautiful.

"It was for me, too. Mostly because you were so happy."

She leaned over, and we kissed for a long time. Her lips made my whole body feel like a surge of wild current was running through it. I rested my left hand on the silky covering of her thigh; it felt smooth and warm. She put her hand on top of mine, and I thought she was going to make me move it. Instead, she raised my hand to cover her breast. It was both soft and firm. That was the first time I felt a breast. It lasted only a moment, and then she pulled my hand away.

"We better stop, Larry."

"Uh, yeah, I guess we should." The last thing I wanted was to stop.

Just as we got out of the car, she said, "Know what? We forgot to get his autograph."

"Wait a second." I reopened the door and pulled out the flat bag Big John gave me and handed it to her.

"John said to give this to you."

She opened the bag and inside was the album *Johnny's Greatest Hits*. The cover was signed, "To Frankie, All my Best, Johnny Mathis." Tears came to her eyes causing her mascara to run again. She gave me a long hug. Some of her mascara got on my shirt but I loved it. I loved Frankie.

8

Lincoln Avenue

Almost hidden in the dark corner of our smoky, cluttered living room, Bud slouched in his beat-up light green Stratolounger. The shadows on one side of his face from the weak light of a black plastic horse lamp made him look like just another piece of clutter. He held a can of Budweiser in one hand and picked at the cracks in the armrest with the other. Two crumpled cans laid next to his chair. He was watching his pride and joy, a blond-wood Zenith television with a small circular screen. Its flickering light danced across his face. That evening it was working. Even when it didn't, Christie sat in front of it with her frayed pink "blankie" and watched it anyway. Once I stopped to tell her there was no picture. She just said, "I know, but I can hear it." I thought that was pretty cute. Maybe she made up the picture in her head.

The rest of the front room was crammed with cardboard boxes and other junk, even under the two end tables. No empty space was safe from the stuff my mom refused to get rid of. Even the carpet was fucked up. Staring up like a misshapen black eye was an iron burn in the middle of it. I couldn't even imagine how it got there. The sofa, with its worn red and gold fibers and broken springs, sat in front of the living room windows. Behind the sofa, tightly knotted, smoke-stained curtains showed windowsills that Christie used to chew on. In the other corner, a small bookcase painted black held several pink and white plaster curios and a yellow porcelain pig from Maxwell Street. Alongside them were the only books in the apartment: a couple of Zane Grey cowboy stories and a few copies of Reader's Digest that belonged to my stepdad.

When I thought about where I lived, I knew I could never let Frankie know about it. I also knew I could never introduce her to my family. Christie was the only person I would ever want her to meet, and then I don't know how I would do that.

I decided to watch TV with Bud while I waited for Dino and his girlfriend, Eve, to get ready. We were going to go to Lincoln Avenue so Eve could be fitted for a prom dress. Eve was pregnant, but you couldn't tell; she still looked like her normal self. They were going to have to get married after her graduation. For some reason, her old man insisted that she go through with her graduation before they got married. Her family was Syrian, and her dad had the biggest belly I ever saw. He loved to eat in their yard in the summer. When he finished eating and there were leftovers, he'd just throw them over his shoulder and say, "Back to nature." Funny guy.

There was a war movie on television, and I could tell from his fidgeting that Bud wanted to turn it off. As I expected, he said, "Turn that damn thing off!" We were watching a scene in which a soldier lay dying, talking to his buddy.

"Oh, people don't die like that," I said.

Suddenly, Bud was shouting at me from the edge of his chair. "You goddamned right they die like that! You goddamn right! Right here, in these arms they died like that! What the hell do you know? Did you ever close the eyes of a friend who just died? You're still wet behind the ears, and you think you already know everything." Tears began streaming down his cheeks. He angrily wiped at them. I never saw him cry before, and I somehow knew he really hated that he was. He quickly got up from his chair and half-stumbled to his room. I was baffled because he hadn't shouted at me like that since the time he came to pick me up from the police station. And he never talked about the war. The only thing he ever said was that he didn't want to talk about it and, "You'll have your own war."

I *always* wanted to talk about it. That shit was what was happening when I was born! I saw a lot of war films, and I liked them. What about Audie Murphy? Man, he was my war hero. He was a real person, and he even played in his own movie, *To Hell and Back*. He really kicked ass over there. He joined the army when he was eighteen and, by the end of the war, he was decorated nine times, including the Medal of Honor. He was the most celebrated combat soldier in World War II.

If it weren't for American soldiers like him the whole world would be one big Germany by now. My mind spilled over with scenes from television, magazines, and newspapers about the invasion of Normandy, with its bloody beaches and piles of skeletons discovered in the concentration camps. They bulldozed bodies into big holes in the ground like piles of garbage. I wanted Bud to tell me about those things and to explain why the Germans would do that. I didn't understand why he wouldn't talk about it. How could he *not* want to talk about that? He was part of it. He was there. He saw it! Damn right, I would have my war; and I would kick ass just like Audie Murphy did.

Dino and Eve finally came out. Eve looked pretty. She was tiny next to Dino. She had long black hair and deep red lipstick. She always looked and smelled fresh and clean like Irish Spring soap. She took good care of herself. I liked her.

"What's the matter with Bud?" she asked.

"I guess I upset him talking about the war."

"Ahh, he drinks too much," Dino chimed in.

Eve looked at Dino with a frown. "He was *crying*, Dino."

"Whatever. Larry, you ready to go?"

"Yep." I was glad to get out of the house. I felt sorry for Bud because he never seemed happy, even when he drank. And the war thing really got to him. If a car backfired in the street while he was sleeping, he shot out of his bed in a split second, running around the house in his underwear with a stunned look.

We drove to the prom shop on Lincoln Avenue in Dino's '54 Olds coupe. It was black on top and light yellow on the bottom and had glass-pack mufflers. The roar of those mufflers followed by their sudden silence always signaled Dino was home.

Dino and I sat in the lobby waiting for Eve while she tried on a couple of pastel-colored dresses. Four guys came in to talk to one of the clerks. They looked like punks, and I thought they were going to try to rob the place, but I guess they knew the clerk. When they were finished talking to her they walked past me, but one of them stopped in front of me, looked down, and said, "Fuck you!"

In those days, that was not something you said unless you wanted your ass kicked. I jumped up and followed them outside; sure that Dino would be right behind me. When I got outside, I grabbed the arm of the guy who said, "fuck you," and pulled him away from the front of the prom shop toward the dinette shop next door. "What did you say, asshole?"

"I said, *'fuck you.'*"

Then I noticed the three other guys standing just behind him. Shit. I knew I had to finish what I started, so I slammed him in the mouth. He went right down, but then his friends jumped in, and we instantly became a jumble of raging arms, legs, and fists. After awhile, I wasn't sure who I was hitting and who was hitting me. I knew I had taken some pretty hard blows to my face and some kicks in the stomach. It was strange because after awhile I didn't feel any pain; the punches and kicks just seemed like dull thuds. I finally went down to my knees and, before I saw it coming, one of them kicked me in the chest so hard I went crashing through the huge storefront window. It must have been eight feet high and at least as wide.

After I went through it, I landed on the inside floor of the store. I turned around and saw a shocked salesman and a woman customer standing behind me. Both of their mouths were wide open. I think they had just been looking at the dinette set I knocked over as I came through the window. I was already a bloody mess; blood and shattered glass were all over the place. When I tried to get back outside the window, I stepped on some glass and slipped back. The fall forced me to sit down on the jagged bottom of the window. Just then I had one of those slow motion experiences you see in movies. I looked up and noticed a large pane of broken glass still hanging from the top of the window—my fall had jarred it loose. I tried again to get up just as the sheet dropped. It raced down at me like a guillotine. I knew that if I hadn't moved fast enough it would have cut my head off. I was halfway out when I felt it slice through the back of my jacket, cutting it almost in half.

As I stood outside the window, the guys I was fighting had taken off. A crowd of people was staring at me. That's when I noticed Dino quietly standing there, his hands in his pockets, smirking—an image I couldn't forget. He never got into the fight; he had just stood there watching the whole thing. I became aware that my pants were sticking to my skin and could feel the warmth of blood running down the backs of my legs. My shoes felt squishy; they were full of blood. Blood seemed to be everywhere. I could taste it.

"That was a lousy fuckin' fight," Dino said. "Let's go."

I wanted to say, "Fuck you!" but couldn't find the words. I felt dizzy, weak, and very tired. I couldn't sit in Dino's car because when I tried I felt a shearing, sharp pain in my ass, so I rode to the hospital facing backward on my knees. My nose felt like it was on the other side of my face. The night was black and getting blacker by the moment. The last thing I remembered was hearing someone say, "We've got a bleeder here." We were in the hospital, and I was hurriedly put on a gurney and wheeled into the emergency room—the same place I brought Tiny after our fight with the Warlords. I must have passed out again because I don't know how long I was there. I woke to the muffled sound of doctors talking. Something about "thirty sutures, broken nose, dislocated shoulder, two pints of blood." Then one of them looked at me. "You awake, son?"

"Yeah, I guess."

"How are you feeling?"

"I have a horrible headache on the right side of my head."

"Is it throbbing?"

"Yeah."

"It's a migraine. We'll give you something for it but, we need to keep you here overnight. You've lost a lot of blood, and we want to make sure you're stable before we release you. We had to remove a lot of glass pieces from your cuts and put in quite a few stitches. You're lucky, you know. From what your brother said about your fight, it could have been worse; you could have been decapitated."

Then I remembered the image of Dino standing there, watching. I wondered if he smiled or laughed when he told them. It wouldn't have surprised me. The bastard watched while I almost got killed. My mind went back to his smile. It was almost as if he enjoyed it. If he had helped me, we could have easily kicked their asses. I once saw him fight four guys by himself, and when he was finished, they were all on the ground.

This shouldn't have happened. I never lost a fight, but I felt stupid for not being more careful. And stupid that I trusted Dino would be there for me. Then I felt ashamed, but more than shame; for the first time I felt like I hated Dino.

My guys came to see me in the hospital. They wanted revenge. They wanted to put together a search party and find the bastards who did this to me.

"What about Dino, man. Wasn't he there?" Eddie asked.

"He was there."

"Didn't he help you?"

"Nope. He was a fuckin' spectator. Didn't raise a finger." I felt ashamed that he hadn't, but I wanted my guys to know what a bastard he was.

"Jesus, he's your fuckin' brother, man. What's with him anyway?"

"I don't know. I really don't know."

When I got out of the hospital, I tried to stay low for a few days. I looked like shit. I didn't want Frankie to see me. School was almost over, and maybe she wouldn't have to see me. She had mentioned a going away party, but I wasn't sure I'd go.

I decided to visit my friend Sal in the West Side projects. I hadn't seen him in a long time. He had heard about my fight and wanted to see me. Sal and I grew up together in the old neighborhood, but his family had moved to the West Side projects to get out of the Near North. We met in the dark and isolated inner courtyard of the projects. There was nothing in it but a concrete basketball court and a few benches.

It was late at night and while we sat on a bench catching up on old times, about fifteen Cobras came into the inner courtyard. They wore their yellow and green gang jackets with a Cobra insignia on the back. Since they were one of the best known and feared gangs in Chicago, I was glad we knew them. Even the police used to avoid the projects because of them. I remembered Sal saying that just the day before they had castrated some guy with a broken beer bottle. As they got closer, it was obvious that they were all really fucked up on drugs and beer. Their eyes were so dazed that they looked like they couldn't see straight. They came walking, half stumbling, over to the bench where we were sitting.

The leader of the Cobras came up to us first. He was a mean bastard called "Scarface" because his face got messed up in one of their rumbles.

Scarface was looking at me. "Well, look at you. You sure got fucked now didn't you?" he mumbled through a twisted smile and glazed half-shut eyes.

"What's happening?" I imagined him shoving a broken beer bottle in my crotch.

"Whaaats happenin' is you are about to get *even more* fucked up," he laughed.

"What's the problem? You know us," Sal said.

"Cuz I know you doesn't mean I like you, Sal. Never have. And I like your pretty-face friend Larry even less."

"C'mon Scarface, he's already been through a lot of shit."

"An' about to go through some more, I would say. Both of you."

He turned to his guys and said, "Who's got two empty bottles?" A couple of them shuffled forward with beer bottles. "Break off the bottoms of those," Scarface ordered. "Now my guys here are gonna hold these bottles by your pretty faces. If you lift a hand to fight back, the bottles go in your faces. Got that?"

There was nothing we could do when Scarface and a couple of his thugs started beating on us. Any time it looked like we might fight back, the bottles came closer to our faces. We just let them beat us until they were finished. They left both of us on the ground in front of the bench. People in their apartments around the courtyard who heard what was going on just closed their windows and turned out their lights.

We eventually limped out of the courtyard.

Sal's face looked terrible; both his eyes were nearly swollen shut. He was enraged. "This is war! We're going to get those bastards, and they're going to pay for this."

"We'll organize it tomorrow," I said. "Rest up tonight. I'll call you tomorrow. I'll get my guys, and you let Smitty know. He'll love the chance to get enough of us together to get Scarface." Our friend Smitty hated Scarface because he had made a pass at Smitty's sister.

On my way home, I noticed my pants and the car seat felt wet. My stitches had broken open. I felt my nose under the bandages and brace. It didn't feel like it was where it was supposed to be. At home, I put some old T-shirts in my pants.

I pulled my nose back to where it should have been, and it caused a massive nosebleed. I wasn't going to go back to that hospital again.

The next day I was too fucked up to go to school and now I was sure I did not want Frankie to see me. Sal and I organized a war on the Cobras for the next night. We went all out and brought in whomever we could. By my count, we had three gangs: a hundred guys and twenty cars. The plan was to keep it quiet as much as we could and take the Cobras by surprise. Late at night, after the Cobras were in the courtyard, we would surround the West Side projects with the cars. Our guys would enter the courtyard from all five possible entrances; twenty guys would come in through each passageway. Sal and I would come in last. Once they were in the courtyard, they would form a tight circle and close ranks around the Cobras. Smitty's guys brought guns, real guns, not zips. I told them not to use them unless they had to. I didn't want a murder beef topping off my troubles.

The Cobras were in the courtyard, drinking beer, and laughing. We streamed quietly into the courtyard, surrounding them. I saw one of them poke his buddy in the ribs and raise his chin toward us. They went silent as the circle drew closer around them. The slamming of a few windows above broke the silence. The sight of a hundred of us surrounding the eighteen of them with baseball bats, chains, and knives, must have scared the shit out of them. I noticed Scarface trying to duck behind some of his guys. "Fuckin' chicken," I thought. Then the circle parted and Sal and I walked in. We stood in front of the Cobras.

"Scarface!" Sal screamed. "Get out here, you yellow piece of shit!"

Scarface slowly crept out from his hiding place.

"Get down on your knees," Sal said.

Scarface just stood there. "Hey, man, we didn't know what we were doing. We didn't recognize you."

"But you do now, right?" I said.

"Sure, man, I know you. I know Sal. Of course, man."

"And because we know you doesn't mean we have to like you, right Scarface?"

"Down on your fucking knees, asshole!" Sal said.

Scarface got down on his knees in front of Sal. "Man, I'm telling you we were fucked up. We didn't know what we were doing."

"Well, I *know* what I'm doing, Scarface. Smitty, give me your gun."

Smitty stepped forward from the circle and handed Sal a chrome snub-nosed .38. Sal took the gun and pushed the barrel into the side of Scarface's head.

"You think your face is fucked up now? Do you know what it's gonna look like when I blow half your ugly fuckin' head off?"

"Please, man, don't shoot me, please."

"Turn around and face the rest of your assholes."

"Please, man, don't do it." Scarface slowly turned around on his knees.

"Tell your guys what a cheap fucking coward you are."

"I…I…I'm a, a cheap fuckin' coward."

Sal turned to me. "Larry, you want to shoot him?"

"Yeah, but first I want him to say he's sorry."

Sal handed me the gun. It felt cool and heavier than I thought it would be. It felt good in my hand. I hoped the safety was off, because I didn't want to seem stupid if I had to look for it. I never held a .38 before.

Scarface turned his head toward me. "I'm sorry, man. Jesus. I said I'm sorry, didn't I? I'm really sorry, man. Please don't shoot me!"

"Turn around so I don't have to see your ugly face." I cocked the gun. The safety was off, and my hand was trembling a little. I hoped nobody noticed.

"Oh no, man, please!" Scarface started crying when he heard the gun cock.

I pointed the barrel of the .38 just to the side of his head and fired. The gun jumped in my hand. He flipped over like he was shot, screaming. The shot was a lot louder than I expected. My ears stung and started ringing.

"You didn't shoot him!" Sal said.

"Fuck him. It's better this way. Now he has to live with it." I knew I wasn't going to shoot him. I just wanted to scare the shit out of him.

Sal went over to him and started kicking him, in the back, the face, all over. I don't know how long he kicked him, but he looked almost as dead as if I'd shot him. When he was finished kicking him, Sal took out his dick and pissed on Scarface. That was a first.

"*This is your leader!*" Sal screamed at the Cobras. "Any of you *ever, ever* fuck with us again—you're dead."

"Let's go, Sal."

Sal waved our guys out.

◆ ◆ ◆

I went home and snuck into my room. For some reason I felt a little afraid. On the streets, I wasn't used to being afraid. Since I was in the Deuces, I don't remember ever being scared. Usually, we were the ones someone feared. I liked the sense of power and style we had. It was an attitude that said, "If you like your life, don't fuck with us." Something about shooting that .38 at Scarface bothered me. The stupid bastard was probably going to be as deaf as I was—at least in one ear. I knew I wasn't going to shoot him, but I also knew if I hadn't taken the gun from Sal he might have.

That night as I tried to sleep, the image of piss-soaked Scarface, screaming and lying on the ground, blood dripping from his mouth and nose, haunted me for a long time. The mask was there again; its buzz grew louder, almost a roar—much more intense than I had ever heard before.

9

Detention Camp

The next morning Bud was at the kitchen table in his underwear hunched over his coffee. The drooping ash from his cigarette fell. "Joe Casellti called."

"Your ash just fell in your coffee."

"So what? You miss an appointment?"

"No, I don't have to go until next week."

"Well, he wants your ass downtown today. You in some kind of trouble again? It's the fights, isn't it?"

"I don't think so."

When Joe looked up and saw me come into the Probation Department, he quickly let the guy he was talking to go and motioned me to come in. He was fingering the bowl of his pipe. He seemed fidgety, which was different for him. "Larry, Larry, what am I going to do?"

"What's the problem?"

"The *problem*, my friend, is you've been contracted."

"By who? For what? Besides, what do you know?"

"Larry, don't insult me. You know for what and by whom. I can't reveal my sources."

"The Cobras?"

"Good guess, my friend. I would have guessed Dino would be contracted, not you. You're going to have to leave the city."

"Right, just go hop a bus somewhere?"

"No, you're going to camp for the rest of the summer. I've made arrangements for you."

"Camp, like a Boy Scout camp?"

"No, not Boy Scout camp. Juvenile detention camp."

"This is like a bust."

"It's not a bust, but technically because of your three fights…"

"*Three* fights? The second one wasn't…"

"Don't interrupt me. I can count. Your three fights and using a gun; you are seriously in violation of your probation so I have the authority to do what I want with you. I'm not doing it as a bust. I'm doing it to protect you from the danger you're in. You obviously don't have the ability, or the sense, to protect yourself. If I send you to Juvie, you'll be in at least as much danger as you are on the streets. Larry, I can't impress you enough with how serious this is. The Cobras are the worst gang you could mess with, and you guys almost killed their leader. They're going to be gunning for you and Sal if it's the last thing they ever do. I'm not even sure your family is safe."

I immediately thought of Christie.

"I'm going to put out a rumor on the street that you left Chicago."

"You're going to lie for me?"

"It's not exactly a lie. But I am going to say it's for good. That you went to live with your natural father in Minnesota."

"My father's in Minnesota?"

"I don't *know* where your father is. I'm just saying that to take the heat off."

"What about Sal?"

"Sal's a dead man unless he voluntarily goes to the camp. Since he wasn't arrested and he's not my charge, I have no jurisdiction over him. He would have to agree to be arrested and put on probation. Then I would have jurisdiction."

"That's a new one, agreeing to be arrested."

"It's his only choice. By the way, did he *really* piss on Scarface?"

"News travels fast. Yeah, he did."

"Jesus. Go home and pack for camp. You're leaving tomorrow. Stay off the streets. A van will pick you up at eight in the morning. I'll call your mom."

"Is this camp fenced, guarded?" I wasn't sure why I asked.

"No, it's wide open, but there is a lot of supervision. You'll also be expected to work a regular camp job. Don't even think about leaving. If you do, I'm out of favors. *Capisce?*"

It's funny, I mean like weird funny, but for the first time I got the feeling that Joe cared about me—even though I was a fuck-up.

I'd never been to a camp before. I'd heard of them. The North Avenue Y had a camp, but we could never afford it. They said Johnny Weismiller used to teach swimming there before he became Tarzan.

◆ ◆ ◆

Early the next morning the van arrived like Joe said it would. Bud and mom were still sleeping. They were up late fighting, so I got some of my stuff together and didn't bother to say goodbye to them. I hated their fighting and name-calling. I couldn't hear what they were fighting about, but a good guess would be that it had something to do with Mickey, Dino, and me getting in trouble again. It wasn't hard to imagine that Bud wondered what he got himself into when he married my mom and adopted three fucked-up kids. I was just as relieved to be getting out of Chicago as I imagined Bud and mom were to see me go—and Dino could go fuck himself.

By the time the van arrived at the camp it was almost noon. The air was a lot cooler than it was in the city and didn't have the sooty city smell. We were dropped off by a semicircle of cabins at the end of the road. To the right of the cabins was a large building on a gently sloping hill and, in the distance behind that, a lake. I was assigned to a cabin with seven other guys. On the front of our cabin, there was a carved wooden sign—"Woody Pines." Fitting, I guess. What else are there, plastic pines? The cabin was pretty simple, but it was squeaky clean. It was like a small version of an army barracks like I'd seen in movies. The entrance to the cabin had whitewashed rocks lining the walk up to it. Inside it smelled like bleach or disinfectant. There were no glass windows, only screens with wooden shutter-type things on the outside that could be opened or closed from latches on the inside. Eight single metal beds lined the walls of the cabin. Each had a mattress folded in half on top of it. On top of each mattress were sheets, several towels, and two olive green army blankets. I later found out that, like a lot of stuff here, all these things were Army surplus.

Not long after we arrived, we met Bob Steinberg, our counselor. He was a P.O. from Chicago who worked as a camp counselor during the spring and summer. He had a white T-shirt and khaki shorts. Written on his T-shirt was *Cook County Detention Camp.*

"OK, boys, listen up. Before you go to lunch, we need to orient you to the camp."

"Man, can't we eat first? I'm starving," a clean-cut white guy standing next to me asked. He looked a little familiar. I hoped I was wrong.

"Nope, first things first. And what's your name, hungry boy?"

"Tom Hagen."

"It's 'Tom Hagen, *sir*.'"

"Yes, sir. It's Tom Hagen, *sir*." He was grinning sarcastically. "What a bunch of crap," he muttered.

"That's better, Tom."

"Do we call you Sergeant Steinberg, *sir*?" Tom asked. We all laughed.

"Not unless you want to be called Private Smartass, Tom. Call me Bob."

"No, sir. Tom is fine, sir."

"OK. First some camp rules. You won't see any walls, fences, or barbed wire here. But that doesn't mean you are not in custody. You are here on the honor system. *No one* is to leave the campgrounds *at any time* without my permission. Understood? If you do, you will be immediately sent back to wherever you came from. And I know some of you came from a lot more unpleasant places than this camp. Chow is served three times a day—seven in the morning, noon, and six in the evening. If you miss any of those times, you don't eat until the next mealtime. Each of you will be assigned to a work detail. This is your job as long as you're here. You will be expected to report for that duty at eight in the morning, you get an hour break for lunch, then you work till five in the evening. You will do this five days a week and have the weekends off. You cannot miss work unless you have a medical excuse from the nurse at the camp infirmary."

He was trying to act like a drill sergeant, but with his balding head, pudgy stomach, and horn-rimmed glasses, he looked more like Sergeant Bilko.

"So what are our jobs?" Tom asked.

"They will be posted on the bulletin board outside the mess hall in the morning. After breakfast, look on the board. A detail will be posted next to your name. Next to the board is a mailbox to send letters out of the camp."

"How we gonna pay for stamps, man? I'm broke," said an obese black guy with a red bandana around his head.

"You will get a stipend for your work on Friday of every week."

"Wow, we get paid, man. My P.O. didn't tell me that," Tom said.

"It's not exactly pay, it's a stipend."

"Like a couple hundred a week?" a Hispanic guy joked.

"More like ten dollars a week."

"Ten dollars!" all the guys said almost in unison.

"Gentlemen, let's not forget you're here in custody."

"More like slavery. This here is a slave farm, man," the black guy said.

"I'm goin' to see the nurse. I feel real sick right about now." That was a tall lanky guy with a Southern accent. I found out later that his name was Herman. I thought for sure it would be Slim.

Bob let us go to lunch. Lunch was in the building on the hill. It was called the Lodge. I didn't know how many people were in this camp, but from the looks of the lodge, there were enough tables to seat an army battalion. As it turned out, not all the guys here were probationers—in fact, most of them were just regular camper types. We were the work force. Somehow, it was easy to imagine Joe Casellti negotiating this arrangement with whoever owned this camp.

All of my cabin partners were at the same table, and the conversation naturally went on about why we were here, gang affiliation, and that kind of stuff. The black guy with the bandana, who was the most outspoken, introduced himself.

"So brothers, my name is Eugene, and I's from Chicago and a member of the Black Kings. You all know that name?"

"I heard of 'em," Herman said. "Buncha racial motherfuckers."

Racist, I thought.

Eugene got up from the table, sliding his chair back. "Say what, white boy?"

"The name's Herman, *black* boy."

I thought for sure there was going to be a battle, but Bob Steinberg came walking up. "Sit down, Eugene." Eugene had just started to reach for a pitcher of Kool-Aid. They called it "bug juice."

"Dis white boy jus' insulted me."

"I don't care who or what started it. Fighting is grounds for sending you back home. We also have a custom here. Anybody who has enough of a beef to fight somebody else does so with gloves in the ring by the rules of the ring, and the whole camp gets to watch. So think about it. You guys want a match; I'll set it up. Otherwise keep your fists to yourselves."

I thought that was a pretty cool way to handle fights because at least one of the fighters could be made a fool of, especially if he didn't really know how to fight by the rules. Tom Hagen looked at me and smiled. I think he knew what I was thinking. I started smiling a little myself.

Eugene was looking at me. "Now whatchoo smilin'at?"

"I'm just musing."

"Musin'? Now that is funny. What is musin'?" blurted a Hispanic kid from across the table. He had a hair net over his jet-black hair. "What's your name, Meester Muser?"

"Larry, what's yours?"

"Fernando. An' I'an fron Cheecago, amigo." He seemed relaxed.

"Cool, we have something in common."

"You fron Cheecago, too?"

"No," I lied. "Both our names end in 'o'."

"Hey, das right, my man. Das right!"

Funny how easy some guys were distracted. Lunch ended without bloodshed. I was glad.

On my way back to the cabin, Tom Hagen caught up with me. "Hey, Larry, wait up." I stopped.

"What's up?"

"Why did you say you weren't from Chicago? You're from my neighborhood."

"Where you from?"

"North, Ogden, Larrabee."

"Keep it to yourself."

"You used to go to St. Mike's, right?"

"Not very long."

"You're the guy who got sent to the Deaf school, right?"

"Yeah."

"And you boxed in the CYA. Lightweight champion, right?"

"You in the FBI or something?"

"Hell, no." He laughed.

"I went to St. Mike's, and we boxed in the CYA, man!" he said.

"You must have beaten me. I don't remember any guys I lost to."

"You were lucky. Beat my ass. You don't remember your wins, either. If I'm right, you never lost a fight," he said.

I felt a sudden sense of shame. He should have seen me on Lincoln Avenue.

"Anyway, I don't fight anymore."

"What'd you do? Kill somebody in the ring?" He laughed.

"Listen, Tom. You can't let on where I'm from, OK?"

"Why's that?"

"Maybe I'll tell you sometime. Just don't let on. Keep it between us."

"Sounds like some pretty serious shit."

"Yeah."

◆ ◆ ◆

The next morning I must have gotten up at five or five-thirty. I couldn't sleep much because I had been thinking about Frankie. I imagined her smiling, laughing, saying my name. Thinking about her made my body ache. I felt bad that I just disappeared. I thought about writing her, but decided against it. I couldn't tell her I was in a Detention Camp, for Christ's sake. She was probably pretty pissed off by now. Maybe it was for the best; I didn't think I deserved her anyway. I got up, dressed, and went out of the cabin quietly. I wanted to take a walk down by the lake. The camp was silent, and it was barely light. As I passed the lodge, I smelled pancakes. I hoped I wasn't going to get the kitchen detail.

When I got down to the lake, the sun was just coming up on the other side. I could hear lots of bird sounds and some funny croaking sounds. The only birds I knew about were pigeons, and I wasn't sure they made sounds. The lake was huge and surrounded by trees. The rising sun made the bark orange-brown. I had never seen so many trees or so many different kinds of them either. In my neighborhood, you had to walk almost to Lincoln Park before you ever saw a tree. Grass? Forget about it. This scene reminded me of when I was a little kid I used to think the rich people owned the park. My mom laughed and thought that was pretty stupid. "Where'd you ever get *that* idea?" I don't know why I thought that. I guess I never imagined poor people could own trees or anything as nice as a park.

Anyway, the lake was completely still and a low mist hung over it. The surface was as clear as a mirror, reflecting the slowly disappearing mist as the sun rose above it. Close to the shore were lily pads and cattails, the names of which I learned later. The only movement was from little black bugs that flitted across the top. It was quiet, peaceful. The smell of the lake was fresh, hard to describe. Marshy? I had nothing to compare it to. Every once in a while something stuck its head out of the still water, making little watery haloes. Then it disappeared. I lay down in the damp grass close to the water. I felt safe there. In a few minutes, I fell asleep. I had a short dream that I was drafted into the army and, in the dream, I wasn't happy about it. I was planning to escape.

I woke up just in time to see an older black guy in the distance with a slight limp trudging toward me. He wore denim coveralls and a white T-shirt. I didn't know what time it was, but I was sure I missed breakfast. I got up and brushed off my moist Levis and T-shirt. I felt hungry.

"You Larry?" he asked.

"Yep, that's me."

"Ya missed showing up for your detail, so I came lookin' for ya. Name's Joshua, and don't be callin' me Goldmouth."

"Hi, Joshua. What was my detail?"

"Yer detail still is. It's wit' me and it jus' time to get started. We is the *Sanitation Engineers*." He laughed.

"Sanitation Engineers?" Good, it wasn't the kitchen. "What's that?"

"Mostly pickin' up the trash. Doin' some cleanin' of the camp. Pretty cushy, if ya ask me. We even got us a truck. No other details got a truck. We even got a radio." His smile showed his gold caps.

We drove around the camp in Joshua's truck: a dirty, banged-up, dark blue '50 Ford flatbed with moveable sides. The back of it was filled with large oil drums. He was listening to music on the radio. "Y'all like the blues, son?"

"They're all right." I didn't know much about blues.

"Best music there is. I come from the blues country, Pascagoula, *Miss-sippi*." He stretched out the word but left out the *issi*. "Ever hear of Highway 61? Peg Leg Sam? Rev. Blind Gary Davis? Scrapper Blackwell? Sippie Wallace?"

"No. None of them."

"Great blues folks, all a 'dem. Da best of the blues."

"Why do they call them the 'blues?'"

"'Cause the blues is about bein' black in the South. Blues is about slavery, cotton pickin,' bein' poor, bein' lynched, and just about anything bad dat happened to the black man—which was a whole lot—and still is."

"About the problems of black people?"

"'Bout the problems white people *give* us blacks. It's about sufferin' an' how black folks feel."

"I get it."

"Where you from boy?"

"Uhh, Chicago. But don't tell anyone."

"I gotcha. Your business, boy, not mine." He smiled, showing his gold teeth again. They weren't completely gold; I noticed a small white heart in the middle of one. You don' seem like no troublemaker tho'. Other boys come here 'cause they in big trouble down in the city. What's you here for?"

"Long story."

"Dat's OK. Blues went up to Chicago, you know. Plenty a places to hear the blues in Chi Town. You ever hear 'em, or you too young?"

"I heard some at the London House when I worked the door."

"Now dat's a mighty fancy place. Poor black folks don' go there, but der's lotsa small blues joints in Chi Town. Most in da South Side."

The truck made its way up to the lodge. "First stop is da kitchen. See dem barrels a trash? We pick 'em up and put down a clean barrel for each full dirty one. Catch my drift, son? It ain't too hard."

"I gotcha." I wanted to talk more like he did.

"I be goin' in da kitchen. You put dem full barrels on da truck an' put down a clean one. An' Jessie, watch yer sore leg."

"My name's not Jessie, and I don't have a sore leg."

"I know, I know. Jus' do what I say, boy."

There were four smelly barrels by the kitchen and heavy as shit. He should have helped me. I could barely lift them up on the truck bed. When I finished I got back in the cab. A few minutes later Joshua came out with carton of milk and a paper plate covered in aluminum foil. He opened my door and placed them on my lap.

"Figured if ya almos' missed da detail, ya sure missed yer breakfast."

Inside were four pancakes covered with butter and maple syrup and four link sausages.

"Ya gotta eat wit yer fingers, boy. They don' allow no silver outta da lodge."

"Thanks, Joshua. I'm starving!"

"I figured. Be my pleasure, boy. Eat up before we git to the dump. Ya'll won' feeling like eatin' once we git der. Take my word."

After we picked up all the barrels from around the camp, we headed out to the dump several miles outside the camp's gate. I finished my pancakes and milk before we got there. They were delicious!

The dump reminded me of the alleyways in my neighborhood where everyone dumped their garbage. Here there were tons of rotting garbage in large piles, some actively burning, others just smoking and smoldering. The putrid fumes made the air so rancid I had to hold my breath so I wouldn't choke. I gagged. I was glad Joshua had warned me.

After we'd finished the garbage detail, it was time for lunch. Unfortunately, I left my appetite at the dump. I was already exhausted but, in the afternoon, we had to clean and hose down the bathhouse, collect dirty towels and sheets, and take them to the laundry where Joshua's "missus" worked. That detail was pretty much the same every day, all week. But Joshua always had stories to tell. Stories about growing up in *'Miss-sippi.'* He never sounded like he felt sorry for himself, but that was the first time I heard that blacks used to be slaves, that there were separate bathrooms for whites and blacks in the South, and that blacks had to ride in the back of buses. I thought poor whites had it bad.

I told him that our detail reminded me of the summers I went "junkin'" with an older man who lived in a stable by one of the alleys not far from our flat. LeRoy had a big wooden cart and a horse named Buttercup. She always had a yellow plastic flower in her bridle. LeRoy used to say things like, "Giddy-up, Honey." He loved that horse. We used to ride through the alleys and go through the garbage for stuff to sell at the junkyard. I did that until I was twelve. Then one summer Buttercup just fell over in the street and almost pulled the cart over.

LeRoy got out and listened to her heart. When he didn't hear a heartbeat, he just hugged old Buttercup and cried.

"Now ain't that da saddest thing ya ever saw?"

It was.

◆   ◆   ◆

On Saturday, Bob Steinberg used Joshua's truck and took us into town to see a movie. For some reason, I felt a little scared. I didn't want to leave the camp. When we got to the town and parked close to the theater, I noticed another group of guys in the distance. All the guys got out of the back of the truck and started walking toward the theater. They seemed to be walking in our direction. I felt I had to get out of there, so I took off running in the opposite direction. I had no idea where I was going; I just knew that I had to escape. I ran like a crazy person from one hiding place to another in the town. At one point, I ended up lying in the dirt under a billboard sign. I was sweating and panting and more scared than I ever felt in my life, but I didn't even know why. Maybe I thought there was going to be a rumble back at the truck. I felt nuts. I don't know how long I lay behind the billboard; it must have been hours. I realized I didn't know where I was or how to get back to the truck. All I knew was that I didn't want to be seen on the street, and I didn't want to be left in this town either. I slowly climbed out from my hiding place and crept around the town. After awhile I found the police station. I went in and offered a lame story about getting lost from my camp truck. One of the cops took me in his car, and we rode around town to find the truck. When we got there, all the guys were already in the truck, waiting. Bob Steinberg was waiting outside the cab with a puzzled look.

"What's he done, officer?"

The cop shrugged his shoulders. "Nothing, no charge. He just came to the station and said he was lost."

"Thanks," Bob said.

Bob knew something wasn't right with me, but he didn't ask. "Let's go, Larry."

I got in the truck. All the guys were just staring at me. Finally, Tom Hagen said, "What the fuck happened to you? You hold up the town?"

"You look like you was in the town mud pits, man," Fernando said.

The guys all laughed. I didn't. I knew I looked like shit. I was still scared. Except for the wind blowing in the back of the truck, the rest of the ride back to camp was silent. I knew all the guys took turns staring at me.

The next day Bob said he wanted to talk to me after breakfast. We went for a walk down by the lake.

"I talked to Joe Casellti last night."

"Oh, fuck! Joe works Saturday nights?"

"No, I called him at home."

"Is he pissed?"

"No, you didn't do anything wrong. He just told me some things about you. He was concerned."

"Want to talk about last night?"

"Not particularly."

"I'm asking because I'm concerned about you, too."

"I really don't know what happened. I just got scared. I had to run."

"What were you afraid of?"

"I don't know. I just saw those other guys coming. I had to run. I don't understand it."

"I think you had a panic attack."

"A panic attack?"

"It sometimes happens after a person has been through some trauma."

"Trauma?"

"Yes, you've been through a lot, Larry. Joe told me you were almost killed in a fight."

I couldn't hold back my tears. I just lost it. "Fuckin' Dino. That *fuckin'* Dino! He's my brother, and he just fucking *watched*!"

Bob put his arm around me. "I'm sorry, Larry. I'm really sorry."

I felt ashamed and humiliated. Some part of me liked the feel of Bob's arm, but it was also uncomfortable.

By the end of summer, Bob and I had had some other talks. Sometimes he would ask me to go with him on errands in town and let me drive his car. But it was mostly Bob who talked and asked questions—mostly about my family, my neighborhood, and my hearing problem. I wasn't used to someone asking me questions about myself, and I felt ashamed that I broke down in front of him when I told him about Dino. When we said goodbye, he handed me a piece of paper with his home address and phone number in Chicago and asked me to keep in touch with him.

◆　◆　◆

I continued doing my detail with Joshua until the end of summer. He finally told me why he always said, "Watch yer sore leg, Jessie."

"If I say, 'Larry,' you heard yer mama say dat name a *millyun* times, so you don' listen. If I say, 'Jessie,' you say, 'Huh, who Jessie?' You listen. An' when I say 'your sore leg,' you think, 'Hey, I could get me a sore leg if I don' watch out.' So, you watch what yer doin'. Das all."

He was funny, and he was right. He also taught me a lot about blues and black folks that summer. Sometimes when I visited him in his old shanty on the other side of the lake, he played some blues for me on his "geetar."

I never looked up Bob in the city. I didn't understand why. I just didn't.

10

The End of High School

Sal told me that the police decided to crack down on the Cobras that summer because one of them blasted the inside of a squad car with a sawed off shotgun. The Cobras and the police got into a huge battle in the West Side projects, and two Cobras were shot. In exchange for less time, the squad car shooter fingered Scarface in the castration incident. So Scarface was doing hard time, and it seemed we didn't need to worry about him.

At the end of the summer I was off probation and continued to lead the Deuces, but it just wasn't the same for me—and my guys sensed it. Like the time we were coming out of the bowling alley on upper Lincoln Avenue. There were no bowling alleys on the Near North. A North Side gang called the Altinos was waiting right across the street, sprawled over cars and at the curb. They probably spotted us earlier in the bowling alley. We were definitely on their turf; all the makings for a rumble. I was scared, but not panicky like at camp. The Altinos were no match for us; they knew it, we knew it, but pride demanded they make an issue of the turf. Even though it would be an easy win, I didn't want this fight.

"Stay here," I told my guys. I ran across the street to the guy who was obviously their leader because he came forward as I approached them. He looked a little off-guard. "Listen," I said, "some of my guys are really fucked up. I don't want a rumble because you guys will probably win. But if you do, we're going to have to come back here with the Aces, cut you guys up in pieces, and stuff you in garbage cans. So we're leaving your turf right now. No hard feelings, OK?"

Their leader just stood still, with a dumb look and his mouth partly open—like he was trying to say, "What?" Then I ran back across the street.

"They don't want to fight. They know our rep, so let's just leave the fairies alone. Let's go." We left with the Altinos just staring at us and each other like they didn't know what the fuck just happened. I noticed my guys looking at each other and me as we walked away. It was as if they were asking, "Did Larry really just duck a fight?"

◆ ◆ ◆

That was the first time I got out of a gang fight. I just didn't have the stomach for it anymore. It just seemed senseless and stupid.

Another thing was drugs. I didn't mind grass, but the hard drugs my guys were doing were dangerous. We bought shit not knowing what it was, where it came from, or who made it. People who made street drugs didn't give a shit what happened to you. They used to say, "If they're stupid enough to take them that's their problem." Once I took a pill of something Sal gave me while on my way to work at the Black Iris. When I got there, the bartender asked me to take his car and pick up some ice. That was usually a 15-minute job. I came back several hours later with a ticket for running a stop sign and the ice melting in the trunk. I didn't remember most of what happened or why it took so long. If it were anywhere else I would have gotten thrown in jail. Besides that, Big John was pissed and I hated to disappoint him.

That summer Tiny and George both died from heroin overdoses while I was at camp. I was really sorry I didn't get a chance to say goodbye to them, especially Tiny. I wanted to get my guys off drugs and have them straighten out their screwy lives. I tried to use Tiny and George as examples of how we were getting fucked over by drug dealers and the shit they sold us. But, despite my efforts, many of them still ended up addicted or in jail. I didn't want to do drugs anymore, and I'm sure talking to my guys about trying to straighten out my life was making me look soft. I wanted to help them but maybe this *was* their way of life—or maybe you had to almost die before you woke up. I didn't know anything for sure anymore.

I didn't feel like a leader anymore and it showed. I guess I discovered I never really was a gang leader and fighter. Like Joe said, maybe the image was a way to get some sense of self-worth. Even if I couldn't get my guys to straighten out, there was definitely something about *my* life that I was supposed to be changing.

So I quit the Deuces. Dino and Mickey quit the Aces but for different reasons. Dino went to work full time on Rush Street; his ambition was to get into the Outfit. Mickey joined the Army with some of his buddies and went to Fort Leavenworth for basic training. Mickey had been kicked out of the house because all he did was sleep and pee his bed. Plus, he couldn't keep a job, *any* job. Not even the one Bud got for him in his factory just nailing boxes together. On his first day, Mickey tried to put a nail through a knot; the nail ricocheted and hit him in the corner of his eye. Mickey said everything wrong happened to him, and it did. That seemed to be the story of his life. I started thinking of him as *Sad Sack*.

I was surprised that I was allowed to graduate from high school. I graduated without even being there. They probably wanted to get rid of me. In the class standing, there were only nine guys below me. The guys under me must have been either addicts or retarded.

◆   ◆   ◆

I finally decided to go see Frankie. I missed her and I needed to see her before she left for the University of Wisconsin. She and her friends were having a farewell party, and she would be leaving very soon.

The party was at her friend Cynthia's house a block west of Lake Shore Drive. When I first walked in, the party was pretty lively. When they saw me, everyone became quiet. I saw Frankie across the room. She was curled up in a chair near the back wall and was wearing a UW sweatshirt and a pair of Levis. I never saw her dressed so casually. She looked beautiful anyway. Almost everyone was having a beer. Cynthia offered me one on my way over to Frankie's chair.

"Hi," I said. I was aware that my nose probably looked different.

"Hi, Larry. Long time." She was quieter, reserved, and seemed a little sad.

"I owe you an apology."

"Well, maybe you do, and maybe you don't."

"What do you mean?"

"I guess it depends on what you felt about us. I thought we had something good together." She was holding a beer with both hands with the neck of the bottle in front of her mouth. "Oh, sorry." She moved the bottle and straightened up in her chair.

"We did."

"I know we did. I thought maybe I scared you off."

"I scared myself off. And I'm sorry."

"I came looking for you over the summer. I even found your house."

My heart skipped a beat. "How did you do that?"

"A friend in school records. Had her look it up for me. Then Mario's, Black Iris, London House. All the clubs. No Larry. I had a good cry with Big John. He tell you?"

"No, I haven't seen him either."

"He was sweet. Told me you had to get off the streets. That it had nothing to do with me. I heard about your fight on Lincoln Avenue, too. It's sad, Larry. Really, really sad."

"I thought about you…a lot. You were on my mind all summer."

"It's hard to have a relationship in your head though, isn't it?"

Cynthia came over and wanted me to see the last edition of the school paper. She had a devilish look. I dated Cynthia a couple of times before I met Frankie. Because Cynthia had always been jealous of the relationship between Frankie and me, I could never trust what she was up to.

"Let it go, Cynthia, please? I don't think he'll appreciate it," Frankie said.

"What is it?"

"You got a distinction in the graduating edition of the school paper."

"Cynthia, please?" Frankie rolled her eyes.

"What's it say?" I was apprehensive but still curious.

"Well, you were voted 'Most Likely Not to Succeed,'" she giggled. "It gets worse. The paper also ran a fantasy story about our ten-year class reunion. At the reunion, you are still parking cars. You even got to park Frankie and Allen Korkow's Mercedes. They were married; he was a newscaster, and Frankie was an English teacher."

Cynthia sure could be a vindictive bitch. "Fuck the paper," I blurted. But I knew it might be right.

"Are you happy with yourself, Cynthia?" Frankie asked. "Larry, you want to take a walk with me?"

We took a slow walk down to Lake Shore Drive and over into the yacht harbor.

"I'm also sorry I missed your speech. I heard it was good and you got a great ovation."

"Yeah, I just wish you'd been there. I thought of you when I wrote it. I was proud to be at the top of my class. But I felt like I was standing there alone. I wanted you to be there with me, at my side," she said.

"That would have been a sight. You and the guy tenth from the bottom of the class."

Frankie was silent. She put her hands over her face. I had never seen her cry.

"I'm sorry I said that." From the feeling in my throat, I knew I was close to losing it.

She spoke; her voice trembled through her tears. "You know, Larry. I was there not because I'm anyone special. I was there because I was lucky. I was fortunate enough to have the love and support of my parents, the right opportunities, and the financial means to get there. Those things fed my desire to succeed. You are just as smart and just as good as I am. In *every* way. But you are Antoine. Remember the Truffaut movie we saw? Antoine, without support, love, money, or opportunities. People are *not* born equal. You were not born equal, Larry. I saw where you live. Have you ever had any energy for what *you* really want? Do you even know what you really want? I doubt you've thought much about what you want."

I reached out to her, pulled her into my arms, and held her tightly. I could feel her body tremble as she cried. I cried silently with her—knowing I might be holding her for the last time. A cool breeze off the lake swept over us, bringing the fragrance of her hair to my face. I was hungry for it and breathed it as deeply as I could. I promised myself I would never forget it.

She pulled back from me. No mascara streaks this time. She had no makeup on, and I could see she had small faint freckles on her nose.

"Well, look at us. A couple of babies, huh?" she said while running her fingers over my face, touching my tears. "I love you, Larry."

"I love you, too." I felt like I would start crying again.

"So bad boys cry?"

"More than you think. More than I like."

"Larry, what are you going to do with yourself? There's a part of me that wants to stay here, be with you, watch out for you."

"No. No way. You have to go. You've worked hard for what you have. I'll be all right…Really. I've just got to get my life together."

"Can you promise me you will?"

"Yes, I promise."

"Cross your heart?"

"Cross my heart."

11

Starting Over

Frankie was right. I didn't know what I wanted out of life. How *could* I know what I really wanted if I had never even thought about it? I never had any energy for what *I* wanted because my energy had gone into making myself an imitation Dino. What good had that done? The bastard almost let me die. I really didn't know who he was, but he wasn't my brother anymore.

I realized I'd been on a path to nowhere. My life had been a misdirected failure; my values were all wrong. Who I was felt pointless, hollow, and trivial. I knew I duped myself. I totally fucked up high school. If all that wasn't bad enough, my headaches were becoming more frequent and more intense. They were getting to a point where I had to go to the emergency room for a shot to make them stop. And after that shot, all I could do was sleep.

For the first time, I thought about suicide. But suicide couldn't be right. Clay killed himself and left me a confused mess in more ways than one. I never did understand what his problem was, but I don't think he solved it. If Mr. Frommer was right and his soul did come back one day, he might just have to start over where he left off. Maybe I could start over without dying—or at least with less dying. Maybe it wasn't too late for me, but I didn't know where to begin. Maybe if I had asked myself what I *didn't* want that would be a start.

So that fall I spent a lot of time thinking about what I didn't want. I didn't want to be Dino; I didn't even want to work for him anymore. I didn't want to be a fighter anymore. I didn't want to be in a gang anymore. I didn't want to live at home anymore. At least if I knew what I didn't want I might have a direction.

If I quit working for Dino, I'd have to get another job even though the money on the street was good. I couldn't leave home if I didn't have money.

At home, Mom and Bud weren't getting along at all.

"You're nothing but a goddamned drunk," she would say.

"All you ever wanted from me was money," he would reply.

"Well, you spend most of your money on booze, and I don't need any more help from drunks like you. I'm going to be a singer. Neal tells me I can sing as good as anyone out there."

She had started taking singing lessons from Neal Epsom, a guy with an undersized studio on Wells Street. Something I learned on the streets is that there's always someone eager to take your money—avid customers make it even easier. Once I bought ten boxed cashmere sweaters straight out of a guy's car trunk for only five bucks each. He was in a hurry, looking up and down the street while telling me what a great deal I was getting. After he left, I pulled them out of the box. All I had were sweater fronts—no sides, no backs, no sleeves. Dino laughed his ass off. Bud seemed to know about people like that, too.

"Neal's a greedy prick and all you'll ever get from him is a snow job."

I was disgusted with my Mom's anger, depression, and make-believe life. She treated Bud worse than a dog, always screaming and swearing at him. Once, as he came up the stairs drunk, she hit him in the head with an iron skillet and knocked him to the bottom of the stairs. A full case of beer and a bottle of vodka went clanging and bouncing down with him. He begged her to forgive him and promised to quit drinking; she answered by whacking him with a Coke bottle and telling him to get the fuck out.

Bud often confided in me, which was mostly complaining about the way mom treated him. He said she wanted a divorce. Later, I told him if he had any self-respect left, he should leave before she killed him. I believed it could happen. The black guy next door shot his wife in the back of the head, and the gypsy lady down the block killed her husband by shooting him in the heart with his .45. Bud hid a .45 in his old Army duffel bag in the closet at the end of the hall. I just hoped my mom didn't know it was there.

◆ ◆ ◆

I found a job in the local hospital as an orderly and told Dino.

"A hospital?" He laughed. "Same one you got your ass sewed up? You'll be lucky to get a buck an hour."

"It's more than that, but I don't care. I'm tired of working the streets."

"You'll be back. You'll see."

I promised myself I'd never go back.

The hospital needed someone to work weekends and holidays. The job would eventually become full time. It was at Alexian Brothers. Yeah, the same hospital I was in after my fight on Lincoln Avenue, and the place I brought Tiny after the rumble. Tiny died there after he overdosed. The Alexian Brothers emergency room was where the police brought a kid who was riding a bike when Dino ran over him. The police made Dino wait while the kid was treated. Dino complained to the cop that the wait in the emergency room was so long that his hot dogs got cold. The kid almost died.

Working in the hospital took some getting used to because of all those reminders of the past. I also wasn't used to being around sick and dying people. It was the first time I saw someone die naturally. I saw a few people killed on the streets pretty close up, but it always seemed a little unreal. Like when I saw the black guy next door shoot his wife in the back of the head as she ran away from him. Even though I could feel and hear the clumpety-clump of her body as he dragged her back up the stairs, I had to go downstairs to see the massive trail of blood before I could believe I had seen him shoot her. It still didn't seem completely real. There was something in the mind that made it that way—as if there was a censor in there trying to make you forget things even as they were happening.

At the hospital, I got a different view of death. It wasn't violent like death on the streets; it was a death my mind wouldn't try to make me forget. I didn't try to walk away from it or forget it because it was more personal—a death I was forced to think about. Well, at least that's the way it was for me.

The first patient I saw die in the hospital was someone I had helped take care of. He was a "charity case." Alexian Brothers took people without money, without families, and without homes. This man had been impossible to know as a person because he was sort of crazy when he was alive. No one came to see him after he died. One of my jobs as an orderly was to prepare bodies for the morgue. It was strange to touch the still warm body of this man who once was and now wasn't. It's difficult to describe the deep impression he left on me. But, for the first time, I saw that at death there is simply nothing there anymore. The utter stillness of his body in the breathless silence of that room made his nothingness a certainty. Whoever and whatever he was just stopped being. That made death more frightening.

I was beginning to think a lot about what I wanted to do, and it terrified me to imagine that it could all suddenly become simple nothingness. It gave me the shivers. So seeing this dead man in the hospital was very different from death on the street. Even though he wasn't my friend, I closed his eyes. Bud was right; people did die like that.

The hospital job was a lot of work. I changed sheets, emptied bedpans, wheeled people to X-ray, and carted people to the morgue. After a few weeks, I started to like working there. I liked wearing the crisp starched white shirts and pants and being part of the excitement you only find in hospitals.

The Brothers in the hospital weren't all the same as I thought they would be. Some were like Brother Matthew, the administrator. He was a huge guy in a long black frock; he was stern and always serious. Others were like Brother René, a very skinny, pale blond-haired guy who wore a white robe. He was easygoing and friendly. One day Brother René surprised me by inviting me to take a break with him in the cast room up on the third floor. When we got there he lifted his robe and pulled out a pack of cigarettes. I was surprised he smoked and that he offered me one. "Did you think *all* Brothers were angels?" he laughed.

"Why do you call yourselves Brothers?"

"Because the Pope likes to think of us as a big happy family. There are Fathers, Mothers, Brothers, and Sisters. Then there are the bosses: the monsignors, cardinals, and bishops. Sort of like a pecking order. Brothers are at the lower end, the workers. Some Brothers, like us, are nurses; others teach, and some even make brandy."

Brother René and I became friends. He had a very kind and gentle way with patients, and they all seemed to look forward to seeing him. He taught me a lot about nursing and showed me how to make rounds with the doctors to assist them. He also told me which of them were jerks and who the good doctors were. One of his favorites was Dr. Keddy, a surgeon. He was the chief of surgery and a professor at the University of Illinois medical school. He had the reputation of being a "no-nonsense" kind of guy. No one ever had to guess what he wanted. He meant what he said. I liked that he was dependable that way. Sometimes he was critical, rarely warm, and even less complimentary. I suspect that if you asked him what life was about for him, he would say something like, "It's a job to be done, and you do it the best way you know how."

As a physician, he was a perfectionist. As I got to know him, I discovered that he had a phenomenal memory. Other physicians in the nursing station or on rounds would often ask him about certain drugs, dosages, and things like that. Without even looking at them, he would reel off what they wanted to know, as if he was talking to himself. He also remembered small details about patients' habits, attitudes, even their addresses! He reminded me of Bud's great aunt, the first woman to graduate from the U of I medical school. Like Dr. Keddy, she was a powerhouse of a person. She worked until she was eighty and, even then, it took a bolt of lightning to kill her. Dr. Keddy's intuition about his patients, other doctors, and even me was remarkably accurate.

One day in the hallway of the ward, he tapped me on the shoulder and asked, "You need some extra money?"

"I sure do. I'm only working part-time."

"Well, how about being my supply tech in the heart lab?" he asked.

I was ecstatic. "That…that would be great!"

"Good. Meet me in the heart lab on Monday morning at seven. Know where it is?"

"Yes, sir."

"But what about my orderly job?"

"You can do both, but the heart lab has priority. I'll talk to Brother Matthew about it."

I was so happy I skipped the six blocks home that afternoon.

◆ ◆ ◆

That Monday I was at the heart lab before Dr. Keddy arrived. It was in an annex building across from the main hospital and had its own self-contained surgical suite.

I showed up at six-thirty.

Dr. Keddy showed up at seven sharp. "Early bird," he quipped.

We went into the lab, and we changed into passion pink surgical suits. He showed me how to scrub up.

"If you're wondering, 'why pink?'" I was. "it's because we keep our laundry separate from the regular surgery scrubs. And always, always shower before you go back to the hospital. I don't want to be another Ignaz Semmelweis."

"Who is he?"

"Was. Ignaz Phillip Semmelweis. A Hungarian physician who discovered aseptic technique while teaching in Vienna. He drove himself crazy trying to get doctors to wash their hands. There's a book about him."

Then he showed me around. He began shooting off all the things he wanted me to get and do.

"Dr. Keddy?"

"Yes?" His "yes" was as quick and sharp as the shot of an arrow.

"Can I write this down?"

He went to a desk in the corner of the room and got me a notepad. "Yes. Write everything down," he ordered. "Everything."

As he was introducing me to the lab, I could barely contain my excitement about being there and being with him. It was a totally new environment; there was equipment I had never seen before. In fact, I had never seen most of what was in the heart lab, but it was still very exciting. In one corner of the room was a large cage with a sign on it labeled "Fido."

"Who is Fido?" I asked.

"Fido and the Fidos are our 'patients.' They are the experimental animals." As if reading my mind, he continued, "And if you like dogs, don't worry. Their lives will save the lives of many children. Our experiments are practice for the new field of pediatric cardiovascular surgery and soon after that, adult open-heart surgery. We also do research on the ancillary effects of our procedures."

"Ancillary effects?"

"Well, we've discovered that just doing the procedure may affect liver function. Things like that. That's why we always save the liver."

Apparently, labs like this were springing up all over the country. Cardiovascular surgery was still in its infancy.

"And in a year or two," he continued, "we'll move this set-up to Children's Hospital and begin doing cardiovascular surgery on many of the heart problems children are now dying from. And if you're still with us then, you can come with the team."

"I…I can?" I stammered. Dr. Keddy looked at me almost as if he was annoyed. I knew that he wasn't. I was beginning to understand that when he said something, he meant what he said and expected that that's exactly how it would be understood—no questions.

So began my time in the heart lab. It wasn't long until Dr. Keddy promoted me from supply tech to extracorporeal perfusion technician. That meant I would be the person who set up and ran the pumps that circulated the blood around the "patient's" body while the heart was being worked on. Dr. Keddy wanted everyone on the team to have some experience with every aspect of the procedure, even me. So I was trained in surgical pharmacology and anesthesia, as well as running the heart pump. I learned to prep the dogs, give the preoperative medications, intubate them, and even administer the anesthetic. I was able to "open and close," that is, surgically open the animal's chest wall, apply retractors to the rib cage, and close the chest wall when the procedure was over.

Dr. Keddy got permission for me to use the hospital library, so what I didn't learn firsthand in the lab, I could read about in the hospital library. I even spent some of my meager money on surgical books. I wanted to do some experiments of my own. I also found the book on Semmelweis at Beecher's on Michigan Avenue. It was called *The Cry and the Covenant*. It was wonderful and the first book ever to make me cry. Since I hadn't read that many books, I guess it was no big deal. I also finally bought Freud's *Interpretation of Dreams*.

Dr. Keddy began kidding me about spending so much time in the library. "The librarian tells me you're becoming her most frequent visitor." I think that amused him. I think he liked it.

As we worked together more, his confidence in me seemed to grow. He began showing me procedures only the surgical residents were permitted to do. He let me start doing procedures on my own after we ran the experiment. Before long, I had done a nephrectomy, thyroidectomy, and some other procedures. I mounted the organs and left them in the lab.

One day he asked me to assist one of the residents in doing a demonstration for some of the surgical staff. The demonstration involved opening a dog's chest, connecting a respirator, and demonstrating the effect of the respirator with the chest open.

When the time came for the demonstration, our "patient" was a huge dog, much bigger than most we had work on. The resident didn't seem at all interested in the whole affair. He acted as if he was insulted to be asked to be there, much less do the demonstration. When I met him at the lab, he said, "You do it. If you do something wrong, I'll tell you."

I rather liked the idea of doing it myself, but I had a difficult time getting the dog out with the Nembutal. I eventually gave him enough to quiet a horse, and he finally went to sleep so I could start the anesthetic. After I intubated him, I opened his chest and connected the respirator. The surgical staff started showing up in the lab almost before I had it set up.

After everyone had arrived, I started to explain the respirator. In the middle of my explanation, the dog gave a start on the table. I couldn't believe it, but the anesthesia wasn't deep enough. The dog jumped from the table to the floor, dragging the respirator with him! The surgical staff was so dismayed that they walked out.

The resident just stared at me and said, "Jesus Christ, Larry!" Lot of help he was.

I was sure Dr. Keddy would fire me for the way the demonstration ended. The next day I got a call from him. He wanted me to come see him in his hospital office. His office was small, but impeccable, not a particle of dust. The walls were lined with mahogany bookcases filled with medical books of all kinds. There were lots of diplomas and awards on the wall behind his desk. When I walked in he didn't look up.

"Sit down, Larry," he murmured with his head still down. On the front of his desk, exactly in the middle, was a large brass desk lamp with a green glass shade. He was making some notes on a patient's chart.

I sat there with the ankle of one leg propped on top the knee of the other one, opening and closing a hemostat on my pants cuff for what seemed like an eternity.

"Please stop that," he said.

"Sorry, sir."

Finally, he capped his fountain pen, closed the chart, took off his black horn-rimmed glasses, and looked up at me. I think he knew how scared I was.

Then he said, "I heard how the demonstration went. I understand it wasn't the resident who did the procedure. Is that right?"

"Yes, sir."

"I asked you to assist. Did the resident ask you to do the procedure for him?"

"Yes, sir."

"Hmmm. You should have told the resident you were only assisting." He was biting his lower lip. "I'll talk to him."

"So your patient wasn't deep enough, was he?"

"No, sir, he wasn't." I think my voice was shaking.

"How much pre-op?" he asked.

"Well, I started with 50 milligrams of Nembutal. When he didn't quiet down, I gave him another 50 milligrams, altogether 150 milligrams. He was a big, probably 45 to 50 kilograms."

"Any trouble starting the Pentothal?" he asked.

"No, sir. That was easy."

"A hundred and fifty could have quieted a horse," he said.

"That's exactly what I thought, sir."

"But why did you stop there? Why not go to 200?"

"Well, I was concerned about the effect of that much Nembutal on his respiration. It seemed like if I overdid the Nembutal, it might affect his respiration and, if it did, there wouldn't be much point in demonstrating the Bennet respirator."

"At what point does Nembutal depress respiration?" he asked.

"Well, it depends on the weight of the dog. I figured he weighed close to 100 pounds and so he could tolerate at least 150. I was thinking in terms of about three milligrams per kilogram."

"OK, OK."

"I'm really sorry, sir. I didn't mean to embarrass you."

"Oh, you didn't embarrass *me*, everyone watching you probably guessed what happened. It happens to the best of us. You know, patients sometimes come out of the anesthetic when they're on the table. Better it happened to you with a dog than with your patient. The important thing is how you *thought* about it. You thought well. The staff walked out because they were disturbed by what they saw, not because it couldn't happen to any of them—including the lazy resident."

I was amazed that Dr. Keddy wasn't upset. He even paid me a compliment. I wondered why he thought I would ever have a patient.

◆ ◆ ◆

Between my job in the heart lab and being an orderly I was finally working full time. That's when I decided to move away from home without telling my mom.

The situation at home was the same except that Bud had moved out. Even though it was quieter, mom turned her anger on me, often threatening to "kick my ass up between my shoulders" when she was pissed off. Her mouth was as bad as some of my guys' were. The apartment was still full of junk, always dirty dishes in the sink, grimy floors, filthy windows, and rats in the walls. One time the sink was so full of dirty dishes, I put them in the bathtub and washed them. That really pissed her off. She couldn't believe I washed the dishes "where she washed her body." She didn't take that many baths anyway. Mom was so full of herself. She thought her voice lessons were going to make her famous.

But I worried about Christie who was only nine years old then. She was so sweet and innocent I couldn't believe she came from the two of them. I wondered what would happen to her if I left her alone with my mom. At least I took her some places and read to her. I even took her to the beauty parlor once in a while to have her hair done.

It was really hard to leave Christie behind. She was my Phoebe and I was her Holden. We both cried, but she knew I had to go. I felt guilty leaving her with my mom, but I didn't know what else I could do. I promised to stay in touch and let her know where I was.

I rented a furnished room in a rooming house up on Fullerton Parkway, only six blocks east of the hospital. That made it easy to walk to work and back. The nicest thing about Fullerton Parkway wasn't just that it was a nicer neighborhood, but that it had trees. Only two blocks to the west was Lincoln Park.

A pharmacist named Phil owned the rooming house. He worked nights in a 24-hour drugstore somewhere downtown. Phil was tall, heavy set, and looked like he could have been a guitarist in a Spanish band. I imagined him in a sombrero. He was a quiet, peculiar guy who sketched a black pencil-line moustache above his upper lip. He drew his eyebrows a little thicker. You could also see that he dyed his hair black because the gray roots were always a little visible.

The place was a bit gaudy. To the left of the front door was a concrete lion with one of its front legs raised. The lobby had a pink vinyl sofa and black wrought-iron lamps sitting on a tacky gray shag rug. On the wall was a matador with a bull painted on black velvet and framed in gold. I guess you could call it a painting. But, that said, the place was clean.

Phil took me up a very narrow winding stairway to the second floor. I was glad I didn't have a suitcase. Off the hallway on the right was a bathroom and shower with pink and black plastic tile. A Filipino guy who wore loud floral shirts and played the xylophone had a room at the end of the hall. Phil showed me a small, simple room with a high ceiling. It had a double bed, a dresser, and a blond wood end table next to the bed with a white porcelain lamp. Opposite the door was an oversized window that looked out on a small church across the street. Since the side street was so narrow, the window of my room was a perfect frame for the church's large circular stained glass window. Another, even smaller, vacant room was on the left. I took the larger one. It was ten dollars a month and included weekly sheets and towels. The view of the stained glass window was worth ten dollars alone.

The first thing I bought myself was a bar of soap from the drugstore down the block on the corner. It took me awhile to decide which one to buy. I decided on a bar of Old English Lavender. I don't know why, but that made me very happy. It was *my* soap.

The first night there, I took a long hot shower with my new soap. When I came back from the shower to my darkened room, the stained glass window across the way was lit up. It was so large it filled my entire window. It sparkled like a massive multicolored glass flower. I looked at it for a long time before I got into bed. I liked the fresh clean smell of the sheets and the fragrance of the soap on my body. I slept well—and there was no mask above my head.

12

Jean

Since I hadn't lived on a street with trees before, it was a treat to see the leaves changing color and floating down to the small front yards, streets, and sidewalks. I had leisurely mornings on the days I worked the PM shift at the hospital. I got into the habit of getting up early, taking one of my new books, and going down to the Golden Cup Coffee Shop on Clark Street.

After that, the walk to work in the early afternoon was refreshing. The breezes coming off the lake replaced the humidity of summer and blew fallen leaves around. I counted the trees on every block along Fullerton Parkway from the rooming house to Halsted Street where they suddenly stopped. There must have been ten in every block. After that, the streets became barren again. In those days, it was still legal to burn leaves at the curbside. I enjoyed watching people standing over their smoking leaf piles with fan rakes making sure the burning leaves didn't go under someone's car. It was one of those sights and smells you never forget.

When I arrived at the corner of Halsted Street, I saw Sal's sister, Jean, waiting for the Lincoln Avenue bus across the street. She wore a tan raincoat with a long, dark blue scarf loosely wrapped around her neck. She looked pretty. I hadn't seen her in a long time and wondered about Sal. I waved and called after her, then ran across the street.

"Hey, Jean, how've ya been?"

"Oh, hi, Larry. Long time, no see. I've been OK."

"How's Sal?"

"He joined the Marines last month. I guess he's doing basic training somewhere."

"Somewhere?"

"You know Sal and me. He only tells me what he wants to. I haven't heard from him since. I doubt I will."

"He can be like that, I know. How are your folks? Sisters?"

"My dad got a brainy idea and moved to Iowa. They're all there, outside Des Moines."

"Iowa? Jesus! Is he going to start a farm?" I joked.

"I doubt it. He just wanted to get out of the city, out of the projects, especially away from the Cobras after what happened to Sal—and you."

"So where are you living?"

"Oh, I found a room in a woman's apartment down by Lincoln Park West."

I saw her bus coming in the distance. "Well, give me your phone number. I'll call you, and we can get together."

"OK." She reached in her purse and scribbled her number on a piece of paper. "Don't forget, Larry."

"Not a chance. I'll call you at the end of the week."

It was interesting running into Jean. She looked older than the last time I saw her. She wasn't a little girl anymore. Her short, dark brown hair, deep brown eyes, and light olive complexion made her attractive. I used to think she was cute, but never thought of her as attractive. Her parents were both Mexican. I guess I always thought of her as "Sal's little sister," even though she was only a year younger than he was. I had known their whole family since I first started going to St. Michael's. Sal and I went to kindergarten together.

◆ ◆ ◆

That afternoon I ran into Dr. Keddy on the med-surg floor. He was making rounds with two residents I hadn't seen before.

"Larry, this is Dr. Montego and Dr. Nelson. They're coming on board. I want you to show them the heart lab and show them how to set up the pump. We'll be doing a procedure this Wednesday."

"I'd be happy to." Both the residents coolly shook my hand. I felt they were looking at me sideways, like "Who is this young jerk?"

"Make sure they understand how important the pump connectors are."

"Yes, sir." I liked his confidence in me. I'm not sure the residents did.

The floor was quiet, and Dr. Keddy had already made arrangements with Brother Matthew for me to meet with the residents that evening. I met them in the lab after dinner. I explained everything I knew about the pump: the importance of the connectors and especially the clamps that absolutely had to be tight around the different stainless steel housings that connected to the polyethylene hoses. I may have overdone it a bit, but I wanted to be sure. At best, they looked bored and above it all. I guess they didn't consider this to be "real medicine."

On Wednesday, the whole team was in the lab, and the residents had set up the heart pump ahead of time. I was busy with prepping, intubating, and starting the anesthesia. We opened the chest wall and exposed the heart. Dr. Montego was the first assistant. Dr. Keddy was getting frustrated with him. "Your hand is on the patient's heart, *doctor*!"

"The dog's heart," Dr. Montego corrected him. He seemed irritated.

"No! It is not a dog's heart, *doctor*. It's a child's heart! And from the moment you begin this procedure until this procedure is finished, this is a child's heart. Don't forget that."

Dr. Montego nodded.

When the heart was isolated from its major vessels and the pump was activated, several of the tubing connectors of the pump suddenly broke loose and, like wild writhing snakes, started spewing blood in regular bursts all over the lab. Just when I pointed and said, "It's the connectors!"—a still twisting piece of tubing turned at me and shot a huge spurt of blood in my face. All the outside circulating blood shot all over the lab. The room and everyone in it was blood splattered. That's the worst thing that could happen in a heart lab because there was nothing anyone could do. The procedure was over.

Dr. Keddy was furious. "Dr. Montego, you just killed a child! Now get the hell out of here." He threw his hemostat across the room into the steel sink. Then he turned to me and said, "Larry, see me in my office tomorrow."

Everyone had left, and I don't remember how long I was there cleaning up. At one point, I just happened to glance up at the large mirror over the operating table and caught a glimpse of my face—it was still covered with blood. For a moment I looked like a scientist gone totally mad. That night I took a very long shower.

The next day I went to see Dr. Keddy. I was sure I was going to be fired. He was at his desk again, writing.

"Have a seat, Larry. I'll be right with you."

This time I wasn't playing with a hemostat.

He finished writing and carefully put his chart aside. "About yesterday's procedure…"

"I'm very sorry, sir, I…"

"I'm not finished, Larry," he shot back at me. "That was a disaster, but that's not why I wanted to talk to you."

He reminded me of Joe Casellti sometimes.

"Oh. I'm sorry, sir."

"I *know* you know the difference between a scalpel and a hemostat. But sometimes when I ask for a scalpel, you hand me a hemostat. You have a hearing problem," he said with absolute certainty. "Why didn't you tell me about it?"

With those surgical masks, it was impossible to read lips. Sometimes if I didn't hear him, I'd give him what I thought he wanted from what I knew he was doing at the moment. I always knew when he wanted *something* because of the way his eyes looked at me above his mask. It was really stupid to hope he wouldn't notice; he never missed anything. "Uh, I was afraid you wouldn't hire me."

"Do you have a hearing aid?"

"No, sir." I could feel my face redden.

"What type of loss is it, sensorineural?"

"I'm not sure."

"When was the last time you had it evaluated?"

"It's been a long time."

He got out a prescription pad and wrote something on it.

"I want you to see this doctor. I'll talk to him. He'll evaluate your hearing and your need for a hearing aid."

"I don't have insurance yet."

"Don't worry about it. Just do as I say. I don't want you in the heart lab until it's done. The sooner the better."

"Yes, sir."

Shit! That afternoon I had a feeling I was washed up. Even if I needed a hearing aid, I couldn't afford one. Besides that, I hated the idea of wearing a hearing aid. It was embarrassing.

That week, I went to see the ear doctor, Dr. Engram. He did a hearing test. The audiogram looked like a chicken had walked across it. He told me I had a "bizarre" form of sensorineural hearing loss. Bizarre because I could hear some sounds in the high frequency range and not others. My discrimination was also bad, meaning I had difficulty making out words when there was background noise.

"How the hell do you manage to hear in Keddy's lab?" He smiled. "You're working with people wearing masks, pump going in the background, several people talking at once. It's remarkable."

"Do I need a hearing aid?"

"You need two, a bicross, actually. One for each ear, but the one on the right will only be a microphone that feeds the sound from that side to the left ear. Your right ear is basically useless, but that way you will get a better sound balance."

"Is it expensive?"

"Dr. Keddy is paying for the consultation and the hearing aids."
"He *is*?"
"That's what he said."

◆ ◆ ◆

I went to see Dr. Keddy the day after.
"Dr. Engram said…"
"I already know. He called me after the consultation."
"I want you to get those hearing aids. When you do, you can come back to the lab. We have a lot of work to do and I need your help."
"I really appreciate what you're doing for me, Dr. Keddy."
"Don't worry about it," he said abruptly. "Another thing, Larry."
"Yes, sir."
"Have you ever considered becoming a physician?"
"Well, actually, lately, I had sort of thought about it. I like working in the lab and the hospital."
"Are you in school?"
"No, sir."
"What are you waiting for?"
"I guess I need to make some money first," I lied.
"Let me know if you need some help. I might be able to help you with the University of Illinois and Marquette. Both have good medical schools. There are ways to do these things. But you just need to want to do it. It's got to be the most important thing."
"Yes, sir, thank you so much. I really…"
"I know you do, son. Get those hearing aids."

◆ ◆ ◆

I couldn't help crying a little as I walked back home that afternoon. Dr. Keddy was so kind and generous; I liked that he called me "son." I was so happy and, at the same time, I felt as if I had ruined my life. I *had* been thinking about becoming a doctor and imagined I would really like medicine, but I always dismissed the idea. How could I ever go to college, much less medical school? I decided to apply to several schools just to see what would happen.

On Friday, I called Jean, and we made a time to get together. We went out to dinner at a small Italian restaurant close to where she lived. We talked a lot. Well, she talked a lot, but it was fun being with her and eating out. All I had in my room was an electric frying pan.

"So what are your plans, Larry?"

"I'm going to be a physician." The words surprised me, but I liked saying them. I realized I hadn't told her about the heart lab.

"You are? That's great, but I thought you really messed up in high school. Do you have the grades to get into college?"

"Probably not, but I'm going to apply anyway. All they can do is reject me." We laughed, but it really wasn't funny anymore. I thought about Frankie, *How do you know what you want if you've never thought about it?* Her words haunted me.

"So?"

Her question brought me back. "So, what?"

"Where will you apply?"

"Oh, University of Illinois, Arizona, Michigan." I made them up.

"Well, Sal went into the Marines. Sometimes you can get money for college from the service."

The thought of going into the service almost made me sick. That was the last thing I would ever do. Besides, with my hearing problem, I would be 4-F anyway.

"You could be drafted, you know. The draft is on."

"Thank God for hearing problems." I also hadn't told her about that.

"Anyway, Larry, another thing."

"Yes?"

"Are there any more rooms where you live? I hate living with Rosie."

The question caught me off guard. Before I thought about it, I said yes. I thought of the little vacant room next to mine.

"But it's a tiny room; you wouldn't have room for anything but a bed and dresser."

"That's OK. All I need is a place to sleep."

"Well, all right. I'll give you my address. You can stop by and talk to Phil."

I didn't know if I should have told her about the room. Something made me think it wasn't a good idea. She seemed too eager or something.

◆ ◆ ◆

I got the hearing aids. Dr. Keddy did pay for them. He said I worked better in the lab with them. And now, if he asked me for a scalpel, I wouldn't hand him a hemostat. Big difference. No wonder he threw so many instruments back on my tray and raised his voice.

I got applications for the U of I, Arizona, and Michigan and sent them off with my high school transcripts. It was embarrassing, but, so what, they couldn't see me. It didn't take long to get replies from Arizona and Michigan. They said about the same thing. 'We regret to inform you....'

Then I got a letter from the U of I at Navy Pier asking me to come and see a counselor. I thought that was encouraging. When I got there the counselor was looking at my high school transcript, almost smiling.

"When is the last time you looked at your transcript?"

"I haven't...for a while."

"Well, I bet the original is in Technicolor. Blues, greens, blacks, lots of red. Right?"

Smartass.

"Larry, it appears from your transcript that you might not even know how to read well."

"I can read fine."

"Well, my suggestion is that you might go to a junior college and pick up some of the remedial skills you missed in high school. Then you could take the standard entrance exams. Then, if you do well, you might consider reapplying. Some schools will consider you if you do exceptionally well on your entrance exam scores."

I went back to my room. It didn't sound as if reapplying would work. I doubted even Dr. Keddy could help. He didn't know how badly I messed up high school. I thought about the word "remedial." I thought I knew what it meant, but I looked it up in my new dictionary anyway. "1. Supplying a remedy. 2. Intended to correct or improve deficient skills in a specific subject; *remedial reading*." I needed a remedy all right. I looked at *remedy* just below remedial. "Something, such as medicine, that relieves pain, cures disease, or corrects a disorder." I thought about how interesting that was! I know it meant medicine such as a pill, but I thought of the study of medicine instead as if "medicine would remedy my disordered life." Dictionaries are great. I often thought the best gift you could give someone would be a dictionary. But then they would be insulted. Oh, well.

I went to the library to ask the question I should have asked the counselor, but didn't. I was afraid I already looked stupid enough to him. Frankie had mentioned them.

"What are entrance exams?"

"They are tests required by many colleges and universities for admission. Not all schools require them. Some just go by your high school grade point average."

"What if you have a lousy grade point?"

"If you do very well on the entrance exams, some schools might admit you even if your grade point is below what they normally require."

"How do you take them?"

"You sign up for them, pay a fee, and take them at a specific place and time. They send the results to the schools you're applying to. But, if you didn't do well in high school, I would strongly recommend that you prepare for them."

"How do you do that?"

"Basically, get a preparation book and read high school books on the subjects covered on the exam. You can borrow all those books here if you like."

I didn't have a library card—never did—but I got one. I took the books she gave me and made a plan to read them all. She was right; they were books I should have read in high school. Despite that, I was determined to read every one of those books. I finally felt as if I knew what I wanted to do, and I started to read as if my life depended on it. I signed up to take the entrance exams. Then I applied to Marquette, a Catholic university in Milwaukee.

Jean did move into my rooming house—right next door to me. She wanted to spend any free time we had together, but studying for the entrance exams became the most important thing to me. After the way I screwed up high school, this felt like my one chance to change my life. It wasn't going to be easy, and I was going to be damn sure I didn't blow it. When I wasn't in the heart lab or working on the floor, I was reading. I think Jean resented that. And I'm not sure she understood how important it was.

"You know I always liked and admired you, for years. But Sal was your friend, and he wanted it kept that way. He could tell I liked you, so whenever you came around, he made me go to the back of the house."

"He did? What did you like about me?"

"Oh, you were always so cool, so composed; you seemed so sure of yourself."

"I was?" I laughed, "I sure didn't feel that way. I never felt sure of myself. I guess looks are deceiving. I *always* felt nervous."

"About me?"

"No, about everything. Life."

"Well, you did a good job of hiding it."

"I'm not sure I was trying to hide it. I thought it showed; that it was just there."

"Sal was always pushing me into the background when you came around. Now I feel like you're pushing me away because you need to study. I kind of hoped with Sal gone, you know, we could get to know each other better."

"Well, I do need to study. It's important because it might be the only way I'll ever get an education. I feel like I have only a few months to learn everything I missed in four years in high school. Now I regret it. I feel like a jerk nobody trapped in my stupid past."

"You're not a jerk nobody."

"Well, go tell that to the asshole at the University of Illinois who thinks I *can't read*, for Christ's sake."

"Hey, I'm on your side, OK? Calm down. You're starting to sound like Sal."

"I'm sorry; I didn't mean to yell at you. I guess I'm just trying to make a point."

"What's the point then?"

"The point is it's now or never. Frankie said…"

"Wait. Who's *Frankie*?"

"Uh, Frankie, is…er, just one of the Deuces."

"I don't remember a Frankie in the Deuces."

"Not Frankie. Frank, Frank McGovern. I'm sure you heard Sal mention him. What I'm saying is that I'm finally thinking about what's important to me. If I don't do this, I might as well drive a fucking truck. But it's not just about education—it's about *who I am*. Sorry."

"What do you mean, who you are?"

"The truth is, I…I don't fucking know right now." I was tired.

To me our relationship was important mostly because we were both isolated from families and friends. I wasn't so sure what it was to Jean. As time passed we became even more dependent on each another. It was like two have-nots trying to make a whole.

Unfortunately, and I guess inevitably, we started having sex. Not making love, just having sex. In the beginning, I really didn't want to. But we were both virgins, very curious, and always right next door to each other. While the physical part of sex felt good, I also had enormous pangs of guilt about it. After the first time, I lay there for a long time in silence feeling vile. Being Catholic didn't help. Sex before marriage wasn't just a venial sin; it was a mortal sin, a real "soul stainer," read *lethal,* punishable by being sent to Hell. My sex education didn't help either. It was a one-liner from mom—"Masturbation makes people crazy." She got that on the unquestionable authority of her mom. I guess her mother surmised that from working in a mental hospital where she saw a lot of patients doing just that. If anything was crazy, that was.

I wanted to do what was "right," but I was totally confused by my curiosity, unexpected sexual feelings, guilt, and shame. But more importantly, I knew in my heart that I didn't feel about Jean like I did about Frankie. I cared about Jean, but when I thought about Frankie, I regretted she wasn't my first lover—and that I wasn't going to be hers. Thinking about Frankie made me feel even guiltier.

◆ ◆ ◆

I sat for the entrance exams. It was hard to tell how I did, but I was afraid to hope I did well. I started watching for the mail on the table in the lobby every day. For many weeks, there was nothing.

One night I returned from the hospital and found a lone letter sitting on the lobby table. It was from Marquette. Not bulk mail either; my name was typed perfectly in crisp black letters. I was enormously excited but afraid to open it. I felt it, touched it to my chest, and looked at it in the light hoping for a clue. It was like trying to open a letter that said I was going to live or die. I didn't want to open it in the rooming house so I took it to the Golden Cup Coffee Shop. It was open all night. I carefully and respectfully placed it on the counter in front of me.

"Coffee?" the waitress was standing there looking at me and glancing at the letter.

"Yes, please." I would be up all night anyway, good news or bad.

"Important letter?" she smiled.

"Yes, very." I moved the letter around as if the counter was a Ouija Board. I unsealed it. That was a big step. Very slowly, I unfolded it, noticed the gold and blue Marquette University letterhead and saw "Dear Mr. Pedersen:" Then even more slowly, I peeked at the first line. "Congratulations. We are pleased to inform you…" With that, I let out a loud "Yahooooooooo!"

The waitress looked at me and laughed. "Guess you got the right answer."

To my amazement and joy, the university had accepted me because of my entrance exam scores. I was so ecstatic I left the waitress a dollar tip. I danced up Clark Street, waving my letter for a long time. I didn't tell Jean.

But now I had a dilemma. I didn't really love Jean as I did Frankie, and I couldn't tell her. I felt a terrible sense of guilt about our relationship because we had had sex and even worse about the idea of leaving her behind. I didn't know if I could do that.

13

Leaving Chicago

I wondered what room Tiny had died in. I asked the male PM nurse on that floor if he remembered Tiny.

"Was he a little skinny kid, Timmy or Tiny? Died of a heroin overdose?"

"Yeah, that was him. What room was he in?"

"I'm pretty sure it was 307. But there's a patient in there. Father Carl."

I went to the room anyway. Even though most of the rooms were pretty much the same, I wanted to see the room where Tiny died. The lights were out, but the night-light on the wall was lit. I could make out that Father Carl was sleeping on his side and covered only by a sheet. He still had his glasses on. There was a small black book with a gold cross on it under his hand. Since it was a cool evening, even inside the hospital, I got a blanket and covered him. I gently took off his glasses, picked up the book, and placed them on the bedside table.

The next evening the male nurse, Hannah, told me Father Carl wanted to see me. I wondered if I was in trouble for some reason. When I got to his room, he was sitting up in bed reading the little black book by the light of the overhead lamp. He seemed awfully young to be a real priest. He looked more boyish than fatherly.

"You wanted to see me, Father?"

"Yes. Was it you who came into my room last night?"

"I'm sorry if I disturbed you."

"Oh, you didn't. I just wanted to thank you for giving me the blanket and taking my glasses off."

"Well, it wasn't a big deal."

"Maybe not a big deal, just a very kind thing to do." He smiled.

"Well, thanks, Father. I actually came in to see this room."

"Oh? Why's that?" His face lit up a bit.

"Well, it's a little awkward to say." I hesitated. "A friend of mine, his name was Tiny, he died in here. I hope you don't mind my saying that."

He laughed. "No, I don't mind. I realize people have died in every one of these rooms. This hospital *is* over a hundred years old."

"Well, sometimes patients ask if anyone ever died in the room they're in. I just lie and say, 'I don't think so.' Ooops, I hope that isn't a venial sin."

He laughed even louder this time. "It's forgivable. And, yes, lots of people are afraid of death. They don't want to be in an *unlucky room*. Don't worry about me. I only have pneumonia, and I doubt I'll die from it. What happened to your friend?"

"He died of a drug overdose. Heroin."

"I'm sorry to hear that." He put his book down. "Did you get a chance to say goodbye to him?"

"No, I didn't. I regret it." I was starting to feel a lump in my throat.

"You regret that you didn't take the time to see him?"

"No. I didn't know what was going on with him. I was in Detention Camp when it happened."

"Detention Camp?"

"Well, it's long story. Tiny was in my gang."

"It's OK, Larry. This isn't confession. But would you like to say a prayer for him with me? Then you can say goodbye."

"Uh, I guess so."

"Well, I'll start and then you just say whatever you want. OK?"

"Sure." I wasn't sure.

He bowed his head and made the sign of the cross. "Heavenly Father, please hear our prayer for Tiny. Go ahead."

I was silent for a couple of minutes. I didn't know what to say.

"Just say, 'Heavenly Father, please hear my prayer for Tiny.' Then say anything that comes to mind."

"Heavenly Father, please hear my prayer for Tiny. Tiny, I'm…I'm sorry I didn't get a chance to say goodbye. I would have if I had known what happened. And I'm sorry about your eye." Tears began rolling down my cheeks. "And I hope wherever you are you know I'm thinking about you. I miss you, Tiny. Take care. Goodbye."

Father Carl put his hand on my head; I liked the feel of it. Then he said, "Amen. You'll feel better, Larry."

"I never thought of actually *saying* goodbye to him."

"Many of us don't."

"I'm sorry I cried, Father."

He smiled. "Larry, never be sorry for your tears. They mean that your feeling comes from deep within your heart."

I liked that.

During the time Father Carl was in the hospital, we talked a lot—especially about my experiences with religion, about violence and death, and about Clay and Tiny. He seemed more progressive and liberal than most priests I knew, but he also admitted there was a lot he didn't know. He talked about faith and said I had had a "crisis of faith" because I lost two close friends when I was so young. He encouraged me to rejoin Catholicism. I still wasn't sure about religion, though. I don't know if I had any faith when Clay and Tiny killed themselves. I was confused about religion even before that. It was just that none of them had any answers. I didn't tell him that Freud thought religion was "the opiate of the masses." I still wondered if it was.

Father Carl eventually left the hospital and gave me his phone number and the name of his parish. It was called *Our Lady Help of Christians*. He asked me to come and see him.

Fall progressed to winter and the Christmas season was coming. We weren't doing as many procedures in the lab then. Because of this, I got a lot of chances to work on the floor since so many of the staff wanted to be off during the holidays. I didn't mind. I liked the chance to make more money. I didn't even mind working Christmas Eve or Christmas Day.

On Christmas Eve, the hospital was quiet and the corridors were dark except for the night-lights in the hallway. Any of the patients who could possibly be sent home had been discharged. I was sitting in the nurses' station reading *The Interpretation of Dreams*. Hannah let me read when the floor was quiet. I was reading more of Freud and glad that Frankie said his name. I was beginning to like the way he could make sense of dreams by talking about the unconscious mind and how things in dreams were different from the way they seemed to be in waking life—as if there was so much more going on in the mind that we didn't have a clue about. Freud was obviously very smart; he made the unconscious seem smart, too.

The ringing phone jarred me back. Hannah got it. When he hung up, he turned to me. "Shit, that was Admissions. They're sending us someone from the emergency room. Set up Room 312 with oxygen and a cut-down tray."

"OK. Right away." I got a cut-down tray from the back of the nurses' station and went to get an oxygen tank from Central Supply. Unfortunately, there wasn't oxygen in the wall of each room, so I had to get a tank and roll it in. I set up the room.

In a few minutes, an orderly from the emergency room came down the hall, pushing a gurney with the patient on it. I could hardly make out what the patient looked like because the halls were dark and the patient was draped in a sheet that covered most of his face. The patient was either unconscious or in a coma. As we lifted him into the bed, I could see his dirty unshaven face was a yellow-orange color. He smelled of urine and cheap wine. I looked at his hospital wristband for his name. It said, "Doe, John." The orderly left. I took off the remainder of his stiff, smelly clothes. His whole body was that same color, and his belly was so big he looked pregnant. His ankles were crusted with dirt, and his toenails hadn't been cut in ages—they were so long they curled like claws on an animal. The on-call doctor came in. His wrinkled whites made him look like he just woke up.

He looked at the unknown man. "Jesus!" he said slowly. Start the oxygen, will you?"

"Yes, sir." I started the oxygen. It made a hissing sound as it passed through the water jar that moistened it. The doctor took out his stethoscope, listened to the man's heart, then his chest. He felt the man's swollen abdomen.

"He's got ascites. Can you get me a setup to drain his abdomen?"

I went to get the setup from Central Supply and hurried back to the room. Just as I got to the door, the hissing of the oxygen stopped. The doctor was pulling the sheet over the man's head. "He's gone."

As the doctor passed me in the doorway, he stopped a second and said, "Merry Christmas, huh?"

I went back to the nurses' station and told Hannah. He said he would try getting someone from the morgue to come up.

I walked to the end of the hallway and looked out the window. A light snow had begun to fall. On the sidewalk, a woman with a red scarf wrapped around her neck made her way quickly but gingerly, her arms filled with Christmas packages. For a second I wondered what my family was doing but, except for missing Christie, I was glad I wasn't with them.

Just then, the doors at the end of the darkened hallway opened. A procession of hooded Brothers came in slowly, carrying lit candles that cast their shadows on the hallway walls. As they walked toward me they started to sing *Silent Night*. The sight and sound of them gave me gooseflesh.

It was approaching midnight as I walked back to my room from the hospital. The streets were empty, and the snow was coming down harder. When I got past Halsted Street, it was beginning to settle in the branches of the trees on Fullerton Parkway. I watched the snowflakes turn silver and sparkle as they passed through the beams of the streetlights. It was a mystical, magical sight and, for the first time in my life, I felt happy to be alive. I thought about going to Marquette next fall. Frankie would be proud of me. I missed her. But whenever I thought of writing her, I put it off. I still loved her, but I never felt I was good enough for her. I knew it sounded kind of crazy, but our worlds just seemed too different—and belonging to hers seemed like something I didn't deserve.

When I told Dr. Keddy about being accepted to Marquette, he said he was proud of me. I still hadn't told Jean and, sooner or later, I knew I had to tell her. We never talked about what we would do if I were accepted.

In my room the stained glass window in the church across the way was lit up, and there was muffled singing coming from inside. It must have been a midnight Mass. I liked just standing there with the baseboard heater warming my feet as I looked at that window.

On Christmas morning, Jean and I got up early to go to the Golden Cup for coffee and doughnuts. Phil had put a small fake Christmas tree with tiny blinking lights on the table in the lobby. Fortunately, the coffee shop was open every day of the year. The streets were almost empty, but there was about two feet of snow on the ground. When we got to the coffee shop, we were the only customers. By then we had become regulars there and knew most of the waitresses. Old Mary, with her messy blonde-dyed hair tied up on her head, was the only waitress. I was sure that when she was young she was a cheerleader, and even more sure she never forgot it. We all said, "Merry Christmas," but, as usual, Mary soon started her complaints about her varicose veins and her daughter's migraine headaches. It wasn't much of a celebration.

Jean and I went back to my room and exchanged gifts. She gave me an orange plastic electric coffeepot for my room, and I gave her a little floor heater for hers. The wall heater in her room didn't work very well, and she used that as an excuse to come stay in my room on cold nights. When she saw the heater, she didn't say anything; she just lowered her eyes. I'm not sure why she got me the coffeepot for my room. She knew how much I liked going out to the Golden Cup.

◆ ◆ ◆

I had to work again in the afternoon, and there was supposed to be a special Mass in the hospital chapel for people who had to work that day. The Brothers were going to sing Gregorian chant—something I'd never heard.

When I got to the chapel it was completely silent and dimly lit. A few of the hospital staff were scattered irregularly among the pews. Some were kneeling with their heads bowed. The gilded altar glowed from the light of tall candles. Rows of red poinsettias and white jonquils lined the steps to the altar. To the right of the altar was a votive stand with tiers of flickering candles inside small red jars. The cool air of the chapel was rich with incense. I sat alone in a pew close to the front.

In a few minutes, the doors at both sides of the altar opened. The Brothers, dressed in their hooded robes, carried long candles as they had the night before. They walked single file into the chapel and lined up in rows in front of the altar. Then they began chanting. There was no music, only the Brothers' voices rising and falling together without beat or rhythm. The singing was simple but very beautiful. The gray stone walls echoed their voices. As I listened, I felt as if a part of me was being carried somewhere far away, to another place, another time. The word *eternal* came to me. At times like this, I was glad I wasn't completely deaf and imagined whatever I heard must be twice as beautiful to a hearing person.

After the Mass, the Brothers joined the rest of us for cookies and hot chocolate in the cafeteria. I sat by myself, the graceful chanting still in my head. Then Brother René tapped me on the shoulder.

"Hi," he said in his usual cheery voice. "Mind if I join you?"

"Of course not. I was just replaying those chants. Did you sing?"

"Yes. I saw you in the front, but you couldn't see me. I was hiding in my hood. Did you like it?"

"Very much. It's unique, isn't it?"

"Yes, and very old. Seventh century. Oldest music in the world."

"Why do they call it Gregorian Chant?"

"Well, first because it's homophonic chanting rather than singing, and Pope Gregory wanted it preserved, so he issued an edict or something that insured it wouldn't get lost. And it never has. It's had about 1,500 birthdays at my last count."

"No wonder the word *eternal* came to me. How do you guys, uh sorry, I mean Brothers, remember all the words?"

"We rehearse a lot. No, I'm kidding. It's part of being a Brother. You sing them so much, they become like Christmas carols. There are some monks who sing them seven times a day, every day of the year."

"Really? How do they have time for anything else?"

"They're cloistered."

"What's cloistered?"

"Oh, it's kind of like voluntary prison, except it's in a monastery."

"How can you be so happy all the time?"

"Probably the same reason you're so curious all the time."

It's a good thing I didn't ask him what 'homophonic' meant. "I'm serious."

"Well, I'm doing what I want to do and what I need to do."

"How do you know that?"

"Larry, if you were a cat, you'd have a very short life span. OK, seriously, you feel it in your bones."

"C'mon."

"Haven't you ever felt something in your bones? Wasn't there something you just knew you *had* to do? That if you *didn't* do it, it would be a terrible mistake?"

"Not exactly. But I'm beginning to feel something like that about medicine."

"Well, even with all your curiosity, you still haven't thought enough about that. Listen, I have to be at Vespers. Let's talk again. Maybe have a cigarette in the cast room?"

"OK, Brother René."

"Hey, maybe it's poetry! Night, Larry." He went off laughing, shaking his head.

I still wasn't sure about God or religion, but there were some pretty sad and pretty wonderful things about Christmas time.

◆ ◆ ◆

Almost before I knew it, spring had come. From the window of my room, I saw that the snow-capped trees were now bare, scraggly black branches tipped with little green buds. The only traces of winter were small piles of dirty ice at some curbsides. I opened my window for the first time since November. A breeze, both cool and warm, blew softly over my face and into the room. For Chicago weather, this was as good as it gets.

I knew I couldn't put off talking to Jean. I felt selfish, but I hadn't really pictured Jean with me at Marquette; yet she was a good companion and one of the few real friends I had left.

That morning, before I went to the hospital, I took her for a walk in Lincoln Park.

"I was accepted at Marquette."

"Really, that's great! Did you just hear from them?"

"Actually, a few weeks ago."

"Why…why didn't you tell me before?"

"I wasn't sure what to do about us."

"About us? I thought you wanted to get married. What have we been doing together all this time?" I didn't remember *anything* about wanting to get married.

"You want to marry a student?"

"Yes, but not just any student—you. I can help you. I can work while you go to school. Besides, Marquette's a private school, and it's very expensive."

Strange as it seems, I hadn't thought much about how I was going to pay for school. "Dr. Keddy gave me a great letter of recommendation to the Allen-Bradley Open-Heart Laboratory. It's part of Milwaukee County Hospital."

"But you can't work full time."

"It's part-time. I thought I could pay my tuition that way. Maybe take out some loans."

"Larry, it sounds like you never planned on taking me. Did you?" She started to cry.

"No, it's not that. I just wasn't sure." I hated seeing her cry.

"Weren't sure about what? Me?"

"No, it's not that. I thought about taking you." I knew I was bordering on another venial sin. Because Jean had no family or friends, thinking of leaving her behind seemed cruel—especially since we had been intimate.

"I tell you what, why don't we talk to Father Carl about it?"

"Why don't *you* talk to Father Carl!" she yelled and ran off toward the rooming house.

◆ ◆ ◆

I called Father Carl and made a time to go see him. We met one evening in his rectory, which was very modern. I preferred older churches, but he had a very large, comfortable, and beautifully furnished room.

"How you feeling, Father Carl?"

He took off his black jacket and white collar while settling back in a leather chair. "I'm great, Larry. Completely recovered; never felt better. Thanks. And you?"

"I'm OK, but I have a problem."

"Oh? Let's hear it."

I explained my situation as best I could. He listened a long time. He asked if Jean and I had been "intimate." Looking away from him, I said we had.

"Well, Larry, all I can say is that you have to do what you believe is right."

That's not what I wanted to hear. He didn't ask me if I loved her. I thanked him for his time and got up to leave.

"And, if you do decide to get married, I would be happy to marry you."

"Thanks, Father."

On my way home, I decided the only "right thing" was to marry her and take her with me. Even though it was different, it was bad enough that I left Christie with my mother. I hated the idea of leaving her behind. For another thing, I didn't think she would survive Chicago on her own.

◆   ◆   ◆

At the end of the summer, on the last day of my job at the hospital, there was a small farewell party for me in the cafeteria. Dr. Keddy was there with some members of the open-heart team, some of the nurses, Brother René, and some of the other Brothers. I was telling Dr. Keddy goodbye.

"I want to thank you for all you've done for me."

"Well, you're welcome, Larry, but in the year or so I've known you, you've come a long way on your own. I'm sorry you won't be on our team here, but you'll be on the team in Wisconsin. They will be doing the real thing before we will."

I wanted to hug him but couldn't bring myself to do it. It would only be uncomfortable for him, even more than for me.

Brother René was the last to say goodbye.

"I'm going to miss your questions, Larry. But the Jesuits at Marquette live off questions so you'll be right at home there. They'll love you!" Then he whispered, "I'm going to miss smoking with you in the cast room." Then in a normal voice, he said, "And here's something to remember me by."

He handed me a roughly wrapped gift with an oversized green bow. I unwrapped the package. It was a phonograph album called *Chants of the Monks of Santo Domingo De Silos.*

"Those are the 'guys' in Spain who chant all day," he said, smiling.

"Thank you so much, Brother René. I won't forget you." I did hug him. I knew *he* wouldn't mind.

14

Marquette

Jean and I were married that fall by Father Carl in a small, simple ceremony at St. Clement Church not far from the rooming house. Father Carl had convinced me to reaffirm my faith in Catholicism and get married in the Church. I wasn't sure I should do that, but I agreed to anyway. Maybe it was because I liked Father Carl and wanted to please him. While he said that getting married was up to me, I got the idea that he thought I should.

Bud and my mom were divorced by then, but they came—separately. Bud brought Christie because she had been living with him since the Children's Protective Services took her from my Mom after their divorce. I was glad for that. Bud had stopped drinking, and he would take better care of her. Christie was the only person I was happy to see. She looked a little older and maybe a little happier. She seemed happy that I was getting married, as if there would finally be someone who would take care of me. Dino and Eve came, but they were late. Mickey couldn't come because he was in the Army brig—undergoing a psychiatric evaluation because he shot a cow with an M-1. Mom brought a wedding cake, but because she took the city bus it was a wreck by the time she got there. She barely made it, and the cake decoration was so smudged it almost didn't look like a wedding cake anymore. Neither of Jean's parents came; they couldn't afford to make the trip from Iowa. She didn't seem to mind. I got the feeling she didn't want them there. We planned a reception at a restaurant where Eve worked, but hardly anyone confirmed—so we canceled it. Anyone who came just went home after the ceremony. Since there was no reception, I threw the cake in the garbage after my mom left.

◆ ◆ ◆

On the drive up to Marquette, we stopped at a small resort hotel in Lake Geneva, Wisconsin, to have our "honeymoon." I went through the motions, but my heart was somewhere else. Other than being afraid to leave Jean in Chicago, I really had no idea why I got married. It was a sad and confusing day for me, but Jean seemed happy. She didn't appear to pick up on my mood. She either didn't want to, or had no idea what was going on with me. I doubted that she even understood me, and I'm not sure I understood her either. I reminded myself to stay focused on school. The next morning I got up early and went to breakfast by myself. Jean slept in. I couldn't imagine that happening with Frankie.

◆ ◆ ◆

As we drove into Milwaukee, the freeway seemed to come to an end just as it approached the outlines of the city. I could begin to see that Milwaukee was a lot smaller city than what I was used to. I felt a jolt of excitement when I recognized the spire of a large church close to the downtown area. From pictures in the university catalog, I knew that this must be Gesu, the campus church.

In downtown Milwaukee, we found a hotel for a few days so we could look for an apartment. I had an appointment to meet with Dr. Stanton in the afternoon. Apart from how I felt about being married, I was full of hope. For the first time in my life I experienced some joyful feelings. It was a natural high. I revisited my dream of making a break from my past—here I could start a new life. I was accepted by a private and prestigious university, had a letter of introduction from Dr. Keddy to Dr. Stanton at the County Hospital for a job, and I was finally out of Chicago—for good! This was the place to get my college degree and go to medical school. That I had absolutely no money for tuition and only a little money to live on didn't even bother me. Dr. Keddy said the job was guaranteed.

Milwaukee was not just another Chicago, either. People said, "Oh, Milwaukee, it's a nice place to have kids and raise a family." Known as the true "heart" of the Midwest, everything about it said middle class. It was a middle-sized city, literally a beer-and-sausage kind of town, thanks to the early German influence. Even its beer was a middle-class drink—not soda pop, not hard liquor. The downtown area smelled of breweries and reminded me a little of Steuben's in the old neighborhood, but I felt safer here.

I had some time before my appointment with Dr. Stanton at the hospital, so I took out my campus map and headed toward the medical school. Its building was a very long, old stone two-story building that excited me just to look at it. Since the semester hadn't started, the medical school was empty, but I tried the door—it was unlocked. Unable to contain my curiosity, I went inside. Close to the front door, I found a large lecture hall with rows of tiered desks and a lecture platform at the bottom. There was a life-sized skeleton hanging next to the podium. I took a seat in the front row, sat up straight and, for a moment, imagined myself with a room full of students in white jackets. An old wizened professor in a brown-tweed jacket and bow tie was at the podium, giving a lecture on anatomy.

The sound of a dragging metal can interrupted my fantasy. I looked up to see the janitor, a black man with a broom and large waste can. "Little early for class, ain't ya, boy?" he smiled. He knew I was enjoying myself.

"Yes," I grinned back. "*Very* early." And then, as if I had made a great discovery, I said out loud, "This is the medical school!"

"Shore is," the janitor smiled again, "and you is one eager young doctor!"

I liked that he understood and that he called me a doctor.

An hour or so later I took the bus down Wisconsin Avenue to the County Hospital. It was a very long ride. On my way there, I started getting the jitters about my appointment. "What if he doesn't like me?" I wondered. "What if he's already filled the position? What if he is put off by my hearing problem?" I tried to reassure myself that these were just normal jitters and decided to enjoy the amazingly clean, neatly ordered houses along Wisconsin Avenue. Milwaukee certainly was a clean city. I thought I was going to like it.

It took almost an hour to get out to the County Hospital. There were expansive grounds around the hospital with lots of trees and grass. I found the Allen-Bradley Laboratories in the back of the main hospital. I was surprised by how large and modern it was. A receptionist at the front desk greeted me and told me Dr. Stanton was expecting me.

In a few minutes, Dr. Stanton came out. He was a tall, handsome, middle-aged man with salt-and-pepper hair. He wore a highly starched white, knee-length lab coat, with his name sewn above the upper left pocket. Under his name was "Heart Laboratory."

"Mr. Pedersen, so nice to meet you. I'm Dr. Stanton." He shook my sweaty hand. "Come on in, have a seat. Would you like some coffee or tea?"

"No thank you, sir. Here is my letter from Dr. Keddy."

"Oh, that's your copy. He sent it to me, and we spoke on the phone."

I felt embarrassed. Of course it was a copy.

"He speaks very highly of you, Mr. Pedersen."

"You can call me Larry, sir." I wasn't sure I should have said that either.

"Oh, good, fine. Larry, then. I was looking forward to meeting you and having you join us."

"Sir, I mean, Dr. Stanton, I am *very, very* happy to be here."

"Good, good. Let me show you around, Larry. We have quite an operation here. One of the best in the country, I like to think. You'll find we are somewhat ahead of Dr. Keddy's facility."

He showed me all around the laboratory. It was a palace compared to our lab in Chicago. They had regular operating suites with all the latest equipment. The blood circulating in the perfusion pumps was warmed electronically, not by warm water. The pressure of the circulating blood also was electronically controlled. They had their own pharmacy and even their own morgue. I felt so happy.

"Dr. Stanton, this place is remarkable!"

"A bit upscale from Dr. Keddy's, isn't it?" He smiled proudly.

"A bit, sir." I laughed.

"Well, we need you here, Larry. Pump techs are hard to find. We are going to be doing pediatric open-heart surgery at Milwaukee Children's very soon. We'll bring you up to snuff in no time. Dr. Keddy said you learn fast, have initiative, and want to go to medical school. That's just what we want in our pump tech. Let's go back to my office and talk about the details."

Back in his office, I was ecstatic. This was the place I wanted to be and, so far, there didn't seem to be any problems.

Dr. Stanton sat back in his leather armchair behind his desk. "Larry, I understand you've been accepted as an undergrad at Marquette. That right?"

"Yes, sir."

"And you understand we will be doing our procedures at Children's very shortly?"

"Yes, sir."

"And you understand that this position is full-time?"

"Full…time?"

"Yes. And when we are at Children's you'll have to be on call twenty-four hours. These babies' hearts don't wait. If we're not there and ready to go, some of them will die."

"But, sir, what…what about school? I was going to go to school full-time."

"Well, for a few years, you can go part-time. We will pay half your tuition as long as you go to Marquette. Dr. Keddy is willing to subsidize your tuition as well. That includes medical school."

I was stupefied. Partly because of their offer to pay part of my tuition, partly because Keddy told him that he would help, and partly because this job was full-time. But mostly because he said, "part time a few *years*."

"Dr. Stanton, sir. I...I just don't know. I don't think I can do that. I wanted to go to school full-time."

"Larry, it seems like you need to think about this. I hope you understand that with respect to medical school, this job is a plum."

"A plum, sir?"

"Yes, a plum. If you work for me, you *will* go to medical school. No questions asked. I am the chief of surgery and a full professor at the medical school. Your acceptance to Marquette Medical School will be guaranteed—and at half the cost. With Dr. Keddy's help, even less than that. Medical school is very expensive. Do you understand what I'm saying here, son?"

"Yes, sir. I understand." I liked that he called me "son." But I was confused. I was very confused—and very sad.

"Well, what do you say then?"

"I'm going to need to think about it, sir."

"Sure. Larry, go home and give it some thought. I want you on our team. Remember that. And remember what I said about medical school."

"Thank you, sir. Very much. I appreciate it. I'll...I'll think about that."

It was late afternoon by the time I left the County Hospital. I decided to walk back to the hotel—I didn't care how far it was. I wanted to rehearse what just happened. In my heart, I knew that I couldn't do it. As I walked, my vision got blurry, and then my head started to hurt. Each step felt like a punch in the side of my head.

By the time I got back to the hotel, it was dark and sometime late at night. My feet felt like swollen, overcooked potatoes, I'd never walked that far in my life. Jean was up, waiting. I slumped deeply into a large overstuffed armchair.

"What's wrong?" she asked. "You didn't get it?"

"Oh, I got it. I just didn't take it. I mean...I don't think I can take it."

"Are you crazy? What was wrong with the job? What will we do for money? I think you're making a big mistake."

I tried to explain everything that had happened, and what I had thought about as I walked back from the appointment. I don't think she understood how I felt. She thought it was a good deal. I didn't. That conversation made me realize how different Jean and I were. Maybe I *was* making a mistake—maybe the biggest mistake of my life. Maybe the marriage was a mistake. I felt my dream was starting to unravel, just as it was getting started. All I wanted was to soak my feet and go to sleep.

The next day I called Dr. Stanton and told him I couldn't take the job. He was disappointed and said if I changed my mind to let him know.

Later that sorry afternoon we found a small, one-bedroom apartment near the campus. It was in a very quiet and clean apartment building just off Wisconsin Avenue. The walk to school would be short.

I hated thinking about money, but I needed a job. I went to the university employment office and found a job at the campus bookstore. It paid a dollar an hour. Jean found a job at Children's Hospital in the medical records department. It paid about the same. Between the two of us it seemed as if we might be able to make month-to-month expenses. Tuition was going to be something else.

When classes started I was very excited. I had signed up for pre-med which meant having a biology or chemistry major. I chose biology. I put the heart lab job out of my mind and tried to focus on my studies.

The first lecture in biology was in a huge auditorium. I had to get a front row seat to hear. A well-known biologist gave the first guest lecture. He spoke about the interface between biology and philosophy. For the first time, I listened intently to what a teacher had to say. "This is an exciting and challenging time for biology. We have advanced to the point where we are on a frontier of being virtually able to create life. Other sciences have also progressed in their own ways to yet another frontier—that of being easily able to destroy life as we know it. As horrific as they were, only eighteen years later, Hiroshima and Nagasaki were child's play compared to the extent of mass destruction now possible. Our country's nuclear capability is such that if there were a nuclear war, life on our planet would cease to exist. The radioactive fallout would be so intense that eventually all ecosystems would cease to function. So we are at a crossroads in science. Science cannot function ethically without the intervention of philosophy's moral point of view. When science goes forward without moral judgment, and when it is exploited for political causes, then its discoveries amount to nothing but harm—to the planet, to its people, and to life itself." He went on.

His speech moved me deeply. This was information I knew little to nothing about—especially our country's insane nuclear capability. How could such smart people be so stupid? Later some of the other students told me that this professor was an ardent antiwar activist. It also introduced me to a way of thinking about science that I later discovered was typical of Jesuit teaching. Regardless of our majors, all of us had required minors in philosophy and theology.

After a few months, I was still enjoying being in school and more convinced that not working for Dr. Stanton was the right decision. My full load of classes was a lot to handle even though I was only working part-time. I still couldn't get the hours I needed working at the bookstore to cover expenses and tuition. I was skirting a thin line between having enough time to study and making enough money. I envied and resented students I met whose parents were paying for everything they needed. What really pissed me off was when they whined about their checks being late. I could apply for student loans, but when I considered the eventual added expense of medical school, it seemed as if I might end up in debt forever. I thought about Rush Street. Making money on the street was easier, even without resorting to illegal stuff. Drugs and prostitution were lucrative, but I would never do either of them. There were lots of other ways to make money down there and a few of the Outfit guys liked me and were willing to give me big tips just for doing them small favors. I decided I would try to see about getting my job back as a hiker on weekends. As much as I hated to work with Dino again, it might just solve my money problem.

15

Back on Rush Street

I swallowed my pride and called Dino. He said that if I came down Friday evenings, I could work thirty hours over the weekend. I made plans to start going down there close to the end of November. I could also work over the Christmas break.

Near the beginning of November, Jean told me she was pregnant. Now that we were "Catholic again," an abortion was out of the question. Not only that, I doubted I could have done that anyway. Jean certainly never would; she never stopped being Catholic. She didn't say so, but I knew she wanted children. Bud shocked me at the wedding when he took me aside and said—almost like a warning—that he thought Jean was going to *try* to get pregnant. I ignored him. It sounded too much like my mother's story about why my natural father left. After they had Mickey and Dino, my real father told my mom that if she had another kid, he was out of there. Of course, she omitted my father's stupidity in ignoring his responsibility if she did. Mom told me that as if it were something I really needed to know. The truth was it felt more as if she was indirectly letting me know I was responsible for his leaving. After all, I *was* that third child.

I was responsible for Jean's being pregnant, especially since we were using the rhythm method, otherwise known as playing "Catholic Roulette."

I hadn't thought of having children any more than I thought of getting married. Yet, with that possibility, a part of me was intrigued by the idea of being a parent. If only to make sure my child would never have the life I did. But that wasn't a great reason to have a kid—and it would definitely worsen the money problem.

◆ ◆ ◆

Before Marquette, the most I knew about politics was that presidents served four-year terms. I barely passed high school Civics. So I was just beginning to learn about politics in some of my college classes, especially in American History. Political conversations also were a regular part of university life, and I was beginning to enjoy them. A little late, I know, but that's where I started.

On the day I was leaving Marquette to work the weekend in Chicago, John F. Kennedy was assassinated. News of the assassination swept the campus like a crackling wildfire. From the little I knew of him, Kennedy had been an inspiration to Americans. He seemed classy, very intelligent, and well-meaning. I got the feeling he genuinely cared about the country. I also liked his accent. As the news of his death spread, the campus went into a state of numbness and mourning. Everyone seemed dazed. Some students held each other and cried openly on the streets.

I was stunned. It was difficult to gather my thoughts when his death was announced during my English class that Friday afternoon. It was my last class of the day. I brooded about it on the train all the way to Chicago. Like everyone else, I wondered who would commit such an appalling act, and why he would do it. My thinking went nowhere. It seemed so momentous an event, yet so childish an act. I knew about death on the streets, but maybe I expected more from "civilized grown-ups."

When I got to Chicago, the city seemed to have also gone into a kind of shutdown. The streets were practically empty. Rush Street, normally a hub of activity on Friday nights, was a ghost town. Andy, one of the brothers who owned Mario's, came out of the restaurant. He was surprised to see me. "What are you doin' here? I thought you went away to school?"

"I'm just going to work some weekends. I'll go back Sunday nights."

He looked up and down the street. "The street looks worse than Christmas Eve," he said matter-of-factly.

"Are we going to stay open?"

"Of course we stay open. The day we close is the day *I* die." He went back inside. Wrong question.

For a Friday night at Mario's, the Outfit guys were conspicuously absent. A little later one of them pulled up. He got out of his still running car and walked over to me. "Larry, come va?"

"*Non c'e male.* It's kind of quiet. Everybody's probably home watching the news of the assassination."

"Fuckin' hypocrites, everybody knows we did it. I'm going to check out the street."

"*Buon fortuna.*"

"*A dopo*, Larry." For a second I couldn't believe what I thought he just said. "Everybody knows we did it." Part of the shock all over the world came from the mystery of who assassinated Kennedy. I had heard on the street that the CIA had approached the Outfit for some hitters to whack Fidel Castro. If that was true, anything was possible, but I was still shocked.

My first night on the street was dead. I parked about three cars. At midnight, I left. Usually I worked until four in the morning. The rest of the weekend wasn't much different from Friday. Dino never bothered to show up, and I went home almost broke. Luckily, the Outfit guy later gave me twenty bucks just to buy him a bottle of bitters.

◆ ◆ ◆

The next weekend Rush Street was in full force. It was as if nothing had happened. A lot of people I knew there were surprised to see me back on the street. Among them were the prostitutes. When they found out I was in pre-med they started calling me "Doc." The bolder ones teased me about wanting to be a doctor and made cracks like, "I know why you want to be a doctor, they're all lechers and most of them are johns." They fascinated me, and I had become a sort of confidant to a number of them. Ginny was my favorite.

The first time I saw her she had just come to Mario's to talk to Ben, one of the other doormen who worked there. She was new on the street and had just finished turning her first trick. I was just a few feet away, watching her as she was talking to Ben in the foyer of Mario's restaurant. I was struck by how young she was but, apart from her age, I was uncomfortably aware of how frightened she looked. She was short and thin. Her hands trembled, and her eyes were wide—as if she expected to be slapped or something. She had long, beautiful, auburn hair, and her red sequined dress clung tightly to her sensuous frame. She was extending a shaky handful of bills toward Ben. I tried to hear their conversation. As he towered over her, he counted the bills, then sneered and said, "What's this?"

His look made her more afraid. Tears welled up in her eyes, and the words faltered from her dark red lips. "I...I thought, you said sixty-forty?"

"I did," he replied. "Sixty for me, forty for you."

Her face grew pale and her eyes even more painfully afraid than before, her words stumbled again. "I'm sorry, I'm...I'm really sorry. I didn't know what you meant."

"Well, keep it straight from now on," he said coldly. "Sixty for me, forty for you."

"Sure, Ben. I'll remember. I promise."

I wanted to throw up. How the hell could he make her pay him more than she got from the trick? I mean it was one thing for her to sell her body for money, but to give Ben more when he just sat on his ass while she took chances with her life totally disgusted me.

That was my introduction to Ginny. Since I started seeing her almost every weekend on the street I got to know her pretty well. Like some of the other hookers, she often stopped to talk to me. With time, she seemed less afraid on the street. She never seemed afraid of me, maybe because she knew that I wasn't a pimp, or at least that I didn't want anything from her.

A lot of hookers had interesting stories to tell, and they didn't have any qualms about telling them—at least not to me. Ginny was no exception. I soon learned she was twenty-three-years-old and had a six- or seven-year-old kid. She got pregnant by her high school boyfriend when she was fifteen and dropped out of school. He promised to marry her so she had the kid rather than get an abortion. A few months later, he took off and she never saw him again. She also told me her boyfriend wasn't her first sexual experience—against her will, her stepfather was.

After one really busy Saturday night, or rather early Sunday morning, just before the restaurant closed at five AM, the street sounds faded as the last of the night's stragglers left the street and the bums from Wells Street came stumbling across Clark Street to search the restaurant garbage bins for food. I was exhausted; my feet hurt, and I was thinking about how far behind I was at school—and why the fuck I ever came back to Rush Street. Then suddenly, out of the dark end of the street, a screaming figure came running toward me. It was Ginny. Her white dress and coat were streaked with blood; she was hysterical. Her right arm was pouring blood. It had a gaping gash in it almost the length of her forearm. I took off my belt and tightened it around her upper arm. Since Mario's was almost closed, and I had no cars left, I rushed her to the Henrotin Emergency Room a few blocks away. On the way, she told me that the owner of Freddy's, a small basement bar down the street, had thrown her against the front glass door. Apparently, the vice heat was on, and he wanted no hookers left in the bar. When she didn't leave immediately, he literally threw her through the glass door.

When we got to the hospital, I remembered that I was in this same emergency room myself when I broke the cashier's cage window in the subway station. The police brought me here with my bleeding hands in handcuffs.

Today the place was packed, and the only two doctors were busy. I was frantic as the ER nurse put a proper tourniquet on Ginny's arm to stop the bleeding. Somehow, the nurse knew Ginny was a hooker.

"Have you got insurance?" Ginny had none.

"Well, honey, it's either pay up front or the County," she said. "We can only bandage your arm; you'll have to go to the County to get it sewn up."

I banged my fist on the desk. "You *have* to treat her," I told the nurse. "I'll pay for it." I remembered I still had my night's receipts.

"Oh, you pimps are so *nice*." Her words were dripping with sarcasm.

"I'm not a pimp…" I started to protest but saw it was pointless to try correcting her *seasoned attitude*. I guess nurses working so close to Rush Street had likely seen and heard it all. To her, the local denizens were obviously a pain in the ass—and they made her work harder.

"Larry, you don't have to pay. Let's just go to the County."

"You ever been to the County, Ginny? The only time it's safe there is when you're already dead. No. We're staying right here till they suture your arm."

"*Suture?*" the nurse said, raising her overpainted eyebrow. "Such big words for a street person."

That was it. "Listen, you don't know what or who you're talking to—just do your goddamned job!" She shut up. It took several hours, but they finally sutured her arm back together. She was lucky; the glass hadn't cut any tendons or nerves. By the time we were finished, the sun was up.

As I walked Ginny back to her apartment, she told me she'd pay me back after she turned her money in.

"What do you mean? I thought in the emergency room you didn't have any money?"

"It's the rule. I can't go into the receipts for anything until I pay my cut."

"I don't understand," I felt really puzzled and must have looked it.

"It's just the rule. Ben said nobody breaks it, unless they want their fingers broken. So it's still not my money until I give him his cut. I'll pay you back tomorrow."

By then we were at her place. She lived in a small, dingy, sparsely furnished apartment on Wells Street not far from the clubs. I wondered why she lived in such a lousy place. If she was turning tricks for a hundred dollars a pop, she should have made enough money to afford something better. Her son was already up. He was playing on the floor between two chairs with a blanket over the top of them.

Ginny introduced us. "Tommy, this is Larry."

He stuck his head out. "I'm in my office," he said. "Wanna come in and talk business?" He was a cute little guy with dark hair and blue eyes.

He reminded me of myself as a kid. I used to make an *office* with two chairs and a blanket. "No, thanks, Tommy. I need to get going home."

"Have you eaten yet, Tommy?" Ginny asked.

"Yeah, I had some corn flakes. What happened to your arm?"

"Oh, mommy just had a little accident."

It was obvious that Ginny didn't have a babysitter. She left Tommy home alone while she worked the street. I couldn't help but wonder why she would leave him alone. She had to make enough money to hire a babysitter. It really wasn't my business, but I couldn't keep myself from asking. "Don't you have a babysitter?"

"Please, let's talk later, not around Tommy." She just didn't seem like someone who would leave her son alone.

By the time I left Ginny's apartment I was exhausted. It was nearly ten in the morning, and I was expected to be back on the street to open at noon for the Sunday lunch crowd. There was an exam on Monday in Biology, and I had to read a shit load of stuff before then. I decided that if I went to sleep now I'd never get up on time, so I went to an all-night diner on Wells Street. I'd have some strong coffee and read a bit there. From there I would go to Dino's house, take a shower, and then go back to the street.

At the diner, a haggard-looking waitress took away a dirty, half-filled coffee cup, wiped the counter, and then glared at me. Through tightly pursed lips, she asked, "Whaddya want?"

I was taken aback and stammered, "Uh, just coffee." When she came back, she banged the cup down, splashing some of it onto the counter, my hand, and my Biology book.

"There's your fucking coffee, you cheap thief." She looked back at the cook who also looked pissed off.

I was flabbergasted and totally confused. "What's the problem?"

"You know the problem, asshole. You stole my quarter tip that was sitting there when you sat down!" That really pissed me off. First, a nurse calls me a pimp. Now a waitress calls me a thief. A quarter thief!

"I did not. I work for tips too!" I sputtered. Then I reached into my pocket, still full of quarters from hailing cabs, bounced a handful of them off the counter, and walked out.

It occurred to me, as I walked out, that like Ginny I wasn't supposed to spend my door receipts either. I decided I would make it up to Dino on Sunday. I also shuddered when I remembered that once someone walked into our bookkeeper's office and shot-gunned his head off. The rumor was that he was skimming the receipts.

◆ ◆ ◆

Later that Sunday evening Dino finally came in. I gave him the receipts from Saturday. "I owe you about a hundred bucks—and some quarters."

"What do you mean you owe me a hundred and some quarters?" He looked surprised and pissed at the same time.

I'm not sure if he was pissed that I spent it, or surprised that I admitted I spent it. I started to explain about Ginny but, no sooner than I got her name out, he began laughing and taunting me. "You little bastard, you mean you paid Ginny for a trick?"

"No, I paid to have her arm sewn together. Freddy threw her through the glass door in his bar. And then I threw a bunch of quarters at a waitress in the diner on Wells Street."

Then he got serious. He wasn't sure whether to believe me or not. "You know about spending receipts. It's bad news."

"I know. Ginny couldn't spend hers either, so I paid the emergency room. She said she would pay me back tonight."

"Well, she better, or it's her ass. And if she doesn't, it's your ass, too. *And besides, you could fuck up my relations with the bosses.*"

By the time I was going to leave, Ginny still hadn't shown up.

When I was about to go home, Dino said, "Well, I guess you worked for nothing this weekend. Your hooker girlfriend didn't show."

"She's not my girlfriend. She's just a friend."

"What's with you and the hookers anyway? They come looking for you like flies to honey. Or maybe you're not getting enough at home? Or maybe you're practicing to be a hookers' doctor?" He laughed.

"That's not it, and you know it. I was just trying to help her."

"Well, don't get to be too friendly with them. They'll just use you if you do. Besides, they're all junkies anyway."

"What do you mean junkies? Is Ginny on drugs?"

"You are so unconscious," he smirked. "*Is Ginny on drugs?*" he mocked. "Ginny and every other whore on the street is on drugs. That's why most of them turn tricks, to support their habit, dumbass."

"What kind of drugs is she on?" I still wasn't sure whether to believe him or not.

"Horse."

"Heroin?"

"That's *right*," he strung out the word "right" for a long time.

"Whatever. Could you at least give me twenty bucks until next weekend?"

"Twenty bucks? I haven't got twenty bucks!"

I knew he did. I saw him take out a very large roll of bills earlier that night. There was a lot more there than the weekend receipts. He always had a stash of money.

"Look, I gotta go back to school. I need at least twenty bucks for the week."

"Sorry. I don't have it."

What a bastard. Fortunately, I had my return train ticket back to Milwaukee. I was tired and tried to read on the train, but my thoughts kept returning to Ginny. Maybe Dino was right. That would explain why she lived in such a dump. Maybe. I fell asleep, and the next time I opened my eyes, the train was in the downtown depot. My body felt like it had been worked over with a rubber hose.

◆   ◆   ◆

Being at Marquette after working long weekends on the street was unreal. I wondered which one was more of an illusion, Rush Street or Marquette. What made it more challenging was that I had theology on Monday mornings at eight o'clock. Father Turtle was my professor for the class *God: The Creator*. He was a tall, stooped, ancient Jesuit. His head looked a little like a turtle's. I wondered when he had last left the shell of his rectory. He almost always opened his class with the question: "Why did God create man?" The first time I heard it, I thought it was a good question. I had wondered the same thing many times. I especially wondered why, if man were created in God's image, why so many of us were ugly, violent, cruel—and stupid. He always had answers; I imagined he must have been giving the same ones for decades. But his answers never cut it with me.

Father Turtle would say it was because man had "free will" that he could choose to be evil. To be honest, the whole free will, free choice thing left me cold. I didn't believe many people were making free choices, so how could they have free will? I wondered if he knew about Rush Street—or if it even mattered to him. The people on Rush Street didn't seem to know about Father Turtle or

"God's generosity" in creating them. I don't think the two worlds ever met, and I don't think his question was really open for discussion. This was not the kind of Jesuit Brother René described. Everything was already neatly printed in the same syllabus he probably had used for years. The stock answer to the class-opening question was, "Because He loved them." Some part of me just groaned and put my head on the desk.

◆   ◆   ◆

Whenever I started enjoying being at Marquette, it was time to go back to Rush Street. It was now close to Christmas, and the weather in Chicago was freezing. With the wind chill factor, it must have been well below zero.

Mr. Gianni, the Outfit's *capo di capo*, came out of Mario's and stopped inside the enclosed glass and wrought iron foyer. I hadn't seen him in a few weeks. He lit his long Cuban cigar. His tall frame made it look like he was standing in a small glass cage. After sneaking a glance up and down the street, he carefully adjusted his elegant black cashmere coat with velvet lapels and smoothed down his white silk scarf. I loved that coat! It must have cost a thousand dollars. He noticed me standing just outside the foyer, then glanced over at his shiny, snow-speckled black Cadillac. It was parked in "his spot" right at the curb. He smiled at me. He liked that I always remembered to leave his car there.

I moved with a start to open the door for him, but before I could reach it, he spread open both of the foyer doors and stood there, blowing out cigar smoke mixed with his steamy breath. He held up his hand, motioning me to wait. Once outside, he walked over to me, put his arm around my neck, and pulled my head hard against the soft fabric of his coat. With my head held tightly against his chest, I could smell the lingering fragrance of expensive cologne mixed with the scent of sweet Anisette, even over the cigar smell. He walked me toward his car with my head still locked against his chest.

"Hey, Larry, how's my boy?"

"I'm fine, Mr. Gianni. Little cold, but fine."

"When you gonna come work for me?" he asked smiling.

"I already work for you, sir." His question made me nervous. It wasn't the first time he asked me that.

"I don't mean this. This is shit." Then he laughed. "What? You think I need a hitter? You're no hitter, Larry. I mean a real job."

"I don't know, sir. Maybe when I finish school." I felt stupid saying that and was sure that he thought I was just a dumb nervous kid.

"School is good," he said. "You got ambition. Don't be a bum like your brother. Always looking for somethin' for nuthin'."

I don't know why, but it frightened me when he said that. It was something I'd heard him say before. "Some day somebuddy's gonna whack him." I was silent. By then we were standing at the side of his car. He released me. I opened the door, reached under the seat for the keys, and felt the handle of a cold revolver. I started his car and got out, holding the door for him. Before he got in, he lifted one side of his long dark coat, and pulled out a thick roll of large bills. He peeled off a hundred. "Here," he pushed the bill into my hand. He patted my cheek with his oversized hand and said, "Buy yourself something for Christmas."

"Th…thank you, Mr. Gianni. Thank you!" Just before he slammed his door, he looked back and said, "It's nuthin'." I don't know if it was true, but I heard that he never carried less than fifty thousand in cash.

I watched the red taillights of his Cadillac fade behind a cloud of white exhaust steam as the car sped from the curb and disappeared into the traffic on Rush Street. I stood at the curbside, firmly clutching the hundred with my cold fingers. I tried repeating his words to myself, "It's nuthin'."

Mr. Gianni wasn't the only Outfit guy who was nice to me. Many of them gave me money or presents for Christmas, like Mr. Bianca. He came in that weekend, too. Sometimes on Sundays he brought his wife. This time he didn't.

"Larry, *come va?*"

"I'm good, Mr. Bianca. How's Mrs. Bianca?"

"She's good, she's good. Home making pasta for the boys. In the back seat are some Christmas presents."

"I'll put them in the trunk and keep the keys."

"No, I don't want them next to the body." He laughed uproariously. "They're for you, Larry. Merry Christmas from the family."

In the back seat of his car were three beautifully wrapped packages: a silk scarf, a white-on-white shirt, and a pair of gray suede gloves.

Besides the money and gifts, the Outfit also saved my life more than once. One time there was a big summit meeting in Chicago, and many of the families from around the country were there. I heard there was a lot of tension and disagreement about something. After the summit, many of them were out partying very late. I got stuck with a Thunderbird when one of the clubs I usually didn't work closed and the car owner didn't return. The custom was to take the car home and leave a note on the club door for the owner to call you when he returned. Then you would bring the car back the same night or in the morning. Whatever they wanted.

The night I did that, I got a call at five-thirty in the morning.

"You little Mother Fucker, who told you to take my car?" the voice screamed.

"I'm sorry, sir. I'll bring it right back. It's the custom..."

Before I finished, he yelled, "No, you little prick. I'll be there tomorrow night. You be there. I'll put you in concrete. You're fuckin' dead!"

I was so scared that when I put the phone down I got an instant headache and threw up. I didn't know this guy, but I knew he meant what he said. The next morning I called one of the bosses from the club.

"What's his name?"

"I don't know. He didn't say. I was too scared to ask."

"What kind of car is it?"

"A white '63 Thunderbird."

"Oh, *that* asshole. He's that *stronzo* from Kansas City. Shot his mouth off at the meeting. He thinks he can fuck with Chicago. Tell you what. Bring the car back to the street, leave it at the club, and put a note on the door saying, 'Ask Big George for the keys to the Thunderbird.' Give the keys to the night man for me. Then take the night off. Don't worry about it. I'll take care of it."

I did what he said and stopped shaking inside.

The next weekend the club's regular doorman told me he had given the keys to Big George. Big George had told him to let him know when the guy returned. When the guy came back, the doorman got Big George to come out of the club. He came out with the keys and walked over to the Kansas City guy. "I hear you threatened my boy."

"I'm going to kill the little prick..."

"No, you're not." Big George pulled out a .38 and put it against the Kansas City guy's forehead. "But I'm gonna blow *your* fuckin' brains all over the street if you don't get in that piece of shit car and get out of Chicago—*capisce?*" The doorman said the guy hauled ass out of there. Fucking bully.

That wasn't the only time they saved my ass. They protected anyone who worked for them. If someone got in trouble with the law, they sent their attorneys—and they were big time. There was a saying on the street that when the Outfit lawyers walked into court, the judge stood up! Another thing I liked about the Outfit was that they were predictable. I always knew what to expect and knew exactly what they were capable of. Something I could never say about the Chicago police.

Once a rookie pulled me over right in front of Mario's because I ran a red light on the corner while I was returning an Outfit guy's car. I got out of the car puzzled because, red light or not, we knew most of the cops in that area and they never bothered us—especially because we paid them. When I bent down to the squad car window, the rookie said, "Who the fuck do you think you are, punk?" Then opened his door so fast the top frame of it almost broke my nose—again. As I stood there bleeding and stunned, the Outfit guy came over, grabbed the rookie by the lapels, and threw him all the way over the hood of the squad car. He said, "You ever touch my boy again, I'll break your fuckin' knees." The Outfit guy gave me fifty bucks and drove off. The rookie got the picture and apologized.

A lot of police pretended to be the good guys who fancied themselves "upholders of the law." But they were unpredictable and—for a price—you could buy their morals. As they say, there's a thin line between cops and robbers.

◆ ◆ ◆

I never did get any money back from Ginny. So I had to give it to Dino from my pay. One of the hookers told me Ginny was found dead in her flat with a needle in her arm. The welfare people took her kid. I missed her and was sorry for Tommy. I wondered what would become of him.

By the beginning of spring I knew I had to stop working the street before another winter. The money was good, but it was just too hard working thirty hours from Friday to Sunday night in that icy cold. I barely got any sleep, and it was almost impossible to study while I was there. I was coming back to school a basket case, and my grades were starting to show it. Jean also was getting close to having our first baby and complained that I was never around. It seemed like the only solution was to try to find a job in Milwaukee.

16

St. Joseph's Hospital

After working in subzero temperatures through the winter on the street, I found the spring weather in Milwaukee a pleasant change. Milwaukee winters weren't much warmer, but at least I didn't have to work outside, right off Lake Michigan, where the wind-chill factor made temperatures ten to twenty degrees colder than they were away from the lake. They didn't call it the *Windy City* for nothing. Even apart from Chicago's lousy weather, I often came back to Milwaukee depressed. Working on the street was good money but made me think the worst of people. Rush Street was an insular mini-world of violence, crime, deceit, and bogus dreams. I missed working in a hospital.

I interviewed at several hospitals around Milwaukee and found an orderly's job on the urology and surgical floor at St. Joseph's. It was a long bus ride to the West Side of the city, but at least I could read on the way. St. Joe's was on the same bus route as the County Hospital.

St. Joe's was a good hospital and except for the uptight head nurse, Mrs. Kink, I liked the nursing staff. Unlike Alexian Brothers, it was a fairly new hospital, and all the nurses were women who cared a lot about the patients. They all seemed like "good people," as Mickey would say. They appreciated the work I did and rarely failed to express it. I worked weekends, holidays, and times when other orderlies wanted time off. I took all the hours I could get. Jean was due with our first child.

On the night Jean's water broke, we took a cab out to St. Joe's. We didn't have insurance so her doctor was a resident. He was easily available and already waiting when we got there. When I got out to pay the driver, I put my Histology book on the roof of the taxi—and forgot it. It must have ended up somewhere on the West Side of Milwaukee. The book cost ten times the taxi fare. The resident met us on the maternity floor.

"You want to be in on the delivery?" he asked.

"If I can, sure. That'd be great."

He told me where to go to change into a gown.

A few minutes later, when I walked into the delivery room, there was a ruckus going on. Several people busily surrounded Jean, doing something I couldn't make out. The resident looked up at me. "Sorry, Larry, you can't come in. We're having some complications. Please go to the waiting room. I'll keep you posted."

Waiting room time goes slower than it does anywhere else. I wanted to read but, even if I still had my Histology book, I doubt I had the concentration. The wait was long enough to give me a chance to review parts of a course I had taken in Genetics—all the things that could be wrong with a newborn. I thought about anencepahaly, Down syndrome, Tay-Sachs disease, thalessemia, and finally, PKU. A little extreme, I admit, but I had read too much genetics to take anything for granted.

Several hours later, the resident finally came out smiling, "Congratulations, you have a baby girl."

"What happened in there?"

"At the start of the delivery, the umbilical cord was wrapped around the baby's neck. We had to untangle it so she could breathe on her own. We're giving her oxygen now."

"She asphyxiated? Is she all right? How was the baby's Apgar score?"

"As far as we can tell, she's just fine and so is Jean."

"As far as you can *tell*? What about the blood pH? The Astrup pH? She could have respiratory acidosis, even metabolic acidosis."

"Larry, you can't have those at the same time."

"Yes, you can. In asphyxia you can! The blood pH can get dangerously low, causing either one, or both."

"Larry, please relax. *I'm* her doctor, OK. All the signs we look for are normal. You can go see them in her room in a little while. But I need to call a pediatrician just to check the baby."

When I finally got to see them, I was relieved. The baby was beautiful. I counted her tiny fingers and toes, just to be sure. We named her Ann, using Christie's middle name. She had dark hair and eyes like her mother—a miniature of Jean. She was a little miracle. I thought of Christie when she was born. She was beautiful, too, except she had blonde hair and blue eyes. Jean looked tired, but otherwise she was fine and happy. I stayed with them all night and through the next day—and missed my histology exam.

Before class the next day, I explained to my histology professor that I had had a baby, I had lost my textbook, and I hadn't been able to take the exam.

"Larry, you know you're going to have to take an oral make-up. I'm sorry, but I can't let you take the same written exam." Every student I knew hated oral exams.

"I don't mind. I think I do better on them." Something about written exams in *any* pre-med course always threw me. Even when I knew the material cold, I just always did poorly on them.

My professor gave me the oral exam after class. It took an hour and a half. The material was on the histo-chemistry and embryonic development of blood cells. It was one of the topics in histology students feared the most. When it was over, the professor put his feet up on his desk. He sat quietly a few moments, looking at me. "Larry, I just don't get it."

"What do you mean?"

"If I wasn't sitting right here looking straight at you, I would have thought you cheated."

"Cheated? I didn't cheat."

"Oh, I *know* you didn't. You couldn't have. Your answers came straight from your head to your mouth. You didn't even so much as pause."

"What don't you get then?" I knew where he was going.

"Up to now, you've only been carrying a C in this class. You just had a baby, so you couldn't have been studying much the last few days, and you just got an A on an oral exam of some of the most difficult material in this course."

"You mean, you're giving me…I got an *A*?"

"Actually, I rarely ever give one, but you got an A+. What's with you, anyway?"

"I know it's weird, but I just never do well on written tests, *if* they're pre-med courses."

"Except for make-ups, *all* pre-med exams are written. And it won't be any different in medical school. You can't get around that. You can't take oral exams unless you miss the written ones. And if you miss many written exams, you'll eventually get thrown out."

"I know. It worries me."

"Another reason to worry is the other students. You just threw the curve quite a ways off. The written average was eighty. But if anyone complains, I'll just offer him or her an oral make-up. See how many takers I get." He smiled.

I thought of my new friend, Tom. He would never take an oral exam. He hated them.

"In any case, I think you should look into this problem of yours, Larry. Maybe talk to someone at the student counseling service. Anyway, congratulations."

"Thank you, sir. I never got an A+ before."

"I meant on your baby."

"Oh, right, of course. Thanks."

I already knew I had a problem. It was becoming more and more common for me to freeze up, or go blank on any written test that was connected to pre-med. Maybe I was sabotaging myself. I decided to make an appointment at the counseling center. I got one for the following evening. The counselor I was assigned to had the same last name as mine. That night I explained my problem to him. He seemed really tired, almost sleepy.

"Did you bring any class notes?"

"Yes, I have my Histology notes."

"May I see them?"

"Sure."

"You have them typewritten?" He seemed to wake a bit.

"Yes, I retype the notes from class, then add notes from the same material in the textbook."

"That must take forever. Why do you do that?"

"I don't always hear well in class, so I have to be sure I'm getting all the material." He looked like he was nodding off again as I spoke. That really pissed me off.

"Why don't you just borrow another student's notes and copy them?" He yawned.

I didn't know what this guy had studied in college, but he had *never* been in pre-med. Asking another pre-med student for his notes would be like asking to sniff his girlfriend's panties. The counselor was still having a hard time keeping his eyes open.

"Look, sir. I think I'll be all right. Thanks for your help." I walked out. Fuck him. He was about as concerned as Dino would be. I'd figure it out myself.

◆　　◆　　◆

That weekend at the hospital I got to know several more physicians by making rounds with them. I enjoyed making rounds with doctors who were good to their patients. Unfortunately, I found a lot of doctors to be pompous asses—like Dr. Stock and Dr. King. They shared a urology practice and looked like the frumpy old cartoon characters, Mutt and Jeff. King was tall with a skinny long nose and thin moustache. Stock was short and fat, with a tiny round nose and a thick moustache. They did everything together, rounds, surgery, and clinic. They probably also had cheap seats at the horse races on their day off.

They always insisted that an orderly come with them on rounds. One morning I made rounds with them, even though they were going to catheterize their patient themselves. That was something we routinely did for doctors on rounds. Their patient was in a coma. In the process, Dr. King dropped the catheter on the floor. Without a blink, he bent over, picked it up, and washed it off in the sink. He didn't have sterile gloves either. Just as he was about to insert it into the patient, I interrupted him.

"Doctor, I can get you another catheter—and some gloves." The unopened sterile gloves sat right next to the catheter tray.

"Oh, this catheter's all right."

"Sir, it's not sterile anymore."

"What? Are you telling *me* what to do?" He glared at me.

"Just suggesting, sir."

"Well, if I *want* your suggestions, I'll ask for them." Then he proceeded to use the unsterile catheter. When he was finished, he and Dr. Stock walked out of the room. They left the patient's gown over his face, right where they put it when they started the procedure. I was outraged. I put the patient's gown back down, straightened the sheets, and picked up the equipment they left.

When I got back to the nurses' station, the head nurse, Mrs. Kink, was waiting for me. "Larry, can I speak to you in my office?"

"Sure." We walked to her small office at the end of the hall. She was a squat, fat woman about fifty with an overstarched uniform and nurse's cap. Her bottom jumped from side to side as she walked in front of me. She sat down behind her desk and told me to sit in the chair opposite her. Her shiny gold nursing school's pin and name tag sat over her large left breast.

"Larry, Dr. King and Dr. Stock made a complaint about you this morning. I know you're fairly new here, the staff seems to like you, and so far you've been doing a good job. But you need to know we don't *ever* question a doctor's judgment on rounds. It's not only disrespectful, but it can undermine the patient's confidence in him."

"The patient was unconscious, Mrs. Kink."

"It doesn't matter. What you did is just not done. Do you understand?"

"May I say something, Mrs. Kink?"

"Yes."

"Dr. King catheterized his patient with a catheter he'd dropped on the floor. He didn't even use the sterile gloves."

"Are you sure?"

"I was standing right next to him. The unopened gloves are still in the utility room."

"That's hard to believe, Larry. Dr. King and Stock are some of the oldest physicians at this hospital."

"I'm not lying, Mrs. Kink."

"Larry, if you're going to be having an authority problem, this job may just not work out for you. Am I making myself clear?"

"Yes, ma'am, very clear. It won't happen again."

Being the oldest docs around didn't make a damn bit of difference to me. In two days, their patient had a raging fever and a bladder infection. Infections like that could easily kill older people. Over time, I found out that King's and Stock's patients had the highest infection rate in urology. I thought about Dr. Ignaz Semmelweis. He would have hung those old farts.

Then there were doctors like MacGillies. He was an exceptional urologist and physician. I actually met him another time I almost got in trouble. I was working PMs and an older man on the floor had gone into urinary retention. He couldn't pass his water and his lower abdomen was terribly distended. The charge nurse couldn't get hold of his doctor and had paged the on-call resident for an order to catheterize him. It was more than an hour and the resident still hadn't responded. The patient was in agony, moaning and rolling around in his bed. I checked in on him every five or ten minutes. The last time I went in, he started sweating and turned very pale. I called the head nurse and told her I thought the patient was going to go into shock. She said I couldn't catheterize him without an order. I got a catheter tray and did it anyway. All told, he had 2,500 cc of urine in him. That's two and a half quarts! I took it out in 500 cc increments; taking out more than that at one time could cause him to go into shock. When it was all out, I asked him not to tell anyone. He said he wouldn't. Except the next day he did. He told his son, who, unknown to me, just happened to be Dr. MacGillies. That day when I stopped by to see the patient, Dr. MacGillies was in the room. They both looked up at me when I came in.

"Is that him?" Dr. MacGillies asked.

"Yes, that's the boy."

I was sure I was going to be reported and fired.

Dr. MacGillies walked over to me and extended his hand. I wasn't sure if he was going to shake my hand or break my arm. "Thank you, son. You added a few more years to my old man's life."

I looked at his father sideways.

"Aww, don't worry, I knew he'd understand."

"From what my dad said, it sounded as if he was starting to go into shock. In addition to his prostate problems, he has a very bad heart. He could have gone into shock, kidney failure, or cardiac arrest—any one of those and it would have been all over. So, thanks."

Not long after that, Dr. MacGillies gave me a small extra job of changing catheters for his homebound patients.

Like a lot of hospitals, St. Joe's started doing code blues—emergency resuscitations of patients in cardiac arrest. In the early days, code blues were indiscriminate and were called on anyone threatening to die. They were also arbitrary in terms of who showed up. Before we created code blue teams, every physician, resident, nurse, and orderly in the area ran to the patient's room. And I mean *ran*. Minutes were precious, so woe to whomever got in the way. Once I came around a corner so fast I ran into an unlucky nurse who had just started down the hall with a full medication tray. When we collided, she went flying down the hall followed by a shower of every pill, injection, and cup of sticky liquid you could imagine. But I had to keep running, yelling, "Sorry!"

One of the early codes I saw was for an eighty-year-old man dying of liver cancer. It was before they had thought up DNRs (Do Not Resuscitate). When the code was called, twenty-two physicians, assorted nurses, and another orderly showed up in the two-bed room, and not a particularly big room at that. It was mayhem. I got stuck between the patient's bed and the wall. A resident who was supposed to start an IV got his foot stuck in a wastebasket. I ended up starting the IV because I was closest to the only free side of the patient. By the time we were finished, the patient was dead, not from liver cancer, but from the procedure. The intern eagerly trying to resuscitate him had crushed the man's chest wall.

That procedure and others like it gave rise to the team concept. After that, code blue teams were trained. From then on, only the team members showed up when a code was called. I became a member of the team. Some of our attempts were truly inspiring and life saving, while others were hopeless disasters. After each one, the team got a short, debriefing coffee break in the cafeteria. Those breaks were some of the funniest times I remember. Often the team would sit together, laughing so hard and loudly that, to others, it must have looked like we were talking about a comedy. It was really just releasing the tension from our desperate struggle to prevent death. Doing codes wasn't pleasant, but there was nothing else at the hospital quite like it.

◆ ◆ ◆

I had two favorite things I liked to do in the hospital. One, I enjoyed was trying to make the patients more comfortable, especially if they were dying. Changing dressings, wet or soiled sheets, rubbing their backs—all those little things felt deeply spiritual to me. They seemed like one of the purest forms of giving—just one person giving freely to another—with no need for thanks or appreciation.

The other thing I liked to do most physicians seemed to have little time for; that was talking to patients and actually listening to them. I never understood why the docs were in and out of patient's rooms so fast. I also didn't understand why they always asked, "How are *we* doing today?" The last place any doc I ever knew wanted to be was in a hospital bed; they were the worst patients. I found out years later in a study of many professions that physicians were among those most afraid of dying. The others were morticians. Anyway, I loved to sit at patients' bedsides, hold their hands, and listen to them talk about themselves. I especially liked listening to the older ones tell stories, not so much about their illnesses but about their lives. I also used to ask them if they had any advice for a young person about how to be happy in life. Some of the answers were pretty funny. One older guy said, "If ya *really* wanna be happy, drink a fifth of whiskey every week, smoke a cigar every day, and have sex as often as possible." How people ended up doing the work they did also fascinated me, so I asked a lot of them about what it was that made them choose what they did in life. Some said they didn't know, some said it was for the money, others said it was just circumstances, and others said because they just *knew* that's what they had to do. That reminded me of what Brother René had said. The last group seemed to be the happiest because they did things they really enjoyed.

I began to wonder about how much of what I really liked doing in the hospital had to do with the practice of medicine.

17

Blood Money

Working on the surgical floor still wasn't providing enough money for all the new expenses. Luckily, St. Joe's had another part-time job for a diener, or pathologist's assistant. It meant being on call every third night. The idea of doing autopsies seemed gross but, at that moment, I didn't care—I needed the money. Blood money. I tried not to think about it until I was actually called.

The first time I was called to do an autopsy was at ten o'clock one night. The call came sooner than I'd expected. I left home immediately and took the long bus ride to the hospital. A few days before, the head pathologist, Dr. Altman, had called me off the floor and briefed me about "the basics."

"Change from your whites to scrubs." The hospital had a strange but strict policy about wearing whites to the hospital, even though you didn't work in them when you got there. That included polished white shoes.

"Go to the morgue. Turn on the lights in the room and above the dissection table." I had already brought a body there from the surgical floor so I knew where it was.

"Get the body from the cooler and put in on the table. Set up the instrument tray next to the dissection table. The doctor you assist will show you the rest. That's it." Seemed simple enough.

The room felt a little damp, dark, and chilly. The cooler in the far corner made a low buzzing sound. I turned on the lights in the room, then the lights above the table. The bright lights reflected off the glistening stainless steel surface of the table and made the room appear even colder and harsher than it was in semidarkness—not a comfortable place to lie down. A large steel scale hung close to the table. Glass beakers with small samples of tissue suspended in a cloudy fluid sat on metal shelves across the room. It was a somber, creepy place. I got a little queasy and light-headed.

The cooler looked like a large walk-in refrigerator. When I opened its huge steel door, the hinges made an eerie, creaking sound. Along with a rush of cool air, an indescribable odor wafted out—one that I'd never smelled before. Inside, the body was lying on a gurney, wrapped in white plastic. When I unwrapped it, the patient was about sixty, an athletic-looking, muscular man. It was strange to think this but, except for being dead, he looked rather healthy. I rolled the gurney over to the dissection table. As I moved the body onto the table, his head banged on the cold steel surface. The sound broke the silence and startled me. I wanted to apologize as I put the customary wooden block under his head. The block was used to hold the patient's head in place—especially if we had to cut into the skull.

Then the door of the morgue swung open with a crash. I jumped a little off the floor. It was Dr. Eneo, a resident I had met on the surgical floor where I worked a few days earlier. I had made rounds with him. He was good to the patients.

He greeted me with a loud, "Hi-ya, pardner!"

"Hi, Dr. Eneo." I was glad to see him, but I wondered how anyone about to do an autopsy could be so cheerful. He was a friendly, stocky guy from somewhere in the South, maybe Texas. He had an amusing, slow, drawling accent. His manner was slow, but he had a great sense of humor and looked more like a cowboy than a doctor. I imagined him in his scrubs with a ten-gallon hat and cowboy boots. That image made him seem a little dumb but, as I got to know him, I found he was sharp-witted and brilliant.

I was counting on his sense of humor and Southern accent to distract me from the gruesome procedure.

"Now, I haven't seen you in this part of the place. You gonna be my helper tonight?"

"Yeah. I just took this job a few days ago."

"So it's your first time?"

"Yeah."

"Well, it's a little unsettlin' at first, but a good learnin' place if ya want to be a doctor," he encouraged. "I'm sure you'd rather be spendin' the night with one of those pretty coeds at school." He laughed.

Studying, I thought, *studying*.

"Now, don't be scared. Are ya scared?"

"No," I replied. "Maybe a little nervous; it's new." I hoped I wouldn't faint when we started.

"Well, y'all'll get used to it. By the way," he added, "can you sew?"

"Suture, you mean?"

Amused by my formality, he said, "Yeah, suture, that's the word I was lookin' for."

"Well, I've done dogs, in an experimental open-heart lab, and some elective surgery on them." I felt better knowing I did have some experience, even if not suturing people. "Damn," he said loudly and happily, "sounds like you might already be a regular little surgeon! Well, let's get goin' then."

He showed me how to open the chest, cut the ribs, retract the chest wall, and expose the heart, which was remarkably similar to opening a dog's chest. Soon we had the man's heart out, and Dr. Eneo was slicing it in sections.

He talked as he worked. "Now, see this here fella had a coronary." He showed me a slice of the heart. "See this little glob of stuff right here?" He pointed to a dark red blood clot inside the coronary artery. "*That* is what killed this man. From the size of it, I would say he was gone mighty fast."

As he talked, I was becoming more interested and less afraid. Now at least I knew I wasn't going to pass out. I was too interested. I could feel my shoulders coming down from around my neck.

Soon we were well into it. We had finished the heart, lungs, the stomach, and the intestines. We removed, weighed, and dissected all the internal organs, taking small samples of each. The small samples would be made into slides and sent to the pathology lab for microscopic analysis.

When we finished weighing and sampling all the tissue, we were done with the formal part of the autopsy.

Dr. Eneo said, "Now, let's close this gentleman back up. Let's see what kind of tailor you are," he laughed. I was glad he called the man a gentleman—it seemed respectful.

As I finished suturing the chest and abdomen, Dr. Eneo ended his dictation into a tape recorder. "Gross anatomical diagnosis: myocardial infarct of the anterior coronary artery." Then he looked up at me and asked, "You done?"

"Yes," I said. "Done."

"Well, let's take a look at your work," he said. He carefully looked over my suturing, running his stubby finger lightly on the suture lines. "You made him look like he was going to come back! Very nice, Larry, *very* nice," he whistled. "You ever think of surgery?"

I liked his approval. "No," I replied, "I'm thinking of internal medicine, maybe psychiatry."

"Don't do psychiatry," he frowned. "Those boys are at the bottom of the peckin' order. Besides that, you go to four years of college, four years of medical school, four years of residency, and what do you do? You end up listenin' to problems you can't do a damn thing about. Now *surgery*," he continued, "that's where you can actually *do* somethin'. It's tangible." After a pause, as if catching himself, he said, "Well, whatever you like, boy. You gotta be the happy person in your life." Then he laughed. "And if all else fails, you'd make a mighty fine tailor." With that he said, "Now let's go wash up and get outta here." I was relieved, and surprised that I hadn't gotten a headache.

◆ ◆ ◆

On the bus going home, I looked at my watch. It was almost one-thirty in the morning. Shit, I had so much studying to do before morning. Maybe *I will* end up a tailor. My thoughts went back to Dr. Eneo. I liked working with him. He was reassuring to be around and his humor and accent had a natural way of lightening things up. But I was glad he was a surgeon; I wouldn't want him as a shrink.

By the time I got home, it was two in the morning. I lay on the couch so I wouldn't wake Jean. I opened my Comparative Anatomy book. We were supposed to learn the anatomical differences of the aortic arch system in vertebrates—cold. Only a few minutes must have passed before I was sound asleep. I woke at seven in the morning when the sun shone through the curtainless windows of the living room. I remembered a bad dream. It left me with a sour feeling. I dreamt I was on a steel table with my insides spread out all over the place. I was dead, but I could see and hear what was going on. An autopsy was being done on me! The two men who were doing it were asking each other, "Who is this guy anyway?" It wasn't a question of concern or even of curiosity; it was simply factual. I was enraged that they didn't even know who I was. I wanted to scream out my name, but I couldn't speak. I was helpless, like a victim.

I got up, made coffee, and was at the comparative anatomy lab by eight. My lab partner and new friend, Tom, was already there. He was always there early.

"Hey, Morning Glory," he called out as I walked in. "You sure do look like shit." He laughed. "Been burning the midnight oil?"

"I wish. I was doing an autopsy till one-thirty in the morning." I yawned.

"Wow, that's great! When did you start doing that? I thought you only worked the surgical floor." He was obviously impressed; he could afford to be. Tom also wanted to be a doctor, a cardiovascular surgeon. He was as determined as I was. Autopsies were something he would love to do.

"Could you get me a job there?" He was enthusiastic, but then quickly caught himself. "Well, never mind. I couldn't afford the loss of study time."

"Tell me about it." I already knew that Tom's father had died when he was quite young, leaving him an inheritance. He didn't need to work or take out loans, not now and not even if he went to medical school.

"Listen," he started with a serious tone, "there's something I have to talk to you about. Can we go to the Student Union for coffee after lab?"

"Uh, sure." I should have gone to the library instead, but I was tired and I needed the coffee to stay awake. And I was curious about why Tom wanted to talk to me. The cafeteria at the Student Union was bustling with students who probably had missed having coffee before their first class. We got some coffee and chocolate doughnuts and found a quiet booth away from the cafeteria line and front doors.

"So what's up?"

He put his head in his hands and mumbled something. I couldn't read his lips.

"I can't hear what you're saying."

He moved his hands down from his face and looked up. "I said, I think Sue's pregnant."

"Oh, fuck."

"Yeah. Her parents and my mom don't know, but they'll kill me when they find out. I just don't know what to do."

"What are your options?"

"Get married. But there's no way that I'm stopping school. It's medical school or die."

"What about an abortion?" I was surprised I said that.

"No way. I'm Catholic; she's Catholic. She wouldn't consider it."

"Do you love her?"

"Sort of. She's been my girlfriend since high school."

"Sort of? Is that enough to get married on?"

"Well, maybe it will grow as we get older."

"And if it doesn't?"

"Well, we'll have the kid, I'll finish school, and we'll get a divorce. People do that all the time."

"'Art thou a man *entitled* to desire a child?'"

"Who was that?"

"Nietzsche. *Thus Spake Zarathustra*. His thing on child and marriage." I remembered that from philosophy class. It struck a deep chord in me when I read it. I wasn't sure *I* was entitled to have a child.

"I like Nietzsche. Superman!"

"I don't think you get it."

He looked at his father's gold watch. "Maybe not. Hey, I've got to go to chemistry. Thanks for your help."

"I don't think you needed it. You've already made up your mind."

"Yeah, maybe. Later, Larry. See you Wednesday bright and early."

He picked up his briefcase, sipped the last of his coffee standing up, then sped off with that funny gait of his. He walked as if he had shit in his pants. The guy was so smart, a straight A student. Book smart.

I went to my Contemporary Existentialism class. Dr. Anderson was the professor, and he covered Nietzsche as well as Jean-Paul Sartre, Merleau-Ponty, Kierkegaard, and a bunch of others. He was a brilliant professor but not pleased that Nietzsche was an atheist. He quoted Nietzsche as saying, "God is dead." But when I read *Thus Spake Zarathustra*, Nietzsche said, "Dead are all the Gods: now do we desire the Superman to live." What that meant to me was that as long as God or Gods were alive, our individual potential to become who we were was dead. I really liked his idea of the *Superman,* but I think a lot of people didn't understand what he meant. I was sure Tom didn't.

What impressed me the most about Nietzsche was how much he emphasized the importance of knowing oneself—psychologically and spiritually. Despite his brush with schizophrenia, or maybe in part, because of it, he was compelled to find out how his mind worked, determined to understand the effect of thoughts and feelings on human actions. "We ourselves want to be our own experiments, and our own subjects of experiment." That was from *Joyful Wisdom* and really spoke to me. As in other courses, my fascination with a certain writer became a "bad habit." I say that because I often read well beyond the required readings, sometimes wanting to read the entire writer. Between reading material I didn't have to know and missing material in class because I didn't hear it, I got in trouble.

Late that night I got another call from pathology. When I got to the morgue, Dr. Eneo was already there. He had put the body on the table himself and was standing next to it waiting for me. When I walked over to him and glanced at the body, I reeled backwards, almost tripping over my own feet. "Oh Jesus! Dr. Eneo, I...I *know* him." The body on the table was my professor, Dr. Anderson.

"Oh, jeez. How did you know him?"

"He's...he was my philosophy teacher. I was just in his class today!"

"Hmmm. You sure you want to do this? I can try to get another diener. It might be hard 'cause it's late, but I can try, if you don't want to do this."

"No, it's OK." I didn't want to, but I didn't want him to go through the trouble of trying to find another assistant. He probably wouldn't be able to find someone else and, if he couldn't, he'd have to do the procedure alone.

"Well, I'll leave it up to you." Wrinkling his brow into a frown and screwing his lips together, he said, "But we're going to have to take his brain. Tell me if you change your mind, OK? We have to do the brain and cord, 'cause this man's doctor thinks he had a massive CVA."

"No, it's OK. Let's do it."

He showed me how to cut the skin around the skull so that it could be pulled over the face, revealing the yellowish bony surface of the skull we needed to cut to get to the brain. Then he showed me how to cut into the skull with the most awful sounding saw I ever heard in my life. It whined at an incredibly high pitch as I cut into the bone—ten times worse than the sound of a dentist's drill. It gave me the creeps.

"Nasty sound," even he admitted.

After the proper cuts were made in the skull, we lifted the skullcap like it was a small helmet. The brain sat underneath. He then showed me how to remove it from the skull case. When I got it out, I stood there holding and looking at the soft mounds of this grayish brain in my palms. There was a large dark mass of blood on one side of it—the evidence of a massive stroke. Here in my hands was the matter that contained all Dr. Anderson's thoughts, memories, wishes, feelings, hopes, and dreams—his whole life. It was an extraordinary moment, but maybe one I could have done without.

Dr. Eneo's loud voice broke into my thoughts, "Now, that's somethin', isn't it." He studied me closely. As if he read my mind, he said, "You're holding the billions of neurons that made this man who he was. Now, put it on that scale there and see how much it weighs. Then we'll get his pituitary and cord. You still doin' OK?"

"Yeah, I'm OK." I was anything but OK.

The pituitary was sitting in the base of the skull in a little bony pocket called the *sella turcica*. It was no bigger than a large pea. He showed me how to take it out with a pair of thin forceps. Then we put it in a large, cloudy jar of formaldehyde with lots of others.

"What happens to them?"

"They send them to the National Pituitary Foundation." He anticipated my next question. "They do an extraordinary amount of research on the pituitary. It's the chief endocrine gland, the powerhouse that tells all the other glands what to do. If the pituitary has problems, there's trouble all over the place. Growth, hormones, metabolism, you name it."

We were then ready to remove the spinal cord. Dr. Eneo said, "Now did you know there was a horse's tail inside of you?" I think he was trying in the best way he knew how to lighten me up. "If you didn't, tonight you're gonna see it!" With that and some effort, he slowly pulled the spinal cord from inside the spinal column. It emerged with strands of long yellowish-white, hair-like nerves streaming from the sides of a thicker column of the same texture and color.

"See," he said smiling. "Now doesn't that look like a horse's tail?" He seemed pleased to be able to show me something novel—obviously a likeness of something from his personal experience. I think he was trying to distract me. But I was thinking that what had once been Dr. Anderson was now nothing more than so many grams of tissue.

◆ ◆ ◆

Tom was in the Comparative Anatomy lab the next morning. We were going to be examined on the anatomy of cats. Each of us had our specimens opened in front of us with little yellow flags the lab instructor had put inside them the day before. Each flag was placed on a specific anatomical part that we were going to have to identify. Tom sat next to me. He leaned over and whispered, "I broke into the lab last night and wrote down all the flags. Any you don't recognize?"

"You did *what*?"

"I just told you. See any you don't recognize?"

"Several."

"Which flags?"

I looked at the flags. There were several I didn't know. So far in this class Tom was getting an A, and I was getting a C. I reluctantly pointed to a couple of flags. He whispered again, "First one is the superior vena cava; second is the femoral artery."

I felt guilty, maybe ashamed as well. I should have known the material but I just hadn't had enough time to study. We took the exam. Tom got a hundred percent, I got eighty-five. The lab instructor was impressed with Tom. If I hadn't been doing autopsies, I would have done even worse.

Afterwards, we went to the Student Union for coffee.

"Are you nuts? If someone found out you broke into the lab, you could get thrown out of school."

"Except no one but you knows, do they?" He smiled.

"I don't know, Tom. It's not fair to the other students."

"Are you kidding? They're our competition! Why do you think anyone is nuts enough to take this fucking course? It's the hardest course in the school. Larry, every asshole in that class is pre-med. It's them or us. I don't know about you, but I'll do anything to get into medical school. Nothing's going to stop me—*nothing*."

"So what did you decide?"

"About Sue?"

"Yeah, and getting married."

"We're going to get married. How'd you like to be my best man?"

"Your best man? What about your other friends?"

"I don't have any I like well enough to ask."

"Tom, we just met this year."

"I don't care, as far as I'm concerned, you're my best friend."

Tom must not have had any guy friends. From the way he talked about high school, all he did was study. Sue was the only girl he dated, and I doubt they went out much, although enough to get pregnant.

Late one night while I was trying to study for an exam, I got a call from pathology. I swore they must have known whenever I had an exam. Dr. Altman needed an assistant because all the residents were away at a meeting somewhere. He was serious, usually quiet, and wore half-glasses. I doubted he had a sense of humor like Dr. Eneo. Altman was all business, but I figured it must take a pretty serious guy to be a pathologist—the last thing I would ever do. I'd park cars before I'd be a pathologist.

The night was cold and rainy, and the trip to the hospital seemed unusually slow. I tried to read on the bus but was distracted by the thunder and lightning, which was unusual for Milwaukee. Heavy splats of rain pelted against the window. Luckily, by the time I got off the bus, the rain had almost stopped. I didn't want to walk the next few blocks in the rain.

I got to the morgue and went to the cooler. There was no gurney, no body. I looked on the shelves for something and found a small plastic bag that looked like it might be a body part. Surgery sent things like amputations to pathology. But since it had a medical chart sitting on it, I was curious. I opened the bag. In it was a small child, a boy. His delicate skin was gray and blotched with spots of red. His light brown hair was matted, and his head seemed larger than normal. To my dismay, this was the "patient." I carefully lifted him up and brought him to the table.

Dr. Altman walked in. "Hello, Larry. Sorry to drag you out on a night like this. But we need to get this done tonight. All the residents are at a surgical conference in Chicago." He picked up the child's medical chart and, with his wire half-glasses pushed down on his nose, leafed through some of the pages. "Now this is going to be interesting! Maybe it'll make your trip worthwhile."

I didn't have the foggiest idea what he was talking about. "Sir?"

"A neuroblastoma."

He was already making the diagnosis. "A neuroblastoma?"

"Yes. You see the perforations in the back of the abnormally large skull? The perforations are from shunts they tried to put in place because of the buildup of fluid in the ventricles-hydrocephalus. It's caused by an embryonic tumor that's called a neuroblastoma. Larry, you don't know how lucky you are to see this."

"What do you mean?"

"You can go to medical school, do an internship, even a residency, and might still not see what you're looking at right now."

I was thinking about the little boy being alive, wondering if he ever got to ride a tricycle, where his parents were right then, what they must be feeling. I didn't feel lucky, I felt sad. My mind went to my precious daughter. I couldn't imagine little Ann being less than perfect. The thought of her with a neuroblastoma or dead made me shudder. Then I thought of Dr. Keddy and felt like yelling, "This is a *child*, Dr. Altman, not a fucking *neuroblastoma*."

We took the child's small brain. It was a lot smaller than Dr. Anderson's.

When we finished, I walked the several blocks to the bus stop. The rain started in again—hard. I hid my Comparative Anatomy book under my windbreaker. By the time I got to the bus stop, the rain was relentless. There was no bus shelter, or any other place to duck into. I stood there, poured upon as if I were under a massive pitcher spilling cold water. I just happened to look down at my shoes and saw very clear repeating circles of white shoe polish surrounding both of my feet. The white, milky pools flowed away from me, down the sidewalk and into the gutter. Suddenly, there was a brilliant flash of lightning and, only a second later, a loud clap of thunder. It was pretty close. Being completely drenched, I felt like something had just been washed off me. At that moment, I *knew* I didn't want to be a physician.

18

Separation

The next morning the rain had stopped, but the sky was still dark with leaden gray clouds. It was nearly as bleak and dark in the apartment. I hadn't slept well and didn't want to get out of bed. Jean was already up and feeding Ann. She called me to breakfast. "You coming to eat?"

"I don't think so." The thought of food made me feel sick.

She said something like, "That was quite a storm last night, wasn't it?"

I don't know why she always talked to me when I wasn't in the same room. I answered anyway—I didn't have the energy to remind her I couldn't fucking hear her. "Yeah."

"I see from your whites you got pretty wet."

"Yeah, I got wet. Very."

"What's the *matter* with you?"

"Nothing."

"Must have been a bad autopsy."

"Yeah, a kid."

"Oh, Jesus. How old?"

"I'd really rather not talk about it."

"Fine. Don't. I'm going out." Jean took Ann out for a walk, and I stayed in bed.

I had made a decision, and I didn't even have to think about it. It felt almost as if it was made for me—and it was final. There was absolutely no doubting it. I didn't even want to go to my classes. What was the point? There was nothing I wanted to do. Deciding to be a physician had given me some direction and excitement; some meaning. But if I didn't want that, what did I want? Not knowing re-created an old crisis; I was all the way back to not knowing who I was.

I spent the entire day in bed reading Nietzsche. Fucking Superman I was. At night, I locked myself in the bedroom and listened to the Gregorian Chants that Brother René had given me.

I did go back to classes, but I really didn't know why.

◆　◆　◆

To make matters worse, only seven months after Ann was born, Jean was pregnant again. During the time of her pregnancy, school became more difficult to manage because working absorbed so much of my time. I was barely making enough money to support us and pay for my school expenses.

I was pleasantly surprised to hear from Don Sitz, a friend who also worked with me at Alexian Brothers. He had finished his undergraduate work in Chicago and had come to Marquette to go to medical school. He was a really fine and intelligent person who I knew would make a great physician. I invited him to come and have dinner with Jean and me at our apartment.

I didn't understand why, but Jean didn't like him. Fortunately, she agreed to have him over.

Don and I were enjoying catching up on things over dinner. When Don started talking about medical school, Jean interrupted him.

"So, Don, now you're going to get a chance to play doctor?"

"What do you mean?" he said.

"You know, now that you're in medical school you can play at being a real doctor."

Don looked over at me, puzzled.

"Jean! Why are you saying that?" I asked.

"Oh, never mind. He knows what I mean, don't you, Don?"

"No, I don't. I have no idea what you're talking about."

Jean continued on with other sarcastic comments until Don pushed his chair away from the table and got up. "Excuse me, but I think I need to get going."

I couldn't stop him, so I walked with him downstairs to the front of the apartment building.

"What's with Jean? That was pretty insulting," he said.

"I'm really sorry, Don. I don't know what got into her."

"That's not the first time she's been like that. I want to be your friend, but the truth is I don't care to spend any time with Jean."

"I understand. Maybe we can meet for coffee on campus sometime."

"Sure. That would be great. Take care, Larry. Good luck with school—and with Jean."

When I got back to the apartment, Jean was at the sink, starting to do the dishes. Don was right, it wasn't the first time she insulted him.

"Did little Don get his feelings hurt?"

"'*Little*' Don? Of course he did. You were rude and belittled him. That was totally uncalled for."

"Well, too bad for him. He's just spoiled."

"So, his parents have money. He's still worked hard to get where he is. Why just not respect him for that?"

"If it wasn't for his parents, he wouldn't be anywhere."

"Just because he's had help from his parents doesn't diminish his accomplishments. Besides, in one way or the other, you've been doing that with all my friends."

"Your friends take time away from us. We hardly have any time to ourselves."

"Of course friends take time, but that's no reason to insult them. They're a part of university life I enjoy."

Don wasn't the first friend Jean pushed away. A married couple we met from down the hall also refused to visit again after Jean criticized them for not having children. Her personality seemed to be changing. She had become increasingly moody, angry, and resented any time I spent away from her and Ann. It was as if my friends became repugnant to her. She became so outright rude to them that eventually they all stopped coming to the house. If I wanted to see them, I had to pretend I was going to the library to study.

I made an appointment to see Father Schraud, the assistant pastor of our church. He had come to see us after Ann was born to celebrate her birth and talk about baptism.

"Thanks for agreeing to see me, Father Schraud. I came because I need help sorting some things out."

"Oh, of course. And congratulations on Jean's new pregnancy."

"That's part of what I wanted to talk about. Being in school full-time, working, and having a baby hasn't been easy on either of us."

"I think I understand, but how exactly do you mean?"

"I've been working every chance I get. Jean also works when she can, but financially we are really struggling to keep it together. Besides that, Jean seems to be changing…"

"Changing?"

"She's moody, irritable, and doesn't like my friends. She has no friends of her own, or any interest in them. When I'm not at school or working, all she seems to want is for me to stay home with her."

"Well, that's probably natural for a new mother now, isn't it?"

"I don't know. I've never done all this before. But neither of us seems very happy. Father, I need to get to my main point."

"Yes?"

"Well, I was wondering if there were any times when the Church would consider abortion." I cringed.

"*Abortion*? Absolutely not. Do you understand your religion, my son?"

"Yes, I do, Father. But sometimes aren't there special—?"

"No, Larry. Never. The Catechism of the Catholic Church states that human life, from the time of conception, must be respected and absolutely protected. From the first moment of his existence, a human being must be recognized as having the rights of a person, among which is the inviolable right of every innocent being to life. Catholics consider abortion to be murder. This is not a solution for failed birth control or unplanned pregnancies. Abortion is like sentencing an innocent to death. That is Satan's happiness, not God's." *That made me feel great.*

"I'm sorry. What about birth control? I heard at the hospital there are some new pills that can help keep women from becoming pregnant."

"Larry, the main purpose of sex is for creation of new life. Sex is a beautiful, natural, and committed act. The Church opposes the unnaturalness of birth control pills. Artificial birth control takes God out of the factor. Those pills can even cause women to abort a fetus. When artificial birth control is used, sex is cheapened. You can choose family planning but only the natural kind. You see, God is sad when life is denied. As a married couple you need to be open to having children."

"So I guess there is nothing we can do?"

"As I said, you can practice natural family planning."

I understood what he was saying, but the conversation seemed pointless to me. Obviously the "natural" method hadn't worked, and I was worried about Jean.

◆ ◆ ◆

Jean and I were sitting on the couch together the day after our second daughter, Lynn, was born. As Jean held Lynn, I noticed Jean's eyes glass over. Her head drooped to the side, and she started to drool from the corner of her mouth.

When I asked what was wrong, she couldn't speak; her only sounds were babble. I lifted Lynn out of Jean's inert arms and put her in her crib, then called the hospital's emergency number. They said to bring her in immediately. On the way to the hospital, I worried that Jean had a brain tumor. Her reaction made it look like that. I got our neighbor to come over and watch Lynn and Ann.

Jean was in the Emergency Room for several hours because they had to call in a neurologist and do some special tests. They also thought she might have a brain tumor. Finally, her doctor and the neurologist came out.

"Mr. Pedersen, we are going to have to send your wife to the County for hospitalization. We don't have the proper facilities here."

"What's wrong with her?"

"She's had a psychotic break, a postpartum psychosis. She needs to be hospitalized."

"Are you sure she doesn't have a brain tumor?"

"Yes, absolutely. There are no neurological signs of that. We're sure of the diagnosis."

It was hard to believe she had had a psychotic break. As we got in the ambulance on the way to the County, she looked like a young child, drooling, and babbling to herself. Seeing her like this was sad, confusing, and frightening. At the County, they told me I should prepare for an extended hospitalization.

◆ ◆ ◆

Jean was in the hospital for more than a month. During that time, with the help of babysitters, I was both mother and father to Ann and Lynn while I continued to work and go to school. Jean finally began talking again, but was never quite the same. Even though she was on antipsychotic medication, her moodiness and isolation only worsened.

Father Schraud came by the house to congratulate us on the birth of Lynn. We showed him into the small children's room, the only bedroom in our cramped apartment. Jean and I slept in the living room.

"Oh my, look at these *beautiful* children." He made goo-goo faces at them and told us what "good Catholics" we were. We came out of the children's room.

Father Schraud looked toward the small couch next to our bed. It was one of the few places to sit in our sparsely furnished apartment. "May I?"

Jean moved some small stuffed toys and motioned him to sit. "Please have a seat, Father. Would you like some tea?"

"No, thank you, Jean. I still have some other parishioners to visit this afternoon."

I was glad he had to leave, but it was becoming difficult to conceal my anger. He got up and moved past me toward the door. I put my hand on his forearm as he reached for the handle. He looked down at my hand, then at me, and raised his eyebrows. I moved it, and he turned toward the door again. "Father, we're trying to do what the Church expects of us, but I'm slowly losing patience with some of its outdated ideas." I aimed the word "outdated" at the back of his head.

He made a half turn back toward me. "Outdated? Larry, are we going to have *that* conversation again? I thought we'd settled that."

"Father, I believe that children have a right to be born, but they also have a right to be born into families and a world that can afford to care for them. Nietzsche asks if we are *entitled* to desire children."

"*Nietzsche*? Let's not cite him. He was an atheist."

"But in school, even Jesuits teach us about the dangers of population explosion. What does God think about a world population of three billion people? If the projections are correct, in only forty years the population will double again—twice the mouths to feed in a world already facing serious shortages of water and food."

"Larry, I'm sorry. But this is hardly the time for an academic discussion." He smiled weakly and glanced at his watch.

"Father, it's not academic. I'm a full-time student. I sometimes work close to full-time, and I have two children and a wife who has just had a psychotic break. What if we have another child? Why can't we use birth control?"

"Larry, we've already discussed that." His face reddened.

"OK, Father, how's this: Jean's doctor is worried that if she has another child she may have another psychotic break and might not recover like the first time. He strongly recommends that she take birth control pills."

"Is he Catholic?"

"Yes, Father, he is Catholic." I must have rolled my eyes.

By this time, I noticed Jean's mouth was wide open. "He what? My doctor never said that!"

I realized she had never been part of the conversation that, in my anger, I had just blurted out. He didn't want to frighten her. "I'm sorry, Jean. But he did say that."

"I'm afraid I have to be going. It seems the two of you have some things you need to settle between yourselves."

Jean was crying. "I'm sorry Larry was so rude, Father. Please forgive him."

"Don't worry, my child, don't worry." He patted her shoulder. "Things will work out. Pray about this."

When Father Schraud left, Jean turned to me—or more *at* me.

"Why did you keep that from me?"

"Dr. Brennan didn't want to upset you. He asked me to talk to you about it. Jean, I don't want another child. It's the wrong time in every way I can think of. You have to take birth control pills."

"I can't. I'm Catholic, we're Catholic, Dr. Brennan is Catholic."

"I hate to say this, Jean. But you know what? I just stopped being Catholic. I don't want any part of it anymore."

"Well, you don't have to be Catholic, but I am. You're going to go to Hell."

"Is that the speech about only Catholics go to Heaven? Or do you mean I can go to Hell?"

"Maybe that, too. I wanted a family and children. Why are you backing out now?"

"Jean, have you forgotten why we came up here in the first place? Maybe for you it was really about having a family and children. But for me it was mostly to go to school, not kill ourselves or ruin your mental health by having babies. What we're doing is not good for the children, and it could ruin my education. You said you would help me."

"I have helped you! I didn't ask you to pick an expensive, private Jesuit university. You could have gone somewhere else. You still can."

"What? I can't believe what you're saying. I'm three years into this. Why can't we just use birth control?"

"Because I'm Catholic. And like Father Schraud told you, 'It's not natural.'"

"You want to know something? Among non-Catholics, birth control pills are becoming the rage of the sixties. It's what intelligent people do to limit the population and make sure they have families they can afford. Catholicism isn't natural. It's abnormal. It's two thousand years of tradition untouched by any kind of progress. Women can't even be priests, for Christ's sake. It's archaic and effete. And it's not fucking *natural* to try to figure out when you're ovulating or not—it's mental, physical, and spiritual roulette! And besides that, do you think I want to watch your mind come apart from having babies?"

"Why do you have to swear and use the Lord's name in vain?"

"Because I'm desperately *pissed off!* I tell you what, you want to be Catholic, be Catholic. I'm not anymore and never will be again. You get pregnant if I look at you sideways. If you don't use birth control, we don't have sex."

"Fine, I'll divorce you."

I didn't want to remind her of the irony of *that* statement.

◆　　◆　　◆

I kept trying to get Jean to use birth control, but she refused. I certainly didn't feel *entitled* to desire children, and it baffled me that she did. I wasn't sure if Jean would divorce me if we didn't have sex, but I knew that our lives would be even more complicated. We didn't stop—and Jean became pregnant again.

During the pregnancy Jean was given even more antipsychotic medication. I was present when Laurie was born—to a confused and unconscious father and a mother who might become psychotic. She was a beautiful, precious soul who entered a world completely unprepared for her. For days and weeks after the birth, I studied Jean constantly, looking for the slightest physical or mental symptoms. Fortunately, this time she didn't have a psychotic break. At least on the surface, she seemed fine.

In three and a half years at Marquette we had three children, and I wasn't close to finishing my degree. We had little money, and my grades continued to suffer because of my long work hours. I felt like a rat on a treadmill. When we moved to a bigger apartment we couldn't afford, I became even more depressed. After the girls had gone to bed, I started locking myself in my room. I began to wonder who I was again. I was married, working, going to school, and having babies without the vaguest idea of *why* I was doing it. This was anything but what I imagined when I left Chicago. My life had become an uncontrolled and bewildering nightmare of frustration, confusion, and guilt. My only comfort was listening to Gregorian Chants and thinking about the girls. They were delightful, precious, and innocent. But I also was beginning to think that the last thing I ever wanted for them was happening; they were becoming the undeserving victims of my unconsciousness. I wanted their lives to be better than mine, and it was agonizing to think they would suffer because of the way I was leading my life.

Two nights of locking myself in my room scared Jean; she called the County Mental Health Services. They told her that I would either have to come in on my own or they would send an ambulance for me. There was no way I was going anywhere in an ambulance. So I went out to the County Hospital and was assigned to a psychiatrist, Dr. Schik.

"Why did you come in, Larry?"

"I was offered a choice of coming in on my own or by ambulance."

"I understand," he smiled. "But what's the reason you're so depressed?"

"Oh, my life is just totally fucked up is all."

"In what way?"

"School, marriage, goals, who I am, my whole life."

"Let's start with school. What kinds of problems are you having?"

I explained as best I could the whole scenario—from high school to the decision not to be a physician. He asked why I had decided against it.

"At first I thought it would be a good profession for me. I wanted to be able to help people. But medicine is just…just too *physical* for me. I'm not that interested in people's physiology, their physical diseases. I mean, it's interesting, but I like to talk to people, hear their stories, understand them, know what makes them who they are. I feel like that about children, too."

"Just like you want to understand yourself?"

"Yes, exactly. But sometimes I have no idea who I am."

"Understanding others begins with understanding yourself. What about your marriage?"

That question made me tear up a bit. It took a few seconds to get rid of the frog in my throat. "I don't really know why I got married. Maybe because I was afraid to leave her back in Chicago."

"Do you love her?"

I hesitated. This was the question I wish Father Carl had asked me. "No. I don't love her. I mean I like her, but I just don't love her. We're very different people. Too different."

"Why do you deceive her?"

"Deceive her? I'm not…" I gripped the arms of the chair, my head started to spin. That question slammed into my head. "Yes, I am, aren't I? I never thought of it like that. That's not…not what I intended."

"You didn't intend that consciously, but that's the end result, isn't it?"

"I guess it is."

"Larry, our time is up. Perhaps you need to think more about that. We can talk again next week if you want to come back."

"OK. Yes, I would. Thanks, Dr. Schik."

On the bus ride home that question kept repeating itself, over and over. Why do I deceive her? It stunned me that I never thought of it in that way. I have no right to deceive her. She deserves someone who loves her. In my stupidity, I thought I was helping her. Maybe I was just afraid to tell her what I really felt. Maybe I didn't think she could survive by herself. I don't know, but whatever it was—I wasn't helping her at all.

When I got back home, Jean was waiting in the living room, obviously eager to know how the appointment went. "Well, what did the doctor say? Do you need medication, too?"

"He didn't mention medication."

"Well, what did you talk about?" She was fidgeting with the hem of her skirt.

"In a nutshell, everything. Me, school, us, the marriage."

"The *marriage?* What's wrong with the marriage?"

"It's not so much what's wrong with the marriage, it's more what's wrong with me." Perspiration broke out on the back of my neck and my temple started to throb.

"What do you mean?"

"He asked, rather bluntly, why I deceive you."

"What do you mean, *deceive* me? Deceive me about what?"

"About my feelings."

"Oh, please, Larry. You're scaring me. What are you talking about?"

"Jean, I…I haven't been completely honest with you."

"What do you mean?"

"I don't think I ever wanted to get married."

"*What?*"

"Just what I said."

"Get the fuck out of here!"

"What do you mean?"

"Just what *I* just said. Now! Get the fuck out of my sight, you lying bastard!"

"I'm sorry. I am really, really sorry, Jean. I never meant to deceive you."

"*Sorry?* That's pathetic! You marry someone, have three children with them, and you just say '*sorry*?"

"It's deeper than that, Jean. Much deeper and more complicated."

"I don't care what it is. I want you out of here. Now! Get out, get out, get *out!*"

"Jean, please. Let's talk about this. I don't want to lose the children."

"The children? *The children?* You just lost them."

In trying to be honest, I felt as if I had just done the cruelest thing I had ever done in my life—as if I had just I killed her. What I said wasn't only an unspeakable blow; after I said it I realized that to her—it was unforgivable. Maybe in the recesses of my mind, I always knew that for Jean, honesty *was* worse than deception.

◆ ◆ ◆

I went to Tom's house. He let me stay with him for a few days. I tried to call Jean every day for several days. No answer. The last time, the phone had been disconnected. The next day I went to our apartment in the late afternoon. The back door was unlocked. When I went in, the kitchen was cold and empty except for some of my clothes and books in boxes. On the sink was a scribbled note on a crumpled piece of paper: "Call Father Carl." The sharp echo of my footsteps followed me across the bare wooden floor as I walked from room to room. Window shadows stretched across the barren rooms. In the children's closet, sitting limply in a dark corner was "Hippity-Hop," Lynn's stuffed rabbit. It would have been like her to leave it for me; she was that kind of little girl. I lay down on the closet floor, held the rabbit, and cried.

19

Chicago, '68

I called Father Carl. He had heard from Jean and wanted me to come to Chicago immediately to talk to him. I made arrangements to see him the following weekend at the rectory.

"She's very angry, hurt, disappointed. I have to say, I am too."

"You're angry?"

"No, not angry, disappointed. Disappointed that you chose to break up your family."

"My feelings for Jean were a lie. I liked her but I didn't love her. I went to see a psychiatrist…"

Father Carl interrupted, "You have an obligation to your family, Larry."

"Yeah, but what about to myself?"

"You made a sacred promise—for life."

"This is awkward, Father, but I don't want to be Catholic anymore."

"Why is that?"

"I just don't think the Church is right about some of its doctrines. Birth control, for example. That was a big source of trouble for us. We shouldn't have been having children. We couldn't afford them. Going to school full-time, having children, and working is almost impossible."

"Well, birth control is meant…"

"I know. Father Schraud and I had a conversation about it. It just doesn't work for me. I don't believe in it anymore."

"That's no reason to give up your faith."

"I don't know if I ever had any faith. I believe there is a God, but Catholicism is just too restrictive for me."

"Well, you still have an obligation to your family. You can't abandon them."

"I have no intention of abandoning them. Jean's the one who left. I don't even know where she is."

"She went to Southern California. She's living close to her mother."

"California? I have at least another semester of school to finish."

"Perhaps you can finish in California."

"Father, I can't do that at this point. Any other school would ask that I be there at least a year or more before they would give me a degree. Besides that, I changed my major to psychology. Actually, I'm completing the requirements for both biology and psychology."

"So you're not going to medical school?"

"No, I decided against it. I'm more interested in people than diseases."

"The people you should be interested in first are your family. I think you should go to them."

"I can't; at least not now. I have to finish my education. I don't know if I can be with Jean again. I think we'll get divorced."

"Jean doesn't want a divorce. And, if you divorce her, you can never marry again—unless she dies."

This sounds like what Father O'Neill said to my mother when I was a kid, except he told her she would go to Hell. I thought he was cruel.

"Getting married again is the *last* thing on my mind."

"Larry, I'm deeply disappointed in you. You should reunite with your family."

"Whether I love Jean or not?"

"Yes."

"I can't do that."

"You *must*."

"I'm sorry, Father."

◆   ◆   ◆

Back in Milwaukee, I finally found a California telephone number for Jean's mother.

"Hi, Mary, it's Larry." Silence.

Finally, in a matter-of-fact voice, she said, "Yes?"

"How are you?"

"Fine."

"How are Jean and the children?"

"As well as can be expected, I guess."

"What do you mean?"

"Well, the children have no father, you know. And Jean has no husband."

I didn't know if I wanted to get into this with her. "Does Jean have a telephone?"

"No." Silence. "She doesn't want to talk to you unless you come here."
"I *can't* come right now; I'm still in school."
"I mean she will only talk to you if you come back to be with the family."
"Jesus Christ."
"Don't use the Lord's name in vain, please."
"Look, Mary, I want to send her some money. Can I have her address?"
After several more moments of silence, she gave me an address. "I don't know how you could have done this, Larry."
"Will you tell Jean I called? Tell the children I love them."
"I'll give Jean your message."
"Tell the children I love them."
"I'll give her the message."
Her mother was such a happy victim. It was agonizing and frustrating—I felt like both of them were punishing me.

◆ ◆ ◆

I gave up the empty apartment and rented a room close to the hospital. That's when I met Grant. He was a new orderly who was also a student at Marquette. Grant came from an entirely different background than me; he was a preppy from a wealthy suburb of Chicago. I learned later that he had been a history major at a private college in Minnesota. Not long before coming to Milwaukee, he had suffered a nervous breakdown and had to be hospitalized.

Even with our different backgrounds, we immediately became great friends. Eventually, we got an apartment together not far from campus. I enjoyed Grant a lot because he was easy to talk to, very bright, interested in politics, and thought religion was something he could do without. He was caring, good to the patients, and enjoyed working in the hospital. We also found many of the same things funny. But he often seemed depressed, or preoccupied about something. I got the feeling from the way he talked about home, that he didn't get along with his parents very well—especially his father. When he wasn't working, he would lump around the apartment, brooding. What was really different between us were the things he had and the things he ate—shit like spinach soufflé and quince jam—stuff I had never heard of before. He not only had a car, but everything else any college student could wish for. Grant's fancy embroidered robe and his wearing plaid pajamas to bed amused me. I neither had a robe nor knew anyone who wore pajamas. Getting dressed for bed always seemed simply weird.

After living together several months, I came back from the hospital one night and found Grant sitting in a daze at the kitchen table. His wrists were cut and blood was oozing from the cuts. I knew he hadn't cut an artery.

"What the fuck happened?"

"I cut my wrists and took some sleeping pills; yours."

"You took *my* sleeping pills?" I went to my dresser and found the empty bottle. "How many did you take?"

"Several."

"Several? The whole bottle is empty!"

"I flushed the rest of them so I wouldn't take them."

"We're going to the hospital."

I drove him out to the hospital emergency room, and they called his psychiatrist. I was shocked when Grant came walking out not more than a couple of hours later. His wrists were bandaged, and he looked more alert. I had been sure he would be hospitalized.

"Let's go," he said.

"You talk to your psychiatrist?"

"Yeah, he's sending me home."

"Does he know what you did?"

"It's pretty obvious."

"Wait for me a minute." I went to talk to his psychiatrist. He assured me he knew what he was doing. Well, fuck it, then.

On the way home Grant confessed that an affair he was having with a medical resident at the hospital had gone sour. He wanted to scare the resident.

"Well, you owe me a bottle of sleeping pills. Next time, take your own fucking pills." He had to laugh.

While Grant was struggling with his sexual problems and relationship, I met Cindy, a new nurse at the hospital. She was petite and very good-looking. She had blonde, curly hair, green eyes, a tremendous amount of energy, and loved to talk. I wasn't sure if she was as attracted to me as much as I was to her, but there was an even bigger problem—she was married.

One night there was a hospital party that her husband didn't want to attend. Since we were practically the only unaccompanied people there, we spent most of the party together. I enjoyed the touching of our knees when we talked and the brushing of our thighs when we danced—each movement surprisingly intimate and easy. And from my lip-reading the whispers of the others, we were being more familiar than we were entitled to be. The obviousness of our mutual attraction was a bit embarrassing. Everyone knew that I was recently separated and

Cindy was still married, so I may have looked like a lech of sorts. A part of me felt guilty, another part didn't care.

At work, we started by taking dinner and coffee breaks together. One night we went to the basement of the hospital, found a bench in the corner of a dark hallway, and talked about her marriage.

"So when did you get married?" I asked.

"Too young. Nineteen. Just after high school. Much too young to know what I was doing."

"Did you love him?"

"I thought so, but what did I know? More likely it was infatuation. He was the captain of the football team, popular, and very into himself. All the girls liked him. Maybe I thought I was lucky that he liked me. Everyone said we made such a *nice* couple. All that well-worn fairy-tale drama of youth."

"Does he love you now?"

"I don't think there's enough room in his heart for the two of us. He mostly loves himself, but sometimes I even doubt that. What's important to him is money and success. Closeness to him is rubbing his shoulders with Ben-Gay."

"What kind of work does he do?"

"He's a salesman. He works for a large company downtown."

"Does he make a lot of money?"

"More schemes than money."

◆ ◆ ◆

I never dreamed I would get involved with a married woman; it seemed tacky and immoral, but here I was. I suppose I rationalized it knowing she wasn't happy in her marriage. Despite myself, after a few months, I fell in love with her. Then we started spending some of our days off together. We often went for long walks at night along the shore of Lake Michigan or just hung out at my apartment. It was a pleasant reprieve from my feelings about Jean and the kids.

Early one evening we were at the apartment while Grant was at work.

"Give me a bath?" she asked.

"A bath?"

"Yes, a nice warm bath—and wash me."

"Sure. A nice bath." She waited on the couch as I drew her a bubble bath with some fragrant stuff Grant used. Anything fancy, that guy had. When it was ready, she went in and, just before closing the door, said, "Give me two minutes, then come in."

It was a long two minutes. When I went in she was in the bath, everything but her head covered with bubbles and her eyes closed. The bathroom was filled with a steamy delicate scent. I took Grant's large natural sponge, dipped it in the warm water, and began moving it lightly over her small body.

"Hmmm. Nice," she whispered.

I felt as if I was performing a ritual ablution. When I finished, she stood up; small bubbles ran down her soft, pink skin. I wrapped her in a large towel, lifted her out of the tub, carried her to my darkened room, and placed her gently in the center of my bed. I went back to the living room and put on a Frank Sinatra album. *Strangers in the Night* began. I walked back to the bed and looked at Cindy. The low flickering streetlight behind the tree outside made small leafy shadows play across her skin.

She spoke softly, "Make love to me."

I don't know how long we made love, but it didn't matter, it seemed like a wordless eternity. Our entwined bodies performed a Mass of love in perfect harmony—as if we had rehearsed a hundred times before.

We lay embraced in silence. Finally, she spoke. "I felt like a virgin on her honeymoon."

"Or the way a honeymoon should be."

"Mine wasn't like that."

"Neither was mine." For the first time I understood what making love meant.

◆ ◆ ◆

During my last year at Marquette I became friends with a student in my Metaphysics class, Tom Marti. He was a Franciscan novitiate when he came to Marquette but dropped out of the order in his second year. Tom was short, gaunt, and already a bit stooped over. He was almost bald, but around the sides of his head hung a mess of long, thinning black hair practically down to his shoulders. Except for his beady piercing eyes, he looked older than he was. Regardless of the weather, he always wore the same clothes—Levis, tennis shoes, and a black turtleneck. He looked like a young version of Einstein and was one of the most brilliant philosophical thinkers I ever met. In class, he was the most articulate and seemed able to match wits with the professor. After we had coffee a few times, he invited me to his rooming house to meet and have dinner with his roommates, Don and John.

Don also looked and dressed a bit strange. Unlike Tom, he had a full head of long dark brown hair and a beard almost as long as his hair. About all that I could see of his face were part of his cheeks and thick, black horn-rimmed glasses surrounding his sparkling, dark brown eyes. Don had a nervous habit of licking the sides of his moustache. John's face was almost child-like. He was a little heavier than Tom or Don with longish straw-blonde hair, round, silver wire-framed glasses, and an Army fatigue jacket. Like Tom, they both wore Levis and tennis shoes. Next to these guys, *I* looked like a preppy.

The four of us had a spaghetti dinner with French bread and Chianti. The round base of the wine bottle was straw-wrapped. They must have drunk a lot of it because many bottles were scattered around their apartment with varying stages of burnt candles dripped over them.

After dinner we sat around in their funky living room on beanbag chairs and a dumpy couch and smoked a joint. The walls had posters of revolutionaries. One was Che Guevara, Castro's head honcho in the revolution. He had been executed in Bolivia the year before. If Che had glasses and Don had a black beret, they would look quite alike. There was another poster of the founders of the Black Panthers, Bobby Seale and Huey Newton, with their fists raised in the Black Power sign.

We talked about Guevara, the Panthers, music, philosophy, politics, and eventually the Vietnam War.

"Where you from, Larry? You've got a strange accent," John asked.

"Chicago. It's not an accent; it's a speech impediment." They all roared with laughter.

"Seriously, I have a hearing problem, so my speech sounds different. I don't hear words like you guys do."

"It sounds pretty cool to me. Sounds East Coast, maybe even foreign," Don said.

I wanted to change the subject. "Do you guys consider yourselves Communists?" I asked.

They looked at each other and smiled. And almost in unison, said, "No. Socialists."

"What's the difference? Don't the two words describe pretty much the same thing?"

Tom spoke, "The answer is historical. There were a number of people who called themselves 'socialists' in the middle of the nineteenth century but, when Marx and Engels came along, they adopted a more radical perspective called Communism. In *The Communist Manifesto,* they spelled out how they differed from socialists by emphasizing the oppressive split between the bourgeoisie and proletariat. The socialists have a different outlook on things than Communists do. Socialists want peaceful and incremental changes; Communists want proletarian revolution. Socialists favor a strong and centralized state apparatus that owns and manages the economy; Communists want no state apparatus whatsoever. The three of us are neither capitalists nor Communists. We make up the middle ground."

"Are you one of us?" Don asked smiling.

"I'm afraid I've just started thinking about these things. But, yeah, I feel like I'm more of a socialist."

"See! I told you guys!" Tom said, looking toward Don and John. Then he turned to me. "I told them I thought you were one of us."

"So are you against the war?" John asked.

"It's funny but my stepdad used to tell me that one day I'd have my war, that every generation has its own war. I guess this is my war, but I hate it. I've learned to hate violence, and I hate war, period."

"Well, join us, then," Tom said.

"What do you mean?"

"We're the leaders of MFC, Mobilization For Change. Ever hear of it?"

"Yes, it's banned on campus, right?"

"Yep. The administration thinks of us as radicals, which we are, so we're considered bad news. Unfortunately, the university doesn't take a stand on the war, but they do take a stand on radicals. For them, radicalism is just a form of Communism."

"What do you do?" I asked.

"Well, we recruit brothers and sisters like you. We write, underground, of course. We organize peace rallies and demonstrate at them."

"What about violence?"

"We're not violent—unless we have to be."

"I don't know about violence; I've had my share of that. And I don't think it helps anything. I like Gandhi's approach. It's ironic that some silly bastard shot him, isn't it? Maybe Freud was right about civilization when he said that culture is just something we invented to keep us from killing each other. Besides, I don't know if I have the time to do much else but work and study."

"You should read Jung. Freud missed the spiritual by dismissing religion altogether," Tom said.

"You've been in violent demonstrations before?" asked Don.

"No. Gang violence."

"Jesus, you were a gang member?" asked Tom. His eyes widened.

"Not just a member, a leader."

"Wow," Don said. "How the fuck did you ever get into Marquette?"

"Long story."

"Man, this guy's a genuine proletariat," John added.

We talked about our backgrounds. All of them were from very middle-class Wisconsin families. I got the feeling that poverty and real violence were almost academic, and I was a bit unreal to them. Unlike Grant, I guessed they gave up their robes and pajamas, but I liked them. I especially liked their passion and commitment. With Jean and the children in California I would have a little more time.

Saying the political climate of the sixties was turbulent was an understatement. The country was paranoid about Communists taking over the world. It was a decade of assassinations of people I considered my heroes. Even before Kennedy's assassination, the situation in Vietnam was getting more and more out of control. When Johnson took over, he escalated the war to insanity. So when he announced an end to his bombing of North Vietnam *and* decided not to run again, a new wave of hope swept through the antiwar movement. When Bobby Kennedy came out as a peace candidate, we all felt he could revive the inspiration created by his brother. He was antipoverty, antiwar, and a fervent supporter of civil rights. But on June 5, just when it looked as if he would be declared the Democratic candidate, Bobby was shot three times. He died early the next day. Just two months earlier, Martin Luther King Jr. had been assassinated, and Malcolm X was killed three years earlier.

I wanted to be a part of restoring the peace. I thought maybe joining MFC would be a step in that direction. My first big event with MFC was demonstrating at the Democratic convention in Chicago. MFC and many other groups of radical students were going to go there and try to disrupt the convention. We thought it would be an ideal place to demand an end to the Vietnam War. The rally was planned many months before the Chicago convention, but little happened the way it was supposed to. From what I heard, a hundred thousand people were going to demonstrate, but the City of Chicago refused to grant permits for any marches and for only one rally. As a result, only a few thousand people participated in the demonstrations.

When we got to Chicago, lists of available places to stay supposedly put out by sympathizers in Chicago turned out to be bogus. Apparently, the lists were a trick by the CIA or FBI who had infiltrated the ranks of students to disrupt the demonstrations. In addition to the infiltrators, Mayor Daley had added more than seven thousand National Guardsmen to the twelve thousand police officers already on hand to break up the rally.

We decided to camp out north of the convention center in Lincoln Park. Just in case there were police patrols in the park, we set up our sleeping bags away from any streetlights or activity. The freshly cut grass was cool and damp. Not long after we settled in, the guys said they could hear rustling in the distance. A few moments later, from where we sat in the dark, we saw the up and down and sideways movement of a lot of flashlights just over a small hill. The flickering lights created an eerie sight. An army of police in black riot gear came toward us from over the hill. They were talking and laughing loudly. Then the beams of their flashlights landed on our campsite. They started shouting, "Get the fuck out of the park, you fucking hippies." It looked as if the police outnumbered us at least five to one. We frantically started gathering up our camping gear and tried to move away from the police, but it was too late. Without warning, they just started pouncing on people with their long billy clubs. It was hard to see, but I could make out that our people were dropping things, tripping, stumbling, and falling in the dark, desperately trying to run back toward the streetlights so we could be more in the public view. I looked back and saw Don's girlfriend, Roz, trip over her sleeping bag and fall. In a second, two cops were over her like two black bears, clubbing her head and body. She was crying and yelling, "Stop, please stop." Roz's face was already bloody when Don came from out of the darkness and threw himself over her. The police clubbed him the same way. I could hear the cracking sound as their billy clubs rained down on them. I ran toward Don and Roz, wanting to kill one of those fucking cops. But before I got over to them, an even brighter light shone on the cops who were still clubbing Don. It was a newsman with a light on his camera.

"Get that fucking light off me," a cop yelled and turned like he was going to club him. The newsman fell backwards. He turned his light off and covered his head. Then I heard the cops calling to each other, "News, News. Let's get out of here."

I wasn't hurt, but many students besides Don and Roz got the hell clubbed out of them even though they had already fallen to the ground. Roz's face was a mess and, in trying to protect her, Don's ear was split.

I walked Don, and he practically carried Roz, about a mile to the Alexian Brothers' emergency room. In the corridor there were many other students waiting to be treated.

"How'd you know where the hell this place was?" Don asked.

"I used to work here."

"Shit, that's right, you told us about that."

We put Roz on a gurney in the hallway. The peculiar smell of the hospital was exactly as I remembered it five years ago. Don was bent over, hugging Roz. He straightened and said, "Larry, someone's calling you." I turned around and saw skinny Brother René coming down the hall, the back flap of his white habit trailing in the air behind him. He looked like Super Brother.

"Sweet Jesus, Mary, Joseph. Oh my God, it *is* you!"

"Hey, Brother René!"

"What on earth happened to you?"

"Nothing happened to me. It's what happened to them, courtesy of the Chicago police."

"But you've got blood on your face."

"I doubt it's mine, for a change. Must be Don's or somebody else's. So what are you doing here?"

"What do you mean 'doing here?' I'm a lifer, remember?" He laughed.

"I know, I just meant, I thought you were doing your vespers, or, oh, never mind."

"They called me to help out. Lots of business tonight. Listen, stick around a bit. Let's have a smoke in the parking lot."

"I'm not going anywhere till you guys fix up my friends."

Roz had a minor concussion, black eye, and a swollen lip. Don had a split ear that needed a few stitches. After they were finished, we went to the parking lot for a cigarette with Brother René. We talked about the past few years.

"How is Dr. Keddy? I never wrote to tell him I wasn't going to medical school."

"He'll be disappointed to hear that. He mentioned you a few times and wondered if anyone had heard from you. He was sure you were going to make a great physician."

"Next to not knowing what I would do with my life, the hardest part of changing my mind was thinking I would disappoint him. Please tell him I said 'Hello.'"

"Oh, Larry. We send you off to Marquette, and you end up back in the emergency room." He put his arm around my shoulder and turned to Don and Roz. "This guy is something. He came to us from the Chicago Outfit, we set him straight, sent him off to become a doctor, and now he's back in Chicago causing trouble again."

"This time I'm fighting for peace, Brother."

"I know you are. And you know what? I'm proud of you."

"It's really good to see you, Brother René. I missed you."

"I missed you, too, Larry. Next time, try writing before you show up."

We all laughed. Even though it hurt her mouth, Roz laughed, too.

We went back downtown and found a cheap hotel. Sleeping in the park was a big mistake. As it turned out, where we camped was one of the major battlegrounds between the police and students. "Battle" isn't really the right word. We simply got our asses kicked. We heard later that even the legal rally in Grant Park ended when police clubbed a demonstrator who was lowering an American flag while his friends tried to protect him.

On another night the police and Guardsmen tried to remove everyone from Michigan Avenue in front of the Hilton Hotel, the convention headquarters. Some people were pushed through plate glass windows because they were caught between Guardsmen and police trying to disperse the crowd. I thought of my last fight on Lincoln Avenue.

By the time the demonstration was over, six hundred of us were arrested and many more injured. Fortunately, for us, television news cameras not only caught our battle in the park but also captured many of the confrontations. When these images were played on monitors at the convention itself, they disrupted the proceedings far more than we could have in our efforts to march. Later on, an official report described it as a "police riot." That report damaged the reputation of the Chicago police more than anything we could have done. Mayor Daley didn't help either. He made a Freudian slip on the news when he said, "Our job is not to *prevent* disorder, it's to *preserve* disorder."

After the convention, the Democrats lost the election to Nixon, and the war not only dragged on, it got worse. We weren't sure if we were making a difference or not. The morale of the antiwar movement seemed to wilt, but the demonstration in Chicago created a strong bond between Tom, Don, John, and me. Roz also was our constant companion. We hung out in coffee houses, smoked a lot of grass, and listened to the Beatles, Joan Baez, and Simon and Garfunkel. We liked to sing verses from "Masters of War" by Bob Dylan like:

> You've thrown the worst fear
> That can ever be hurled
> Fear to bring children
> Into the world
> For threatening my baby
> Unborn and unnamed
> You ain't worth the blood
> That runs in your veins.

While we kept our passion for the peace movement, our last year at Marquette was demoralizing. Tom got his draft notice. The day he went for induction, we all went with him, arm in arm. Tom wore his Sgt. Pepper jacket. When the other recruits took one step forward, Tom took one step back. I knew he was scared because the back of his jacket was shaking. Actually, it was a little funny trying to imagine a guy as sweet and small as Tom in the military—if his drill sergeant didn't eat him for breakfast, he still wouldn't have lasted through the first day of boot camp. To underscore that war was a crime, but not refusing induction, we all burned our draft cards outside the induction center. Because of my hearing problem, I would have been classified 4-F, so I couldn't have been drafted anyway—but I really enjoyed burning my draft card.

The antiwar activities took some of the sting away from my missing the children. But Jean continued not to answer my calls, using her mother to relay messages.

"Well, Larry, all I can do is give her your messages. She doesn't want to talk to you."

"What's the point? What's she trying to accomplish? Can't you talk to her?"

"I don't think she wants you to see the children unless you come to California."

"I'm *planning* on coming to California! Does she give them my cards?"

"Uh, I'm not sure."

"You're not sure? Why doesn't she send any pictures?"

"She just wants you to come back."

"It's all about what she wants, isn't it? What she's doing isn't fair to the children."

Talking to her mother felt hopeless. It was becoming a source of torment. Jean's mindset was a side of her I never saw before and never would have guessed she had. I understood her anger at me, but I couldn't accept that she would be so mean to the children.

◆   ◆   ◆

I switched majors after deciding not to go to medical school, so it had taken five years to graduate, but the day was approaching. I had a degree in psychology, actually nearly two degrees, because I almost finished the one in biology, too. With two majors, I had enough minors to fill an ice chest. But their significance was ambiguous at best. While it felt good to have graduated, I was still uncertain about who I was and where I was going. What I knew for sure was that I wanted to move to California to be able to see the children.

As graduation grew closer, I began putting pressure on Cindy to divorce. One day she was going to her hometown for a friend's wedding. Her parents would be there, so it would be the ideal time to tell them she was leaving her husband. I took her to the train station. We sat on a bench on the noisy platform waiting for her train. It was very hard to hear.

"I'm planning on going to California, and I want you to come with me. I need you to separate."

"I can't do that. My parents would kill me."

"Your parents? Whose life is it, yours or theirs?"

"It's mine, but I can't tell them I failed."

"You didn't fail. Your marriage is *dead*."

"I know it is, but I still can't face them. They're Catholic, you know how that is. I don't want to disappoint them. They think everything's fine."

"Disappoint *them*? You're entitled to your happiness. You can't let your family or the Church dictate whether you stay married."

She took my hand, held it tightly, and moved close to my face. "Then let's just run away. I'll go anywhere with you. Please don't make me face them."

"What? Run away like felons? Eventually you'll have to face them anyway."

"I know, but I just can't do it now."

Stupidly, I gave her an ultimatum. "OK, then it's them or me. If you don't tell them, I'm not going to wait around."

"Please don't say that. Say you don't mean that. I need you to stand by me." She begged me through her tears not to insist on separating.

Her train arrived. "Please, Larry, *please*!"

I was silent. Still crying, she got on the train.

I felt sick watching the train pull out of the station. I knew that was a foolish tactic as soon as I said it.

When she returned, I gave her flowers at work with a card apologizing for what I said. But my ultimatum backfired; it had only broken her trust. So much so, that she refused to talk about it or to see me away from work. All she would say was that she was going to try to make her marriage work.

I later found the flowers upside down in the trash.

20

Pork Department

Although I was eager to move to California after graduation, I had no money, so I decided to stay in Milwaukee a little longer to save some. Now I could finally get a job for more than minimum wage. I found a position as a social worker with the County Welfare Department. Tom, Don, and John also started working there. Another advantage was that there were already members of MFC there, and we could join them in the antipoverty movement. The Welfare Department didn't know MFC members worked for them. They suspected that there were radicals in the department, but they didn't know who they were—at least not yet.

Even Grant got a job there, but not for the same reasons. He just needed a job.

"You know, now that you have some extra time, it would be good if you joined us," I said.

"I just want some peace for a change."

"That's what this is all about." I smiled.

"You know what I mean. Personal peace. It's been difficult finding some serenity in my life. Now that school's over, I just want to relax."

"I understand that, but there are a lot of people looking for that, too, like the Vietnamese."

"Larry, the war will be over soon. There'll be peace."

"And when it comes, don't you want to say you had a part in making it happen?"

"I'm too tired. It's just not for me, at least not right now."

"Have you ever rebelled against *anything* in your life?"

"I guess not."

"Maybe that's a problem."

"What do you mean?"

"Joining the peace movement might give you some spirit. Loosen you up, get you yelling, pissed off. Like you don't have to accept everything that someone else says is right. Tom, Don, and John will be happy to have you join us."

"I don't know about them. Their politics are too radical for me."
"*Too* radical? You don't have a fucking rebellious bone in your body."
"I don't like subversive or underground politics."
"I think you just don't like passion, action, or commitment."
"You might be right."
"Besides, you and those guys are the best friends I've ever had."
"I don't think they like me anyway."
"They like you OK. They just think you're a little uptight."

Grant's lack of interest puzzled me. For the first time things between us became tense. It created a serious rift in our relationship. He moved out of our apartment, bought some expensive furniture, and got a fancy place on North Lake Drive.

Since childhood, I had fantasized about belonging to a secret or underground group. I often wondered who else I would want to be in it. I would have to trust them. Except for Christie, certainly none of my family would have made it. Brother René would be one. Tom, Don, John, and Grant were the only other people I trusted. I not only trusted them to be in my underground, I would trust them with my life. MFC was like that underground.

One of my jobs for MFC was to write for the underground newspaper *Change!* under the pseudonym, Zara. It was the first writing I had ever done outside of school assignments, and I loved the freedom of expression that anonymity provided. I soon discovered that radicals loved and praised my articles, and conservatives hated and condemned them. Most of my articles were discussions of poverty, attacks on welfare department policies, and ridicule of their administrators. *Change!* had a fairly wide circulation; it went out to local colleges and universities, Welfare Department waiting rooms, and was stealthily placed in the mailboxes of all welfare employees. Because of that, the Deputy Director denounced Zara as a fanatic and initiated a search to connect the name with someone who worked in the department. Thanks to the First Amendment, my writing wasn't a crime but, if I ever were found out, I would certainly be fired and made an example.

Working in the Welfare Department was sometimes difficult because it reexposed me to poverty. Seeing single mothers living with several children in cramped, cold apartments with barely enough food or clothing to subsist reminded me of Blackhawk Street. Even with those memories, I enjoyed working with my clients. At least I was in a position to help them a little and maybe have some impact on the welfare system. Unlike the stereotypes promoted by wealthy conservatives, my clients were good people who would have taken jobs if they could have found them, had the skills for them, or had affordable childcare. For some, working was simply impossible. I also met people when I visited my clients' neighborhoods like my mother, whose pride kept them from applying for welfare or even food stamps. Rather than be thought of as less than others, they and their children suffered even more.

It was curious how the rare stories of welfare fraud so easily made news, but the everyday plight of poor people was seldom newsworthy. Those most critical of the poor were wealthy conservatives who used welfare recipients as scapegoats for their property taxes. Because of that, I took on another MFC activity—working in a public awareness project. This one was above ground only because administrators didn't know MFC organized and ran it. They gave the project lukewarm approval. We tried to enlist the help of business owners, public utility administrators, and politicians by increasing their awareness of poverty. To do that, we explained the program to our clients and asked their permission to bring these people into their homes to see first hand what poverty was really about. After these home visits, we took the guests out to dinner to discuss their reactions to what they saw and how they felt.

One of my guests was the president of the Wisconsin Electric Power Company. I took him to see a Hispanic family with five children living in one of the poorest areas of Milwaukee. He was a fortuitous guest that day, because when we arrived the father was talking to an employee of the power company who was there to turn off the electricity. He didn't recognize the company's president.

"I'm sorry, but I don't care what you say. I have orders to turn off your power today for nonpayment of the bill."

"But it's Friday. I won't be able to have it turned on again until Monday, maybe later," the father protested.

I interrupted the conversation. "Excuse me, sir. But I'm Mr. Francesco's social worker."

"So?"

"Well, I've already issued a utilities voucher for this family. The Welfare Department will pay his electric bill, so you don't have to turn it off."

"Look, I have my orders, OK? They say to turn off the electricity at this address for nonpayment. Maybe you issued a voucher, but I don't know anything about it."

"If you turn off this family's electricity that means their refrigerator will go out, too. Their food will spoil over the weekend. The voucher guarantees payment."

"Look, it's late. I've got a job to do, and I have to do it. You can straighten it out on Monday."

Then the president spoke, "Excuse me, my name is Bill Fulton. You *will* leave this family's electricity on."

"I don't know who you think you are, but like I just told this guy, I have a job to do and I'm going to do it. It's none of your business."

"It happens that it is very much my business. I'm the president of the Wisconsin Power Company."

"Right. And I'm Paul Revere. I'm sure our president doesn't hang out in neighborhoods like this. Just let me do my job, OK?"

"If you turn this family's power off, it will be the last job you do for this power company, I assure you. What's your supervisor's name?"

"Jesus. Frank Willington."

Mr. Fulton turned away from the employee. "Mr. Francesco, may I use your phone?" When he came back outside a few minutes later, the electricity was already off. Mr. Fulton walked over to the utility man's truck and told him to turn the electricity back on and to call his supervisor.

Ten minutes later the lights came back on. The employee was at the door, embarrassed and apologizing to the president. "I'm sorry, sir, I thought you were kidding."

"Oh, I wasn't kidding at all. Not a bit. I don't think you're the kind of person to be in this position."

Later that evening at the guests' dinner, Mr. Fulton was the first to speak. He expressed his shock at the behavior of his employee and acknowledged that this incident would never have occurred if the family were not living in poverty.

On Christmas Eve that year, the president and his family visited the Francescos and brought them a station wagon full of food and presents. It was one of my most successful public awareness visits. There were other positive visits, but overall the results were small and, unfortunately, the effect of the program was minimal.

That summer, millions of people watched the first moon landing on television. Several social workers brought TV sets so they could watch the historic event. Right after watching it, I had a scheduled office visit with a client. She was a favorite of mine, a likeable, big, black, poverty-hardened mother of six. As she often did, she brought me a piece of her sweet potato pie.

"I just saw the moon landing," I said.

"*Moon* landing? Like landing on that moon up *there?*" She pointed above her head.

"Yes, on the surface of the moon."

"Sheee. There ain't no one on that moon, they makin' that sheet up."

"It was just on television."

She leaned back in her chair, wiped her sweaty forehead with a handkerchief, and adjusted the brightly colored muumuu that covered her large belly. It was a hot July afternoon. "I don' care what you *think* you saw, or what they say they did. I tell you, there ain't nobody on that moon. No, sir." Then she laughed and slapped her thigh. "Ain't *no way* anybody way up there!" I was struck by her ability to keep a sense of humor. She reminded me of the lady who moved upstairs from us on Blackhawk Street after Mrs. Kemper and Harvey moved out.

"Well, that's what they said. I guess it is hard to believe."

"An' besides, who got that kinda money to send somebody to the moon when the welfare tell me there ain't nearly enough money to feed my kids?"

She had a telling point. The spacecraft alone cost more than $355 million. I wouldn't dare to guess the cost of the twenty thousand other industries that worked on the project. The crew was going to have to leave several million dollars' worth of cameras and other equipment on the moon to lighten their journey home. That, along with a flag, human waste matter, and some footprints that would last a half-million years, created an expensive cosmic junkyard only America could claim as their legacy to the moon. Looking at the moon would never be the same for me.

The expense of the war was another hunk of misspent money. Because the administration kept war costs from the public, few knew how much of their taxes had been spent on it. A later "rough estimate" was more than $150 billion—not including $2.5 billion in aid to France even before we fought there.

Then in November of that year, the press finally released the story of the My Lai massacre. It had happened in March of '68, but because of various military cover-ups—including the intercession of Colin Powell who whitewashed the report—it took more than a year to make the news. American soldiers led by Lieutenant William Calley massacred five hundred or more Vietnamese civilians—mostly elderly people, women, and children. Soldiers raped some of the older girls and women before they shot them. When I heard about it, I went to the bathroom and threw up. Just thinking about my girls in such circumstances was devastating. It was, by far, the single most barbaric act I had heard of in the Vietnam War. My Lai so clearly personified the insanity and inhumanity of the war that it turned a few hawks into doves. It further poisoned the antiwar group against soldiers. My feelings about American soldiers in Vietnam vacillated: sometimes I was angry; other times I felt guilty that I didn't support them. More than anything, I felt sorry for them. Fortunately, only the rare soldier was the heartless animal Calley was. The majority were well-intentioned but misguided nineteen-year-olds misled by American propaganda and with little understanding of foreign policy. I doubt most of them even knew where Vietnam was until they got there. On the other hand, maybe they just thought it was "their war" and were doing the right thing by being there. My Lai left us even more deeply discouraged, but we continued our work in the antiwar movement. The phonetics of the name of the village were stunning: "me lie."

◆ ◆ ◆

Although I was saving my money, I didn't have enough to move to California yet, but I had enough to make a weekend trip there. I was eager to see the girls. When they heard I was going to see the kids, Tom and Don wanted to come too. John was going to go to a peace march in Washington. Jean and the girls were in Los Angeles, but Tom wanted me to see San Francisco. He had been there before; Don hadn't. We booked a red-eye flight to San Francisco for Friday, but I made a connecting flight to LA on Saturday afternoon with a return to Milwaukee on Sunday night. It would be a short but, hopefully, sweet visit with the children.

When we arrived in San Francisco, Tom took us directly to "the most beautiful place in the world," Golden Gate Park. It was four in the morning, and the park was deserted, partly darkened, and bathed in fog, but that only made its beauty all the more striking and mysterious. There were many smaller gardens within the park, as well as the deYoung Museum, the Japanese Tea Garden, and an arboretum. I had never seen such a variety of trees in one place.

At sunrise, we walked over to the Haight-Ashbury district, *Summer of Love's* epicenter. I had never seen anything in the Midwest like the Haight's pastel-colored Victorians. Compared to the brick and gray of Middle America, the colors and decorative details of the houses seemed almost unreal. Next, we went down to Ghirardelli Square on the San Francisco Bay. We sat at an outdoor café and had espressos. Except for the clanging bells of cable cars over on Hyde Street, the square was still quiet and peaceful. As the cool morning fog dissolved, the Golden Gate Bridge came into view and the bay sparkled in the early morning sunlight. It was a spectacular sight. Looking out over the water from where we sat, we also could see the infamous Alcatraz and Angel Island. Once a federal penitentiary, Alcatraz had been home to some of America's most celebrated criminals. Our long-haired waiter said Native American Indians recently took it over, claiming it as their rightful heritage.

San Francisco was the most beautiful city I had ever seen. Its rolling hills, quaint pastel Victorians, and its closeness to the bay and ocean made the Midwest seem lifeless, flat, and dull.

I turned to Tom and Don and asked, "Do people really *live* here?" They laughed because they knew exactly what I was feeling. "Know what? I'm going to move here."

"So are we."

"No, I mean it. When I move to California, I'm going to live here."

"We'll be here waiting for you."

"What do you mean?"

"You didn't hear Don and me talking in the park? We already decided to move here. And I said, 'Watch, Larry's going to join us.'"

"You're right on. I can't wait!"

"We're not going to wait. We're going back to Milwaukee to get our stuff."

"What? When are you talking about?"

"Just what I said. We're going back, pick up our stuff, and move right out here."

"What about an apartment? A job?"

"Maybe we'll find an apartment while you're in LA. We'll get jobs when we come out."

"What about your jobs in Milwaukee?"

"We'll quit when we go back. Our heads are on the butcher block anyway. So is yours."

"What are you talking about?"

"The department is onto MFC big time. Someone in the department has been letting on that we lead MFC. The department also suspects that you're Zara."

"Fuck. Why didn't you guys tell me this on the plane? How long have you known about it?"

"The word was out just before we left. We were going to tell you out here. Like we're doing now." They both smiled at each other.

"Jesus. You're sure about this? And sure you're moving?"

"Yep. Aren't you?"

"I'm very serious, but I have to get a job here before I move out. I can't afford to take a chance of not having a job. It's not just me, I've got my girls to think of."

"Whatever. Do what you need to do. We'll be here waiting for you."

"Shit. I think I need a drink. We're actually doing this?"

◆ ◆ ◆

I left for LA the next afternoon. I was eager to see the kids but nervous about seeing Jean. I told Jean's mom when I would be there, and she seemed pleased. I just hoped she didn't think I was coming back to the family. I didn't know how I would get to their apartment. LA was one big, goddamned city.

When I arrived in LA, Jean was at the airport with the girls. I couldn't help crying when I saw the children jumping up and down as I got off the plane. It was wonderful to see them, and they all looked healthy and so beautiful. As I walked toward them, they came running and started jumping all over me, yelling, "Daddy, Daddy!" Then I noticed Jean, a statue in the background, unsmiling, cool, and silent. I gave her a light hug when I got to where she stood—she felt stiff.

"Hi," I said.

"Hi. Long flight from Milwaukee?" Still deadpan.

"Actually, I came from San Francisco." I braced myself.

She tightened up even more. "*San Francisco*? A layover?"

"No, I came out with a couple of friends from Milwaukee. We arrived last night."

"What *friends*?" She made "friends" sound like it was a dirty word. I knew I shouldn't have mentioned them, but I didn't want to lie.

"Friends I…I met in Milwaukee after you left. They're very nice."

She stared at me intently, tensed her jaw. I felt burrowed through, as if she were interrogating me. "What happened to your *hair*?" Her brow furrowed, her lips crooked with disapproval.

"I was letting it grow a little." I tried to smile but it didn't work. Then I tried a half-smile. That didn't work either. I wasn't passing inspection.

"What, you're going to be a hippie now? Hang out with the druggies in San Francisco?" She looked and sounded like someone's angry mother.

"Uh, where's your car?"

"In the fucking parking lot." I was shocked and angry that she swore in front of the children. Their frightened little faces just looked up at me. I wanted to say something but bit my tongue. This was going badly enough.

To my surprise, she had a red '64 Mustang. I didn't know how she could afford it, probably her mother. When we got to the apartment, Jean seemed to calm down a bit. The apartment was small, but clean and comfortable. All the things we had in Milwaukee were there—and some new things. I was relieved that it was a nice apartment. We had an early dinner, and the children were chattering away to me the whole time about anything and everything. They were happy, and it was good to see them; I almost couldn't take my eyes away from them. Jean sensed that, and I knew she was uncomfortable.

"Well, girls, it's time to go to bed."

Their little faces dropped. "But daddy just got here!"

"I know, but daddy and I have to talk. So go get ready for bed. Now!"

I really hated the way she talked to them. They slunk off to their room. "Come and say goodnight, Daddy," one of them called from the hallway.

I went to their room and said goodnight and kissed them one by one and tucked them in. I said goodnight to Ann last.

"Daddy, why don't you live with us like you used to? Don't you like us anymore?" Ann asked.

"Of course I do, Sweetie. Why do you think that?"

"Mommy says you don't like us anymore." I winced.

"I don't think Mommy meant that. Maybe she meant Mommy and Daddy are having some troubles. But I love you and your sisters very much, and I want you to always remember that."

"Why don't you write to us?"

"I write you all the time. On your birthday, I wrote and sent presents. And sometimes I just write to see how you are. And I think about you all the time."

"I never got a birthday card—or a present."

"I have to talk to your Mommy about that."

"It makes me happy that you think about me."

"Of course it does, Sweetie. You and your sisters are very important to me."

"Can you take me to the mountains tomorrow?" She had a darling way of saying *mountains*.

"We'll see. We'll ask Mommy. I would like that, and it would be fun. Goodnight, Sweetie. I love you."

"I love you too, Daddy."

In the living room, Jean was sitting on the couch. She had changed into a sexy light blue nightgown. That was subtle. The gown was like a bright red blinking light. I wasn't going to play that game anymore; it wasn't even tempting.

I cleared my throat. "I guess I better go find a hotel."

"You can stay here—*if* you've made up your mind." Her stare was hard, intense, cold, and meant to be indifferent.

"Made up my mind?" I played dumb.

"Yes. To come back and be with us."

I was hoping we wouldn't have to talk about that. "I don't think I can do that."

"You mean you don't *want* to do that?" Her jaw started clenching again.

"Jean, I'm sorry, but I don't want to be married. But I want to have a good relationship with you and the children. We owe it to them."

"As far as I'm concerned *you* don't have any children anymore." Her eyes glared.

"Jean, please. That's not fair to them. They need me as much as they need you."

"I don't think so. We can get along fine without you."

"Why aren't you giving them my cards and presents?"

"As far as I'm concerned, they don't have a father."

"You can't do that."

"Oh, no? Watch. And now you can leave. Get out!" she yelled.

"What about the rest of the visit?" My heart sank when I thought about the children.

"It's over. Leave."

I knew I didn't love her and now I was starting to dislike her. Her character was repelling. I didn't think she cared about the children or me; she cared about herself. I didn't know what that was about, but it wasn't love.

I left the apartment and walked around for what must have been miles. I didn't even know where the fuck I was. My plane departure wasn't until Sunday, and I had no hotel. Finally, I found a taxi on a large boulevard.

"Take me to a hotel."

"Which one?"

"I don't care, the first one you see with a vacancy sign."

"OK."

At the hotel I got something to eat and took it to my room. When I got there, I couldn't eat. I felt nauseous and knew I was about to get a headache. Jean could make my life miserable. She also could make the children suffer—and I was afraid she would.

◆ ◆ ◆

When I arrived back at the department on Monday, I sensed my redneck supervisor, Bill Watson, was waiting for me. He was a pathetic guy whose only idea of a good time was backyard barbeques and drinking beer with other Colonel Blimps from the department. I went once; once was enough. I guess because their own lives were so shallow, they enjoyed making fun of the clients, joking and laughing about how pathetically they managed their lives. I hated their demeaning and condescending stories. Because he reminded me of a squat snowman, I called him "Fats" behind his back. His abdomen pushed out his lackluster tie about four inches from his chest. He kept glancing expectantly toward my desk with a silly smile. I waved to him and then looked down at my desk to avoid him.

Finally, he rolled on over and stopped in front of my desk. He began tapping on a copy of one of Picasso's earlier paintings, *Maternity*, taped to the side of my file cabinet next to my desk.

"You know, Larry, that painting must remind you of this place." He continued tapping it with back of his finger.

I pretended not to hear him. Then I looked up, "Huh? What do you mean?"

Well, it's kind of like the clients and the department. We're like a tit for them to suck on."

"Jesus. Can I ask you a personal question?"

"Sure."

"Why do you work here?"

"It's a job; it's secure, pays good money."

"Is that all?"

"That's it. I'm not a bleeding heart, if that's what you mean. Well, how was your weekend?" He had the piggy impish grin of a minstrel of misfortune. What he really hoped was that my weekend had been as tedious and uneventful as his. He wasn't only obese; he was obtuse.

I was all too happy to shock him. "I went to San Francisco." That was something totally outside his imagination. I doubt he traveled farther than his back yard.

His loud laugh made his belly shake and his face redden. "San Francisco, huh? That's a good one."

"It's true, Faa…, Bill. San Francisco and Los Angeles. It was great."

"For the weekend? You're kidding." Anyone else's happiness made him uncomfortable.

"Nope."

"Where are your comrades, Kline and Marti? They didn't show up this morning."

He was trying an alternate approach to find misfortune. He always referred to Tom, Don, and John as my comrades. "I don't know. Maybe they're still in San Francisco."

"*They* went, too?" His chubby face reddened more and contorted in disbelief.

"Yep. That's where I saw them last." I knew he was flabbergasted because his neck got red. I think rednecks all have high blood pressure.

"Well, whatever. The unit supervisor told me she wants to see you first thing today." He gave that stupid smile again.

"What about?"

"I don't know. Why don't you go see her and find out." His radar finally zeroed in on some misfortune.

I went to the unit supervisor's cubicle. She was a heartless bitch who didn't hide her officious disdain for welfare clients. She motioned me in.

"Sit down, Larry!" she shot at me.

Before I was halfway down to the chair, she was out of hers, screaming through her over-red lipstick. I thought she was going to crawl over her desk with a hammer. Many faces at the sea of desks outside her cubicle perked up as she shrieked, "Just who the *hell* do you think you are? You think I don't know you're Zara? Your stupid writing and misplaced sympathy don't impress me, and it's going to cost you your job!" I had never seen her so unglued. I glanced over across the room and saw Fats standing on his tiptoes behind his desk.

I tried to keep my self-assurance. "Er, how do you know I'm Zara?"

"Everyone in the department knows it's you! The deputy director knows!"

"But my question is, how do you *know* it's me?"

"We have information on what you've been doing here *and* your Communist antiwar activities."

"*Communist*? What information?"

"I can't tell you, but the deputy director wants to see you this morning. You can ask him."

Shit. The deputy director never talked to anyone below a unit supervisor. I don't think Fats ever talked to him. There had to have been a major leak. Don and Tom were right. I went to the director's office—the only real office in the whole department. His secretary seemed to be expecting me. I was still a little shaken from the first meeting. I could lose my job.

"Have a seat, Mr. Pedersen. The director will be with you shortly."

The director came out in a few minutes and pointed me to his office. He was a biggish, older guy who always wore suspenders and gray vests with a large matching moustache. He smoked stinky cigars, and his office reeked of them.

He plopped down in his leather chair behind a huge mahogany desk and pointed his stubby finger at a chair on the other side like I was a dog.

"Mr. Pedersen, it's come to my attention that you write for the underground newspaper, *Change!* Is that correct?"

"No, sir. It's not. Besides, I don't think it's illegal even if I did."

"No, it's not illegal, but I would say disloyal for an employee to criticize the hand that feeds him. And apart from that, we also have information that you are, uh, fraternizing with your clients." He let out a belch of cigar smoke.

"What does that mean?"

"You are reported to have been seen coming from a client's house early in the morning." The raggy wet end of his cigar must have tasted like shit.

"That's ridiculous. Which client?"

"I can't say, but since that *is* against department policy, we're going to have to let you go."

"With all due respect, sir, I don't believe you can do that."

"Oh, I can't? Just go clear out your things. You are terminated, Mr. Pedersen." Now *that* was going to make Fats very happy.

I went back to my desk, called the social workers union rep and explained what had just happened. He said I was probably right; they couldn't let me go on hearsay. He also said he would call the deputy director and then call me back. Luckily, the rep also was a member of MFC.

I was at my desk looking for a client's file when Fats came over again. "Cleaning out your desk?" he asked with that same stupid grin.

"No, I cleaned it out last week."

"Last week?"

"Yeah, it was pretty messy so I tidied it up a bit. I'm just looking for a file."

"Oh." His smile weakened. "How was the meeting with Miss Winkle?"

"She was very upset. Said she thought I was writing for the nasty underground newspaper. I think she needs a vacation. Probably working too hard. You know."

"And the director?"

"Pretty much the same." Fats didn't know what more to say. He just scratched his bald spot and waddled back to his desk.

The rep called me back. "You were right, and you're safe for the moment, but your ass is really on the line this time, Larry. The deputy director himself is on the warpath. I think it's only a matter of time before they come up with something they can get you on. Might not be your writing; it could be anything. That they didn't get you on these charges is just going to piss them off more. I would lay low if I were you. The ax could fall any day. That's the best I can do. Good luck."

"Thanks, I appreciate your help."

Before I was fired or just left, I wanted to have another job lined up. I sent for applications to the welfare departments in San Francisco and Oakland.

Don and Tom came back a few days later. They hadn't even called in, so they were on their supervisor's shit list, too. They came over to my desk—all smiles. They had gotten an apartment in San Francisco and were going to hand in resignations that afternoon. John was disappointed that they were leaving but happy for them. He wanted to come to San Francisco too, but he felt he still had work to do in Milwaukee. He had just made some important contacts with a new, much more radical group that had broken off from SDS, Students for a Democratic Society, called the Weathermen. Three hundred of them had recently carried out a violent and destructive demonstration in Chicago called the *Days of Rage*. The police shot six of them and arrested seventy.

Before Tom and Don left, there was to be a big MFC meeting to talk to the some of the Weathermen. Part of that meeting also was a farewell party for Tom and Don, who had already hooked up with the San Francisco Peace Coalition before they came back. They didn't seem particularly interested in this meeting.

As we expected, the Weathermen wanted the use of more violence in our movement. One of their first plans was to bomb the Welfare Department. That's where I drew the line. I had to speak out.

"Did you guys think of what the impact will be on services to our clients if we bomb the department?"

The leader of the Weathermen spoke. "It'll be temporary. The positive impact of our attack will far outweigh the disruption of services."

"Depending on how much of it is destroyed, I don't think the department will be rebuilt for a long time. The administrators will be happy to collect their wages while the department's put back together. It's the clients who will suffer. How will they get their food stamps, their checks, and their special needs? I grant you what we have now is shit, but it keeps the clients fed. Do we, or you guys, have the means of providing what the clients will lose if the building is destroyed?"

"The department will likely provide interim means of issuing checks and food stamps."

"I don't think you guys understand the Welfare Department. You can't guarantee they will do much of anything. My guess is that they will be more than happy to take their time and blame the bombing on the recipients. My clients and their children may starve while they're waiting. I say, No!"

Someone suggested taking a vote. Then the leader of the Weathermen spoke up again. "If you people want to join ranks with us, you're going to have to resort to more violent means for change. Otherwise, you'll be at this shit for the next hundred years."

I had to speak again. "You know what? I don't know about MFC, but this isn't for me. I don't want any part of it. The line between the good guys and the bad guys blurs when it comes to violent solutions. Isn't this the same thing the country is doing in Vietnam? Don't they have all kinds of crazy reasons for destroying that country? At what point do we become the same?"

A lot of the MFC people seemed to agree. The Weathermen didn't. I knew it was time for me to get out.

A few days later Tom and Don left for San Francisco. Just after they left, I heard from the Welfare Department in Oakland. They had a position for a social worker available in November. Thank God, they didn't ask for recommendations or references. I wrote and accepted the position. I had a few weeks' vacation coming, and I wasn't going to resign until Fats signed my vacation request. He agreed, so I typed out my resignation, folded it like a paper plane, and went to see Miss Winkle. When I knocked on her door, she looked up with disgust.

"What do you want?"

"Could I please have a minute of your time?"

"Make it quick. Sit down!"

I didn't bother to sit down. "Miss Winkle, I just want you to know that I'm filing a harassment complaint with the Board of Supervisors. Your behavior has caused me a great deal of emotional distress. I was going to tell you to take this job and shove it up your ass, but I don't want to lower myself to your level. And besides that, I doubt it would fit. So I've decided to resign." Then I sailed my resignation right onto her desk. Her mouth was still open as I walked out.

I told Fats I was leaving the department.

"Leaving? I thought you were just taking a vacation. Where're you going? Do you have another job?"

"Have you ever found yourself in an airport wondering if you could buy a ticket and go anywhere in the world, where you might go?"

"No. I always know where I'm going, how long I'll be there, and when I'll return."

"Well, maybe you wouldn't understand, but that's sort of what I might be doing." He didn't know what to say.

After I cleaned out my desk, I left Fats a kid's Porky Pig birthday card in his mail slot. It said: "Dear Fats, I'm off to a new venture. I hope I have done some little measure of good for my clients. I enjoyed working with them, and I will miss them. You might try and invite some of them to one of your barbecues. I think you'll find them just like the rest of us, rather interesting and decent folks who just happen to be poor, a sad fate that could happen to even the best of people. Larry."

Of course, I knew he wouldn't. That would be too much of a stretch for a guy like Fats.

21

El Intermedio

Grant was also taking a vacation. He was going to Portugal and Spain and offered to take me with him—at his expense. It was a mind-boggling opportunity. I'm sure he meant his offer as a peace gesture to mend our rift. The closest thing to a vacation I'd ever had was Detention Camp. Since I didn't have to spend any money and didn't need to be in California until November, I took him up on it.

True to his class, Grant ordered champagne for us on the plane. We got to Lisbon late at night and found a hotel with a room several stories *below* the street level—tiny and dark with two beds and a toilet. Not much, but it was exciting just to be in Lisbon. Early the next morning we had coffee and croissants at a sidewalk café next to a noisy, diesel-smelling boulevard just outside the hotel. The coffee was dark, strong, and more flavorsome than any I'd had in the States. I was very happy to be away from everything back home, and it was a good time to reconnect with Grant.

That afternoon we walked up the esplanades to the castle of Sao Jorge and climbed its ramparts. Inside the grounds were gardens of olive, pine, and cork trees. An occasional peacock strutted by while swans with white bodies and black necks paddled silently in a small lake. The piercing scream of a rare bird occasionally shattered the peacefulness of the courtyard. From the castle walls, we could see the quarters of Baixa and Alfama, the historic parts of the city. We walked down and along the banks of the Tagus River to the downtown area. Baixa had been rebuilt after being destroyed by an earthquake in the eighteenth century. Then we visited the Moorish quarter of Alfama crowned by the magnificent Sao Jorge Castle. Most of Alfama escaped the earthquake. The colorful street markets had lots of bananas and pineapples; the air was fragrant with scents of garlic and freshly grilled sardines. Its narrow cobblestone streets, cages of chirping canaries, and strings of peppers hanging in front of old taverns made it appear as medieval as it had been hundreds of years ago. Its houses were so close together that in some places your stretched arms could touch houses on both sides of the street.

On the western extreme was the harbor of Belém with its sentinel tower looming over the Tagus River that once used to protect the entrance into Lisbon. In another quarter, Mouraria, we had a delicious lunch at a simple, lime-washed restaurant called *Algures*. They served exotic, unheard of dishes from Angola. Grant had chicken cooked with ginger; I had spicy beef stewed in palm nut oil. We toasted our trip and our reunion with a full-bodied Portuguese red wine.

After lunch we walked to the Jerónimos Monastery, a spectacular sixteenth century edifice and one of the few surviving structures of Manueline architecture. It was a mass of high arches, impressive columns, ornate spires, monastic rooms, a refectory, a church hall, and several chapels. The chapels housed the tombs of royal descendants of King Manuel I. The last part of Jerónimos was the cloister with many extraordinary galleries.

The monastery was the best part of Lisbon. It kindled a fascination with monasteries and cathedrals. It didn't matter that I had never seen anything even close to places like these—somehow they felt familiar. Seeing Jerónimos made me want to visit *Santo Domingo De Silos* in Spain, the monastery of the Gregorian Chants that Brother René had given me.

We left Lisbon and took the train to Madrid.

"You know, I have some apprehensions about visiting Spain," I told Grant.

"Oh, no. Here we go."

"Franco is a fascist."

"I know he is, Larry. I thought we came for a vacation."

"We did, but it's hard to still my social and political conscience."

"Tell me about it."

"I'm not going to go on about it. I just wanted to let you know is all."

"I *was* hoping you wouldn't bring it up."

"It's pretty hard not to notice the National Police Corps and Civil Guard since they're everywhere. Doesn't that bother you?"

"Actually, it doesn't. But go ahead. Indulge yourself for a few minutes so we can get on with our vacation."

"You know the militia is out because the ETA-M is terrorizing the country."

"Who are they?"

"A militant offshoot of the Basque Nationalist Party."

"I thought I was the history major."

"You are, but this isn't history yet. It's what's happening right now."

"OK. Now could you please tell me one thing positive about Spain?"

"Hemingway covered their Civil War."

"I said *positive*."

"There's a restaurant in Madrid called Café Botin. Jake Barnes ate there with Brett Ashley in *The Sun Also Rises*."

"OK, let's go there for dinner tonight."

"Great, but I don't know if it really exists."

"I'll ask the concierge at the hotel."

It did. It was still there since 1725. Grant made me promise to enjoy myself. The restaurant was on a small street, *Calle de Cuchilleros,* in a beautiful old stone building just off *Plaza Mayor*. We were seated downstairs, but I wanted to be upstairs where Hemingway ate. I assumed he ate there because he said Jake Barnes did. Upstairs, the delicate scent of saffron floated through the Castilla Room where we sat under wood-beamed ceilings with ornate black-iron chandeliers. The walls were lined with blue and white Castillan tiles. I ordered what Hemingway had, *cochinillo asado,* roast suckling pig and a bottle of *rioja alta*. In the corner of the room a few *tuna* played subdued Spanish songs on their guitars.

"You know, Grant, I could be sitting *right* where Hemingway sat?"

"I'm sure you are. Are you having a good time?"

"Great!" I think he was relieved. "Hey, maybe I should be a writer."

"Larry, you could be anything you want."

"Think so?"

"I *know* so. You're just one of that kind."

"What kind?"

"It's hard to explain. There are just certain types of people who can do anything they want. They just have to know what it is. Once they do, they do it. It doesn't matter what it is."

"Thanks. That's encouraging. Maybe I'll find out one day."

"You will."

"How can you be so sure?" Our dinners came.

"Larry, eat your little pig."

The suckling pig was juicy and roasted to a dark brown with rosemary potatoes. It was delicious. "It's wonderful! I didn't know a pig could taste so good."

We both laughed.

"Larry, this is awkward, but I've been thinking of going up to Scotland. To see Susan."

"Who's Susan?"

"An old girlfriend from high school. Do you mind?"

"No, not at all. Want to rekindle an old romance?"

"Maybe. I don't know."

"It's fine with me on one condition."

"What's that?"

"We go to a bullfight together tomorrow."

"Let me guess. Hemingway."

"Yep. *Death in The Afternoon*."

The next day we went to the *plaza de toros*. Every time the matador hurt the bull, the people stood up and yelled, "*Olé*." Reading about a bullfight was not seeing one. I don't know what I was thinking about, but this was a disgusting spectacle. "What's the fucking point to this?"

"It's the bullfight you wanted to see, remember?"

"It's slow torture. I don't want to see them kill this poor bull."

"It's their sport. It's what they do here. Like baseball in America."

"Baseball! What if that was somebody's dog?"

One of the *Olé!* yellers, a portly guy in a black beret sitting in front of us, turned around and gave me an irritated look.

I didn't say anything to Grant, but for a moment I was back in the old neighborhood. It reminded me of how much I had come to hate violence of any kind. "Let's get out of here."

Grant laughed. "You may become a writer, but you'll never be Hemingway."

"Did I tell you he committed suicide?"

"Jesus, Larry. Lighten up."

Grant and I made plans to meet in New York when we returned from Europe and take a connecting flight back to Milwaukee together. Without waking me the next morning, he went off to Scotland. On the dresser was a pile of cash and a note. "Here's some money to find another Hemingway haunt. See you in New York. Love, Grant." I hoped he did find his old girlfriend; he deserved to be happy.

I went to the Prado Museum. There were works by Goya, such as *Naked Maja,* and the celebrated *Las Meninas* by Velázquez. Others by Hieronymus Bosch, Goya, Caravaggio, Fra Angelico, and Botticelli were paintings I had only seen in art books. The richness of the originals was staggering and overwhelming. I had seen so many famous paintings that I had to sit down and rest. I fell asleep on a bench in the museum. It wasn't long before a museum guard woke me and said something like, *"No echar la siesta, Señor."* I got the idea and left the museum. The fall weather was beautiful so I spent the rest of the day walking down the *Gran Via* and practically all over Madrid. That was an exhausting accomplishment, especially after the museum.

The next morning I woke from a bad dream feeling anxious. I was having a lot of them. Someone was asking me, "What do you do?" I answered, "I don't know.

I don't have a job." That was all I remembered, but it was a reminder that I didn't know what I was going to do with my life. I got up and had some of that great coffee in the café downstairs. It fascinated me that something inside of me kept bugging me about what I was doing—*or not doing*. I decided to try not to think about what I wanted to do until I got back to the States.

◆   ◆   ◆

I took the train to Barcelona and stayed in the Sant Martí District, close to the water. That day I wandered around *Les Rambles* starting at the top of a tree-lined boulevard that cut through the heart of Barcelona's oldest district and ended up down by the sea. It was such an intriguing and beautiful boulevard that it made Madrid's Gran Via seem almost dull. That night, I found a place to see Flamenco dancing—a new club called *Tablao Flamenco Cordobes*. It was a night of the most passionate and energetic dancing and guitar playing I'd ever seen. This was not the stylized, contained Flamenco. The barefoot gypsy dancers and singers were tireless and obviously deeply in love with their work. Their piercing music made my ears ring.

After Lisbon, Madrid, and Barcelona, I felt overstimulated and overwhelmed by the culture, paintings, and architecture. All these things were beginning to run into each other. I thought that finding a nice quiet place to spend the last week of my vacation would give me some time to think and rest. I wasn't sure I could put off thinking about what I wanted to do with my life. That just wasn't my way. Besides that, I wanted the anxiety dreams to stop.

I bought a train ticket that would take me as far as Cadaqués, almost to the French border. I figured I would get off at the quietest town I came to before I reached France. I'm not sure what class ticket I bought, but my train had more chickens than people. It went north along the Costa Brava to the little fishing town of Callela. It wasn't even on Frommer's map. It looked very quiet and peaceful and, because the smell of chickens was becoming a bit much, I got off. There were several men standing around a few dusty black Mercedes at the depot. I asked them in broken Spanish if they could take me to a hotel. They looked at each other and laughed, at my Spanish, I guess. Then one man picked up my bag, put it in his trunk, and motioned me toward the passenger seat. The driver whistled and smiled all the way to the hotel. "You American, no?"

"*Si.*" It wasn't long before he turned onto a street called *Carrer de l'eglesia* and pulled up in front of a small hotel, the *Express*. I noticed there was no taximeter, so I asked, "*Quanto?*"

"I no taxi, *Señor*," he laughed. He got out, lifted my suitcase from the trunk, and put it on the curb. I offered him money, but he just laughed and pushed it away. "*No. No dinero, Señor.*"

"*Gracias, Señor. Muchos gracias,*" I said. He drove off still laughing.

Inside the hotel was an undersized lobby with a tiny bar. A jolly fat guy in a white apron stood behind it. "Welcome to Callela, *Señor.*"

"Hello. Do you have a room?"

"*Si.* For how long?"

"I'd like to stay a week."

"Fine, no problem. I have a nice room with a balcony. It's quiet and has a view of the sea. You want *la pensión?*"

"Sounds perfect. I'll take it. *Si, la pensión.*" The room and meals were incredibly cheap. I could stay here for the week and still have money left over.

"After dinner, the guests come to the bar and talk. You are welcome to join them."

I went up to the room. It was a small narrow room with a single bed and double window-paned doors covered with chiffon curtains. From the balcony was a spectacular view of the sea. I decided to walk around the town and down to the sea before dinner. Although it was fall, the weather was still warm and balmy. I wandered just up the hill from the hotel and found a small sixteenth-century parish. The interior was dark, silent, with a lingering of frankincense. Except for an older woman in a black lace shawl praying in front of a statue of the Virgin Mary, the church was empty. I went inside and sat in an ancient wooden pew. Then I lit a candle for each of my girls, Christie, and for Tom, Don, John, and Grant. I prayed for the end of the war. And I prayed that I would figure out what I was supposed to be doing with my life. Once outside, I walked down narrow twisting streets, past old whitewashed houses with red geraniums in window boxes toward the sea. Across the *Carrer de Josep Anselm Clavé,* the beach met the crystal-blue water of the Mediterranean. The smell of fish and the sea was heavy, pleasant. Several fishing boats dotted the sandy beach, next to them, some fishermen worked on their nets. I lay down in the warm sand and took a nap. Several hours later, I woke to the crashing of the surf and cool salty air on my face. The sun was almost below the horizon. I was starving!

Back at the hotel, the barman smiled at me as I walked in. "*Siesta?*"

"*Si,* on the beach. It's a lovely little town."

He read my mind. "*Hambriento?*"

"*Muchos!*"

"Dinner is not till ten o'clock, but I can give you some *tapas* and wine."

I sat at the bar, and he brought out bite-sized *tapas* of cured ham and chorizo, a bowl of a cool, spicy gazpacho, a decanter of red wine, and a glass. "Now we are a *tasca*," he laughed." These will hold you over until the dinner hour."

"This is wonderful. The wine is delicious."

"*Bueno, Bueno. La sangre de toro, no?*" I didn't like the association to bull blood, but I laughed. He had such a good spirit.

That evening at dinner, I was surprised that I was still hungry. The other residents gathered in the bar area at several tables. Normally, I would have felt shy, but Gustavo, the barman, had a way of putting everyone at ease. He pranced around the tables bringing out more and more food. "Eat, eat," he said. "Enjoy."

Gustavo brought out more gazpacho, dishes of paella, potato tortillas, warm bread, and finally, flan for dessert. Each table had two pitchers of sangria with orange slices floating in them. It was an amazing dinner and for the small amount of money the *pensión* cost, even more remarkable.

After dinner everyone gathered around the bar for more wine or after dinner drinks. I was the only American. The conversations were an intriguing hodgepodge of English, German, French, and Spanish. My contribution was a smattering of German I hadn't used since college and tour book Spanish interspersed with English. To my surprise, I was able to hear and get along with the others. German was a handy language in Spain. People talked about where they were from, why they came to Callela, and spoke a bit about Franco and the Vietnam War. I got the sense that many of the guests had been here before. In my limited polylingual repertoire, I told them the story of the "taxi" at the train station. Despite my struggle to tell it, they thought the story was pretty funny.

Finally, when most of the talk had died down, a German guy about my age turned to me and said, *"Du bist aber kein Amerikaner."*

At first, I didn't understand why he thought I wasn't an American. I tried to correct him. "Yes, I'm an American. I tried my German, *"Natürlich bin ich ein Amerikaner."*

"Nein, nein! Du bist wirklich kein Amerikaner. Du bist eher ein Europäer. Du redest und benimmst Dich nicht wie ein Amerikaner. Du denkst nicht einmal wie ein Amerikaner!" Everyone laughed and agreed. I think he was trying to say I was more like a European and that I didn't even think like an American.

Finally, I agreed with him. *"Du hast recht. Ich bin kein Amerikaner."* Everyone laughed again.

The barman yawned and said he was going to bed. "Take what you want. Pay me in the morning."

This was my kind of place and my kind of people. I don't know what time it was when I finally went up to my room. I was still awake from all the stimulation of the guests and more than enough wine. I had brought *Catch-22* and decided to read it awhile in bed. It was one of the funniest and saddest books I'd ever read. I laughed out loud and hoped no one heard me. War was absurd, but maybe the antiwar movement was absurd, too. I really didn't know what my place in it was. I was beginning to see that movements, or trying to make external political changes, might not be for me. Maybe Grant was right about just wanting some personal peace. I wanted to stay in the peace of Callela. Then I developed a cough and spent a good part of the night either laughing about the book or coughing before I fell asleep.

The next morning I woke to the sea breeze blowing the billowy white curtains into the room. I still had that damned cough. I went to the bathroom and took a serious look at myself for the first time in two weeks. I had already started to let my hair grow longer in the States, and I hadn't shaved since I left. I was surprised to see my hair was almost to my shoulders, and my face lightly bearded and what showed of it was tan. I looked different.

At breakfast, I sat with an elderly German woman who didn't speak a word of English. She had the room immediately adjacent to mine. She looked at me with a devilish grin over her coffee. "*Du hast, ein lustiger Gast vielleicht?*"

I laughed. She thought I had an amusing guest in my room. "No. *Nein, ein Buch.* A very funny book."

She took some small pills from her purse and handed them to me. "*Du hast auch einen ganz schlimmen Husten?*"

"I'm sorry you heard my coughing and laughing through the wall. And thank you for these pills. I'm sure they will help."

"*Bis zum Wiedersehn beim Essen.*"

"*Ja*, see you at dinner, Frau Müller."

Each day and each dinner in Callela was as pleasant as the last. The week went by too quickly. On Sunday I bid the barman and several guests goodbye. He made me promise to return. I thanked him and promised. I took the train back to Barcelona, then to Madrid, then flew from Madrid to New York. By the time I reached New York, I must have been traveling eighteen or twenty hours. I was exhausted.

I went through customs quickly since I hadn't declared anything. All I really bought were some nifty sunglasses in Portugal, some trinkets for the kids, and a small bracelet for Christie. As I walked out of customs, two burly men in trench coats stepped in front of me. I moved to the side, and they moved in front of me again. I tried the other side. Same dance. Finally, I looked up at them. "Is there a problem?"

"We need you to come with us."

"What for?"

"Just come with us."

"Look, I have another plane to catch and have to meet my friend."

They took out gold-colored federal badges. "Come with us."

"I've already been through customs. I didn't declare anything."

"You're under arrest."

"*What*? What for?"

"Suspicion of smuggling."

God bless America. Did I look like a smuggler? Actually, maybe I did. Sunglasses, long hair, bearded, black leather jacket, black turtleneck sweater, and Levis. But this was still ridiculous. They took me to a small, barren interrogation room with two folding chairs and a steel table. On the wall hung a large black-and-white clock with a long red second hand and, below it, a picture of Nixon. How reassuring. With my bag open on the table, they made me declare that anything I brought into the country was in my bag. I did. Then I had to take off my clothes. They proceeded to dump my whole bag on the table and search through my clothes, and even emptied little matchboxes from Madrid. In my jacket pocket was the container for the sunglasses. Inside, in little gold letters, it said, *Lisboa, Portugal*. Shit!

"Did you buy these in Portugal?"

"Yes, I did."

"But you declared that anything you brought into the country was in your luggage."

"Sorry, I forgot."

Then they found the few little pills I was given in Callela.

"What are these? They're unmarked."

"They were given to me by a very nice old lady from Germany."

"What are they?"

"Cold pills. She said they were for a cough."

The agents looked at each other and smirked. "Little old German lady, huh?"

"It's the truth. Hardly enough to sell in the States."

"Watch your attitude. We'll have to confiscate them—and your sunglasses. What kind of work do you do?"

"Uh, at the moment I don't have a job."

"What did you last do for work?"

"A social worker. Milwaukee County Welfare Department."

They looked at each other again. They must practice this shit.

"Is the address on your passport your current residence?"

"Ummm. No, I'm moving to California. It was my last address."

"You have no job, no residence, and you're moving to California?"

"That's right."

"How did you afford your trip to Europe?"

"Well, this is going to sound strange, but my friend paid for it."

I think they enjoyed looking at each other. "The friend you're supposedly catching a plane with?"

I glanced up at the clock. "Not supposedly, I was. It *was* because that plane just took off."

"You can get dressed. We need to check some things. We'll be right back."

I dressed and waited in the interrogation room another fifteen minutes or so. They came back in. "Put your things in your suitcase. We're going to release you, Mr. Pedersen."

"Thanks so much." I didn't think I was becoming paranoid, but I wondered if this had something to do with MFC. I also wondered if the Welfare Department had been bombed.

I had plenty of time after I remade my reservation back to Milwaukee. Since the next flight was in three hours I bought a copy of the *New York Times;* I hadn't read a newspaper in three weeks. Then I went to a hectic terminal restaurant for a good old American hamburger. A front-page article announced, *"U.S. Battle Deaths Reach 130 In Week."* A harried waitress with a pencil sticking out of her messy hair slammed a glass of lukewarm water on the counter. "Whaddya want?"

The hamburger was small and burnt to a cinder. Welcome to America.

22

Turning Inward

All that remained for me to do in Milwaukee was to pack everything I owned in the car I bought and head for California. I stayed at Grant's on my last day and planned to leave later the next morning, but I was too excited to sleep. At four in the morning, I stopped trying. I made coffee, dressed, and woke Grant.

"I'm leaving, my friend."

He was groggy and in his silly patterned pajamas. "What time is it?"

"Fourish."

"So this is it then?"

"Yep. This is it."

"Well, good luck in California—and with your girls."

"Thanks. I'll keep in touch. You too?"

"Absolutely."

"And thanks again for Portugal and Spain."

"Sure, we'll go again one day." We hugged goodbye. I felt relieved that any differences Grant and I had about the antiwar movement were resolved. Our relationship was more important than any political differences anyway.

Driving would be a good time to think about what I wanted to do, and I looked forward to it. I was going to miss Grant and Christie, but I had no doubts about leaving the Midwest. I was on my way to a new life.

I must have been running on pure adrenaline. In the middle of the night, I passed through Cheyenne, Wyoming. I still hadn't slept. I figured I was about halfway to California. Suddenly, a magnificent multicolored shooting star roared across the sky above Cheyenne. I figured that was a good sign. I kept driving. By the time I got to Sacramento, I was periodically slamming on my brakes to avoid gigantic jackrabbits hopping in the middle of the highway. I had read about hallucinating from lack of sleep, but I continued on to Berkeley where I finally stopped at an all-night gas station for directions. The attendant was a young guy with a long ponytail, beads around his neck, and reddened eyes.

"I've come from Wisconsin, and if this is Berkeley, then I've passed San Francisco. I don't know how I did it."

"Man, what are you smokin'? You're not even *close* to San Francisco yet. Just keep going down Highway 80 and across the bridge. *That's* San Francisco across the bay," he pointed and shook his head.

Thankfully, another jolt of adrenaline jerked me awake as I drove across the Oakland Bay Bridge. The bridge lights sparkled through the fog that filled San Francisco Bay. By the time I got to Eleventh Avenue in the Sunset District, it was not quite morning. Tom and Don lived in a typical narrow San Francisco Victorian painted orange and white. I rang the bell, waited, then knocked. Finally, Don came scrambling to the door. His bearded face peered through the crack in the door. "Larry! Oh my God, you're here! Hey, Tom, get up! Larry's here!"

Little Tom came stumbling down the hallway in his underwear with that slight sweet smile of his and yelled, "Larry!" We all hugged for a long time. Then we had coffee and scones on the back deck looking out over the cool, fog-filled back yard. It felt wonderful to be there.

We sat there through several cups of coffee, catching up. Then Tom raised his cup to me, "You're here. Welcome to San Francisco."

"Yeah, I'm really here. It's good to see you guys."

"We planned a welcoming event for you," Don said.

"What's that?"

"Tomorrow we're going to Altamont!"

"Altamont? What's that?"

"The Stones' free concert. It was going to be in the city, but they just moved it to Altamont Speedway. Just too many people for the city."

"That's great! I heard about it on the radio. Grateful Dead, Jefferson Airplane, right?"

"Yeah, and Santana, Crosby Stills, and the Flying Burrito Brothers. It'll be the Woodstock of the West."

The initial excitement on that cold, wet December afternoon at Altamont eroded into one of the worst disasters of the Sixties. While looking for somewhere to sit, we waded through a human sea of tie-dyed and naked bodies that rolled across and up and down the cloudy hills of Altamont. I saw enough drugs passed around to send another ship to the moon. Pungent puffs of grass and hashish wafted through the air. Kids staggered and stumbled all over the place, spoke unintelligibly, and many looked like blank-eyed zombies. The scene was more like an outdoor insane asylum than a concert. In the distance, I could see the front of the stage, stupidly built too close to the ground. Hell's Angels in their bandanas, black sleeveless jackets, and tattooed arms—the security for the concert—armed with pool cues, surrounded it. To control the front of the stage, they threw full cans of beer at the audience. One can bounced off a guy's head and hit his girlfriend in the face, bloodying her nose. The Angels beat others and pushed them around like animals. While Mick Jagger's contorted mouth screamed out a song about "how groovy it was to be Satan," the Angels converged on a drunken spectator, beat him with pool cues, and then stabbed him to death. It wasn't clear to me whether the drunk was just being a nuisance, or trying to get on the stage, but whatever he did was no reason for the Angels to kill him. Their barbaric tactics didn't need much provocation. At the end of the concert, three more people were dead; an old swerving car with a totally stoned driver ran over a couple in their sleeping bag. Another person lay face down and still, drowned in a pool of muddy water.

I had smoked some grass, but the disturbing sights around me were sobering. It was one thing to see shit like that back on the streets of Chicago, but these were supposed to be my kind of people. I wondered what part of human nature it was that led us to justify bullfights, murders, and the stupidity of war. I kept thinking of a quote from Gandhi: *We must be the change we wish to see in the world.* Altamont was anything but that—it was a mad, violent nightmare.

I joined the San Francisco Peace Coalition with Tom and Don, went to demonstrations in Golden Gate Park, and did my small part. But after Altamont, my ideas about how to make the world a better place changed. The antiwar movement had mixed success. A draft lottery was introduced, student deferments ended, and Harris Polls showed that more and more Americans were turning against the war. Congress submitted ten bills to withdraw all the troops, while Nixon was secretly bombing Cambodia. Two steps forward, three steps back. *I wanted to be the change I wished to see in the world,* and I wanted to find a way to help others change, not from the outside—but from the inside. Maybe then, the world would change.

The deathblow to my belief that outer change is possible came with the publication of Robert McNamara's "Pentagon Papers" in the *New York Times,* which was published regardless of attempts by Nixon and Henry Kissinger to suppress it. Its eight thousand or so pages detailed thirty years of deception and incompetence of the American government's involvement in Vietnam. Its history of duplicity and outright lies spanned the administrations of Truman, Eisenhower, Kennedy, and Johnson. It documented the CIA's ouster and assassination of Prime Minister Diem; that the Gulf of Tonkin Resolution was drafted months *before* the incident there ever occurred; and, that Lyndon Johnson committed more infantry to Vietnam while telling the country he had no plans for doing so. If that wasn't enough, Nixon ordered a break-in of Daniel Ellsberg's psychiatrist's office. Ellsberg, once a hawk but disillusioned with the war, gave the papers to the *Times*. The study showed violations of every principle of democracy—it was the worst indictment of America in history. It made the antiwar movement seem like spit on a forest fire.

At Christmas that year, Tom announced he was going to Canada—immediately.

"Why do you have to go to Canada?"

"The FBI is looking for me." He looked pale and scared.

"How do you know that?"

"Jesus, Larry, they issued a warrant for me. They're tracking down all the draft dodgers. I'm not going to jail."

I couldn't imagine Tom in prison any more than I could imagine him in the Army.

"Where will you go?"

"I'm thinking close to the University of Toronto. There's a group of sympathizers there and some people from the Committee who help resisters find a place to crash."

"I'm going to miss you."

"Same here."

A day later, at the airport, Don and I hugged Tom goodbye.

◆ ◆ ◆

I decided to try to visit the children for Christmas. I called Jean and, surprisingly, she agreed. I was looking forward to seeing the girls and told Jean I wanted to take them to Disneyland. Don came with me and agreed to be a buffer of sorts in case Jean pulled another of her stunts.

It was too good to be true. When Don and I got there, Jean picked us up. She saw Don walking beside me.

"Who's *this*?" she asked with scorn.

"This is my friend, Don. Don this is Jean."

When Don went to shake her hand, she turned away from him to face me. "Why did you bring *him*?" She turned back to Don, looking him up and down with a disgusting stare.

"I thought he might enjoy meeting the girls."

"I don't want another hippie around the girls."

"Another hippie? C'mon, Jean, he's not a hippie, he's a good friend." She took us back to her apartment and dropped us off.

"If he's not gone by the time I get back, you can leave, too."

Jean's younger sister, Carrie, was at the apartment watching the girls. They were taking a nap. I introduced Carrie and Don.

"I'm going to pray for you, Larry."

"Pray for me?" Carrie was a born-again.

"Jean told me about the commune and your drug problem."

"What drug problem?"

"I know it's heroin." She tried to give me a knowing look.

"I don't have a drug problem. I've never touched heroin."

"Denial is part of the problem, Larry."

"Carrie, this is bullshit."

"Please don't swear."

Then Jean came back. She stood in the doorway with her hands on her hips. "I said I want him gone. Now!"

"He's my friend, for Christ's sake."

"Don't use the Lord's name in vain, Larry," Carrie chimed in.

"He's not a friend of *mine*. I don't want him here."

I knew if it weren't Don, Jean would find something else to ruin the visit. I felt badly for the girls; they didn't deserve another disappointment.

Don and I looked at each other. "I'm sorry, Don, I guess we'd better go."

"I'll give you a ride," Jean said.

"Can I see the girls before we go?"

"No, they're taking a nap."

"Wake them, for just a minute."

"No, I'll tell them you were here."

I knew she wouldn't tell them, and I shouldn't have accepted the ride, but I hoped she might change her mind. She drove fast and in silence. I didn't know LA, but I suspected she wasn't taking us to the airport.

She screeched to a halt in the middle of a large avenue, "Get out!"

"Where the fuck are we?"

"I guess you'll have to figure it out, won't you?"

We got out and she sped off, tires squealing.

Don stood there, shaking his head, dumbfounded. "Jesus, Larry, now I know what you were talking about. I'm sorry you didn't get to see the children, but I think your wife is seriously nuts."

◆   ◆   ◆

Back in San Francisco, Don decided to return to Milwaukee. He missed Roz, who wrote and said she wouldn't be coming to San Francisco after all. She had two kids in Milwaukee and her family was there. Our happy reunion was over.

I had to move from the San Francisco apartment immediately and decided on Berkeley to avoid the commute from San Francisco to Oakland. Fortunately, I not only found a nice apartment, the company that owned the building needed an apartment manager. In exchange for managing the building, they gave me free rent.

My new place was a studio in a white Spanish-style, adobe building. It was on the third floor and there was no elevator, but the apartment had a tiny balcony with a nice view of the Oakland-Berkeley hills. I made it cozy with the furniture and things that Tom and Don left me from our apartment. I added several maidenhair ferns, some coleus plants, candles, incense, and some Indian throws from Cost Plus Imports. The couch was a foldout bed that was a little bumpy, but it fit the studio just right.

I was enjoying the morning of my first Saturday in my new place with some coffee on the balcony when the loud buzzer I installed blared from inside. I looked through the peephole and saw a tall, husky blond-haired guy in a nice tan suit. If he wasn't so Anglo looking, he might have been from the Outfit. I doubted he was looking for an apartment. I opened the door.

"Morning, Mr. Pedersen. I'm agent Ron Stewart of the FBI."

Shit! "Er, Hi."

"You're Loren Pedersen. Born in Chicago, July 4, 1941."

"Right."

"You were a member of MFC in Milwaukee; you came to California in 1969; you work for the Welfare Department in Oakland, now you're…"

This guy was scary. He was going to keep going, but I interrupted him.

"Excuse me, but how do you know so much about me?"

"I know a lot more."

"Yeah, but *how*?

"Well, you have a dossier at the bureau."

"I was never arrested by the FBI." I thought about the airport in New York.

"I know, but as I said, you were a member of MFC in Milwaukee, which was taken over by SDS. Now you belong to the San Francisco Peace Coalition. Go to any meetings?"

"Well, some, but that's not a crime that I know of."

"No, of course it's not. But the bureau keeps track of organizations that have Communist members."

"I'm *not* a Communist."

"I know that, but you've been associated with others who are. But that's not why I'm here."

Fuck! I thought it was probably about Tom! "So?"

"You do manage this building?"

"Right."

"I'm not sure if you're aware that some of your tenants are card-carrying Communists."

"They are? No, I didn't know that."

"Well, as the manager you should be aware of that."

"The management company didn't tell me they lived here, or that I should know if any did."

"Well, the reason I'm here is that the bureau would like some cooperation from you."

"Cooperation?"

"Yes, regarding the Communists."

"It's not a crime for them to live here."

"No, it's not, but do you understand the nature and intentions of the Communist Party?"

"I know some about the Communist Party."

"Well, the Communist Party is dedicated to the violent overthrow of the United States government. Did you know that, son? Do you understand, son? Their means are *violent*. And that is an illegal activity in the United States of America."

"And the FBI, the CIA, the military are *not* violent? Aren't we using *violent* means to overthrow the Communists in Vietnam?" I thought I better shut up before I augmented my dossier, but this guy was really pissing me off.

"The United States is trying to stop the spread of Communism in South East Asia. The government of South Vietnam has asked for our assistance…"

This was pointless. "I'm sorry, Mr. Stewart. What exactly did you come here for?"

"What we would like from you, let's say as a service to your country, is to just do some simple record keeping for us."

"Record keeping?"

"Yes, what we would like is that you record all the license plate numbers of any visitors to the tenants in 203."

"You mean spy on them?"

"Well, it's not technically spying. It's just keeping a simple record."

"Of license plate numbers?"

"Exactly. The bureau would really appreciate your cooperation here."

I couldn't keep from smiling.

"This is not funny, son. It's a serious matter. These Communists may be planning the violent overthrow of our government in this building, right below this apartment."

"I'm sorry, I just couldn't help thinking about your dossier on me."

"What about it?"

"Seems like someone spied on *me*, maybe thought I might be a Communist—at least something enough to keep a record of me. Can I see my dossier?"

"It's classified, son. That's not why I'm here."

Now I really had to smile. "Let me see if I have this right. You have a dossier on me because of my possibly being a Communist, or at least for associating with Communists. And now you're asking me, as a service to my country, to spy on my tenants because you think they're Communists?"

"We don't *think* they are, son. We know they are. They are card carriers. You can be of service to your country. Besides, it's not that complicated. Remember what President Kennedy said, 'Ask not what your…'"

"Yes, I heard that. But I have a job, as well as managing this apartment building. I really don't think I'd have time to spy on the tenants."

"We're only asking you to observe and record license plate numbers of these tenants' visitors when you're at home."

"I don't know. Besides, isn't that your job?"

"We sometimes ask citizens to do small services in the interest of their country."

"You ask them to *spy* for you?"

"It's not espionage, son. Espionage is another matter."

"Seems sorta like what the KGB is doing in Russia, doesn't it? Everybody spies on everybody else. Isn't that why you couldn't prosecute the Weathermen? Illegal counterintelligence information gathering?"

"This isn't Russia. What the Communists do in Russia is not our concern. We *are* deeply concerned with what their activities are on American soil. We are simply asking you for a little service to your country. You're entitled to refuse."

"And if I refuse, does my lack of cooperation go in my dossier?"

"I don't know, son. But here, take my card. Think about it. You can call me or come in and talk to me anytime. There is a bureau office in the building just down Telegraph Avenue."

"OK, let me think about it."

"Have a good day, son."

After he left, I couldn't help but wonder if they thought "son-calling" was a tactic to get people to cooperate. I was glad he hadn't asked about Tom. I would've hated to say he was in Canada. Fuck, they probably already knew he was in Canada.

◆ ◆ ◆

Before he left, Tom's Christmas gift to me was a copy of Jung's recently published biography, *Memories, Dreams, Reflections*. It was not only a remarkable story about Jung's life, but he also stressed the importance of listening to patients' stories. He said, "…the patient who comes to us has a story that is not told, and which, as a rule, no one knows of. To my mind, therapy only really begins after the investigation of that wholly personal story. It is the patient's secret, the rock against which he is shattered. If I know his secret story, I have the key to treatment. The doctor's task is to find out how to gain that knowledge. In most cases exploration of the conscious material is insufficient.… In therapy the problem is always the whole person, never the symptom alone. We must ask questions that challenge the whole personality."

I thought about how much I enjoyed listening to people's stories. Sometimes just seeing an interesting-looking person on the street made me curious, made me want to know more about him.

It occurred to me that I could make a living doing something I really enjoyed *and* contribute to changing the world—from the inside out. I already had a degree in psychology. With more study, I could become a psychologist. Going to medical school to become a psychiatrist didn't make any sense. I didn't want to study medicine for four years when I could spend that time studying psychology. Besides that, I didn't want to end up a pill pusher like so many psychiatrists. I decided to apply to graduate school at San Francisco State.

I had heard that while San Francisco State had one of the best clinical psychology programs, it was difficult to get into. They accepted only twelve students each year out of several hundred applicants. I applied anyway. If I could get into Marquette, I could find a way to get into State.

Acceptance letters usually went out by April for the class beginning the following September. April came and went. No letter. Finally in May a letter of acceptance arrived. I was elated. It reminded me of getting the letter of acceptance from Marquette. The letter requested I contact the Psychology Department to learn who my advisor would be and gave a date when all new graduate students were to meet with the graduate school dean.

I called the Psychology Department.

"I'm very sorry Mr. Pedersen, but there's been some mistake. You haven't been accepted, but you should have gotten a letter saying you were chosen as an alternate, Number thirteen."

"*What*? What does that mean?"

"We accept twelve students and twelve alternates. As the first alternate, you would gain admission only if one of the first twelve declined. So far, every one of the first twelve have agreed to enroll. I'm sorry."

"But you sent me an official letter of acceptance!"

"I'm really sorry. I don't understand how it happened. The department has a budget for only twelve students."

I asked to speak to the chairman of the department. Same answer. "Sorry, but…" I decided to go to the graduate students' meeting with the dean anyway. It might have been a far shot, but I figured maybe the dean could do something. When he finished his welcome and speech, I went up to him and explained my situation. He asked me to come with him to his office. He called the Psychology Department chair. "Hi Steve, this is Dean Raskin. I've got a student here with an official letter of acceptance, and he says your secretary told him that he wasn't *really* accepted." Pause again. "Yes, he told me he spoke to you. What's the story on this?" There was a pause. "Yes, I understand. Yes, I understand. I know. Yes. I know. Nonetheless, you have to honor the reality that you did send him a letter of acceptance. Oh yes, you do. We can't be sending official letters and saying they're mistakes. I know about your budget, but it's too bad, you're going to have to make do somehow. OK, thanks."

He turned to me with a big smile and extended his hand. "Congratulations, you're in. Call them back; they'll assign you an advisor."

"Thank you so much, sir. I really, really appreciate this." I was overjoyed.

"You're certainly welcome. See you in September."

◆ ◆ ◆

I continued to work at the Oakland Welfare Department through the spring and summer. I quit when school started in September. I found a part-time orderly's job in a hospital in Oakland. It was right across the street from my apartment. On my first day on campus, I found an ad for a research assistant. It was for one of my professors, Dr. Seeward, a Jungian analyst. Between these two jobs, I could get through the first year of graduate school. I didn't do any research for Dr. Seeward, but I organized his office, his library, and his professional articles. He was gray-bearded, very soft-spoken, and wore beautiful tweed suits. Whenever we were both in his office, we had some interesting talks about Jungian psychology. He didn't seem to mind that I asked so many questions. He encouraged me to consider going into analysis.

Finally, I felt as if I was on the right track. Graduate school was promising and exciting. My involvement in the antiwar effort began to wane. There were some demonstrations on the San Francisco State campus, especially after the catastrophe at Kent State where students protested Nixon's bombing of Cambodia. National Guardsmen bayoneted two men—one a disabled veteran—then shot and killed four unarmed students: one who gave a Guardsman the finger, another who was standing four hundred feet in the distance, and two who were on their way to classes. Nixon called the students "bums." The Guardsmen were never punished. That tragedy increased my belief that trying to change the outer world was futile.

My life began turning more and more inward; I wanted to understand the psyche and what it was that made people so angry and violent. As Dr. Schik said back in Milwaukee, the first step in that direction was to understand myself. While my anxiety dreams diminished, I was beginning to feel more and more depressed. That surprised me because I thought I was headed in the right direction. I asked Dr. Seeward about analysis. I couldn't really afford it. He recommended that I call a person at the Jung Institute in San Francisco and ask about sliding scale fees. An analyst called and said he might be willing to see me if my therapy could take place at the hospital where he worked. I would go anywhere for a low fee. We agreed to meet once, explore what I was interested in working on, and see if we were a "good match."

The following week I went to meet him at the hospital. While there were several parking places close to the hospital, I was so anxious that I drove around the block four times before I decided to park and go in.

I registered at the desk and tried to appear casual, as if I wasn't a *real* nut case; the receptionist seemed indifferent anyway and told me to take a seat. I was fidgeting in my seat when Dr. Burns came to get me from the waiting room. We shook hands and introduced ourselves.

He motioned me to walk ahead. "It's the third room on the right just down the hall." The hallway smelled a little like Paraldehyde.

"I'll follow you if that's OK."

"Oh, sure." He walked toward the room and showed me to his office.

Shit. He probably thinks I'm paranoid. In his office, we sat down across from each other. I was relieved that there was no couch. "I'm sorry, I just don't like people walking behind me."

"It's not a problem, but why is that?"

"If I'm walking in front of you, I won't hear what you say. Other than that, I don't really know. I'm like that even in the supermarket, always shooing people in front of me. They think it's terribly polite. If I sense that someone is behind me; it gives me the shivers."

"I see."

He wasn't going to touch that. He probably *does* think I'm paranoid. Nice beginning.

Then he went over the fee schedule. Because of my limited income and child support payments, he could see me without my paying a fee. That was a relief. I felt deeply grateful. Like Dr. Seeward, Dr. Burns was soft-spoken. He was about fifty, tall, heavyset, with dark-framed glasses. He dressed very plainly: a dark blue suit, white shirt, and an average tie. The simplicity of his clothes made him seem less intimidating than I imagined he would be. His manner seemed like a cross between a quiet butler and a big teddy bear. The room was also plain: an undecorated generic hospital room painted light green with sparse and simple institutional furniture. A heavy metal screen covered a solitary window and underneath it a large gray metal desk with a red copy of the *Physician's Desk Reference*. I imagined that a lot of therapists used this room.

Then he crossed legs, adjusted a note pad in his lap, and said, "So tell me about yourself."

I sat up straighter in my chair. "My story?"

"Yes, your story." He smiled.

"I'm not sure where to begin."

"Well, Jungians don't typically take an anamnesis as Freudians do, if that's any help. We like to think a person's history will come out in time. Maybe you can start by telling me if you have any particular problems."

I had to laugh. "I have more problems than I can think of."

He waited quietly and patiently for me to go on.

"Well, I used to be anxious, but now I'm depressed. Or maybe I'm both."

"Do you know what you're depressed about?"

"Not specifically. I can guess, though."

"Why don't you try to tell me about what you guess is wrong?"

"Well, I've always had this feeling that there is something I should be doing. And I'm never really sure if I'm doing it."

"Something like?"

"Like what I'm supposed to be doing with my life. When I was a kid, I thought I was a tough guy. I was a punk, a gang leader. Then I was nearly killed in a fight. I fucked up high school. After high school, I thought I wanted to be a physician, but decided I didn't want to do that. I got involved in the antiwar movement, still am some, because I wanted to stop the war. Now I think I want to be a psychologist, and I'm pretty sure that's what I want to do. It's a feeling inside of me. I don't know where it comes from or why it's there, but it feels very compelling, like if I don't do it there will be serious consequences. A friend of mine back in Chicago once told me about that feeling. I'm sorry. I don't think I'm making sense."

"Oh, I think I understand what you mean. That was quite a switch, from a gang leader to wanting to be a physician. What made you want to be a gang leader?"

I talked a long time about my childhood, parents, about Dino, Mickey, and Christie. I told him about my first memory and my first dream on Blackhawk Street. Then the time was almost up. The hour went quickly, too quickly.

"Well, you've certainly had a fascinating early life. How does it make you feel to talk about it?"

"Dirty."

"Dirty?" His eyebrows were quizzical.

"Yeah. I don't talk much about myself. But when I do talk about being a kid, I always feel dirty, as if I need to take a shower."

"I'd like to hear more about that next time. I would especially like to work with you on your dreams. If you'd like, we can meet next week and pick up where we left off."

A nice way of stopping the conversation, I thought. I got up and shook his hand. It felt warm and soft.

"Well, see you next week then," he said.

It was a great relief that he seemed to understand. His gentleness, warmth, and especially his genuine interest surprised me. I wondered if he liked me. I was always pleasantly surprised when someone did.

When I returned from that appointment, there was a message from my stepfather's new wife, Maggie, asking me to call her immediately. Bud had had a heart attack.

23

Starting Psychoanalysis

When I reached Bud's wife, she told me he had had a fairly serious heart attack. I recommended she contact Dr. Keddy since he was not only an internist, but also an authority on cardiovascular surgery. Then I left for Chicago.

By the time I arrived in Chicago, Bud's wife had contacted Dr. Keddy, and Bud had already had an angiogram. He was in bed, as pallid as the sheets, and shrunken since the last time I'd seen him. His room smelled foul—like a mixture of antiseptic and shit. Bud was self-conscious when I walked in because he was sitting on a bedpan waiting for a nurse to come and get him off it.

"Sitting on a bed throne?" I asked.

"Yeah. Waiting for the damn nurse."

"I'll get you off it."

"Larry, you don't have to do that."

"I've done it many times and for people I didn't know. It's not a problem." I took out his pan and cleaned him up.

"Jesus, Larry. This is embarrassing."

"Better get used to it. You'll be on and off that thing a lot more before you get out of here."

"I mean having you do it."

"Think of it as payback for the time you bloodied my nose," I laughed.

"Christ, the things you remember."

Dr. Keddy came in. He looked the same as always. He was surprised to see me. He put his arm around my shoulder. "Larry, nice to see you. It's been awhile, hasn't it?"

"Yeah. A *long* time. It's good to see you."

"Your dad told me you were in graduate school in California? I heard you gave up on medicine," he said, faking a frown.

"I thought you might be disappointed, but I think it's for the best. I really like psychology. So what are we going to do with this guy?"

"Well, he's got a couple of occluded coronary arteries, but I think his heart is strong enough to do open-heart surgery. I've scheduled him for tomorrow. Want to assist?" He smiled and looked at Bud. "Larry would make an excellent assistant, Mr. Pedersen."

Bud cracked a smile, but he was tired and weak.

The next day Bud underwent the procedure. I was in the cafeteria where Dr. Keddy told me to wait for him. He wanted a chance to catch up a bit. I almost dropped my coffee when I heard, "Code Blue—Recovery Room. Code Blue—Recovery Room." I ran up two flights of stairs and watched helplessly as several doctors and nurses rushed through the swinging doors. It was all too familiar. I looked through the glass hole in the door. They were working hard on someone whose face I couldn't see. After ten minutes, they all backed away. I knew that motion. Except for the ringing of the flat-lining heart monitor, the room became quiet. Then I saw Bud's lifeless ashen face just before the nurse pulled the sheet over it.

Dr. Keddy came out to the hallway. "I'm so sorry, Larry. Your dad had a massive hemorrhage. He went into cardiac arrest, and we couldn't bring him back. We did everything we could, but the hemorrhaging couldn't be stopped in time. It's one of those possible complications you just hope doesn't happen."

"I understand. I know you did your best. You always do."

I went to see my mother and told her Bud had died.

"Well, he might be gone, but he's in my heart," she said flatly.

I wondered just what the fuck she meant by *that*. Her rage and abuse of him was hard to forget. Somehow, she could make anything about herself.

At the funeral home Bud's brother, Darrell, stood in the doorway, scowling at me. "How could you come to your father's funeral with long hair?"

"Nice to see you, too."

Christie was there and so was Mickey. It was good to see Christie again. Dino didn't come. When I talked to Bud's wife, she told me that he made her promise to tell Dino he wasn't to be at Bud's funeral. Hearing that Dino had become a burglar really pissed off Bud. The last Bud heard about Dino was that he'd become a made guy in the Outfit. For Bud, that was Dino's coda. I don't know if it was true, but that was Dino's great ambition.

As part of the service, I read a poem from Kahlil Gibran, *The Beauty of Death*: "Let me sleep, for my soul is intoxicated with love, and

Let me rest, for my spirit has had its bounty of days and nights…"

I'm not sure how well the poem went over, but the listeners were pretty quiet when I finished. I guess they don't clap at funerals. Well, Christie liked it, and a sweet elderly woman I didn't know came up to me afterwards and thanked me for reading it. Things like that were hard to tell with Bud's family anyway. I thought Bud might like it.

◆   ◆   ◆

Back in California, I went to analysis again. Dr. Burns asked about Bud's death and our relationship.

"We weren't very close. I know this sounds superficial, but what stood out for me about his death was that I felt sorry for him. I just don't think he was ever happy. Sorry because even if he finally quit drinking, he didn't accomplish his most important goal—to own a home."

"For some people, that's a very important goal."

"I guess. I'd like to as well, I just don't want it to be at the top of my list."

"What's on your list?"

"I know more about what I don't want. I don't want my life to be about commuting to a rat race, gossipy barbeques, or having friends who wear backward baseball caps. I guess I want to make a difference in the world. I want it to be a little better off than how I found it, better than how it's been for me, and better for my girls. I thought I could do that in the antiwar movement or the antipoverty movement, but now I'm sure that's not the way to go. I think people have to change from the inside out."

"Yes, I think that's true. Is that what you meant when you said you needed to know what it is that you're supposed to be doing?"

"Exactly. It's so strong it haunts me. It's as if someone is watching me, except I know that *whatever* it is, it's coming from somewhere inside of me."

"Perhaps it's something like what Jung meant when he described individuation."

"Meaning?"

"Meaning that the something inside of you is *purposeful*. But, generally it means the growth of the person throughout his or her lifetime. Becoming all of who one really is, as opposed to living only through the *persona*, one's social mask. As part of that, a person may also feel a powerful sense of vocation; as if there is something they really need to do in life. It may express that a large part of what you feel you need to be doing *is* part of your personal growth. Does that make sense?"

"Yes, very much."

"Why doesn't everyone have that?"

He smiled, "They do, but not everyone listens to their insides. When they don't, individuation can turn life sour. Depression is like that."

"Depression is part of individuation?"

"Yes, it grabs you by the seat of your pants, gets your attention, and says something isn't right. So depression may come when a person isn't growing."

"That reminds me of a dream. I dreamt that there was a mass inside of me. Something dark, ugly, crushing my insides, threatening me. It was as if the outer me grew up around this mass inside."

"Perhaps, like depression, it's ugly because you don't know what it is."

"I wanted to kill it. I had my stiletto pointed right at it, like I could cut it out."

"Your stiletto?"

I laughed to myself. I couldn't believe he didn't know what a stiletto was. Probably thought stilettos were high heels. "It's a switchblade I've had since I was a kid. I used it to defend myself against my brothers more than enemies."

"If you cut out the mass, you would also kill yourself, wouldn't you?"

"I guess, but it would make the pain stop."

"What is the pain like?"

"It's agonizing. It's similar to physical pain, but it's not physical. It's mental, emotional, spiritual."

"Do you know what the source of that pain is?"

"I'm guessing, but it feels like the pain of not being cared for, not being loved, not being held. Stuff like that. It's embarrassing to admit that."

"That would be very painful. So you're aware of feeling unloved?"

"I try not to think about it. I don't like feeling sorry for myself. But, yes, I don't think I ever felt loved. My mother was never affectionate. I don't remember her hugging me or telling me she loved me. This is going to sound pathetic, but I used to like throwing up because it was the only time my mother touched me. Sometimes when I threw up, she touched my forehead."

"It doesn't sound pathetic. You were desperate for her touch."

"Yeah, maybe that's why I sometimes I liked holding patients' hands when I worked in the hospital."

"You wanted to give them something you were missing yourself?"

"Maybe. But it also felt like a very spiritual thing to do—to comfort them."

"It's interesting that you were able to get beyond yourself in that way."

"What do you mean?"

"Well, I suppose you could have become bitter and withholding rather than giving."

"I guess. I'm not sure I haven't."

I went away from that session feeling exposed. As if I'd said too much. During the session, all the time I was talking, my hands were cold and clammy.

That night I had a dream that my room was broken into. A crowbar and a man's hat were left on my couch. Three items of my favorite clothing were stolen from my closet.

At the next session, I told Dr. Burns the dream. He said the dream might express feelings about starting analysis and of feeling broken into. And the theft of my clothing was like losing my persona. I respected Dr. Burns, but, frankly, I thought that interpretation was hogwash.

When I returned from that session, I was shocked to find that my room had been broken into. There was a crowbar and a hat on the couch, and the same three pieces of clothing were missing. I called Dr. Burns immediately.

"Guess what happened."

"Your room got broken into?"

"Yes!"

"Jung called dreams like that anticipatory. They are examples of what he called synchronicity. We can talk about it next time."

I hung up the phone and felt dizzy. How could he be so matter of fact about this? I had dreamt something and it came true—in every detail. Then I read everything I could find that Jung wrote about synchronicity.

At my next session, we talked about the "break-in" dream. Dr. Burns said again that feeling "broken in upon" was a natural response to starting analysis because my ego wasn't yet ready to be exposed. He also explained that Jung's thinking about synchronicity was influenced by his conversations with Einstein about the theory of relativity. For Jung, synchronicity didn't really have a cause in the ordinary sense, but was an acausal principle, a significant coincidence in which an outer event occurred to underline an inner reality—meaning that in the unconscious, past, present, and future were relative. That dream profoundly changed how I thought about the unconscious. It occurred to me that I had adopted Freud's "garbage dump" view of the personal unconscious, yet my dream revealed a very purposeful function of my unconscious. I thought I would try to be less skeptical of Dr. Burns' interpretations. He also was right about feeling exposed. My feelings vacillated between fascination with the unconscious and a frightening vulnerability.

I decided to take a night class on dreams at UC Berkeley. That's where I met Greta. Greta was a native Californian, Berkeley graduate, and worked at a disabled children's center. She had long light-brown hair, blue eyes, and was the first woman I dated who didn't wear a bra; her breasts were large enough to draw attention with a bra. Greta was liberal, but not radical, and involved in the Berkeley antiwar movement.

Our first date was dinner at her place. She lived close to the Berkeley campus in a small flat with a bed in the middle of the living room. During dinner we talked about the war in Vietnam, her travels in Europe after she graduated from Berkeley, and my time in Spain and Portugal. As soon as we finished dinner, she turned on some music, and we made love. I was astonished by how quickly Greta and I started having sex; it seemed almost like dessert.

"Wasn't that a little fast?" I asked while we lay in her bed afterwards.

"You're the first guy to complain."

"I wasn't exactly complaining. Well, I was raised Catholic."

"So was I."

"Didn't you get the usual rap about sex and masturbation?"

"Sure, but I never took it seriously. Sounds like you did."

"Of course. The first time I did it I felt guilty as hell. I thought I was a damned sinner. Didn't you?"

"No. I was mostly worried about getting pregnant; we didn't use anything."

"How old were you?"

"First time?"

"Yeah."

"Fifteen."

"Jesus."

"Don't start bringing Him into it again," she laughed and rolled over on her side, her long hair covering her face.

"Can I ask you a personal question?"

"Sure. But let me guess…"

I didn't hear the last part of what she said. "What? I didn't get what you said."

She turned back to me and smiled, "You want to know how many guys I've slept with?"

"Do you mind?"

"No, I don't mind. Would you mind waiting while I counted them?"

"No."

She giggled. "I was kidding, you dummy. Do you really want to know?"

"Yeah."

"OK, so I don't waste your time counting, I would guess, hmmm eighteen."

"Jesus!"

"You really *are* Catholic, aren't you?"

"No, not any more. I don't know what I am, if anything."

"Since this is *True Confessions*, how many girls have you slept with?"

"Including you?"

"I *do* count, don't I?"

"Of course, you do. You're, you're the third."

"Larry, you're still working on your virginity. But I'm surprised only because you're a wonderful lover."

"Well, thanks."

"Maybe Catholicism's different back east. Welcome to California. Wanna do it again?"

"Sure. Then you'll be my fourth."

"Fourth! I thought you meant *people,* not times!"

"Now you're the dummy. I was kidding."

"I know." We both laughed.

I really liked Greta's humor, and I was glad she hadn't taken Catholic dogma seriously—I wished I hadn't. She seemed more confident and much freer than I was.

Greta was responsible for my changing my first name back to what it really was, Loren. She liked it better and said it was more sophisticated and sounded more like me. Although no one in Chicago ever called me Loren, I always liked my real name but could never bring myself to change it. Since living in California seemed like starting a new life, a new identity felt appropriate. I also thought of the tradition of a Native American Indian tribe in which a name change guaranteed that old bad luck wouldn't follow one around.

We spent part of our time at antiwar demonstrations in Berkeley, even though I didn't believe they were doing much good. We were tear-gassed a few times on Telegraph Avenue, once along with an older couple who got caught in the middle of the demonstration. They held each other and almost fell over from their coughing. We stopped and shared our wet face towels with them. It also enraged me that Greta couldn't even see for a few minutes. The fucking cops didn't care who they gassed; the gas sprayed from under their cars while they drove through the middle of the demonstration.

When breaking windows and trashing businesses on Shattuck Avenue became part of demonstrating, I convinced Greta that our time would be better spent at the movies and talking about dreams. Getting tear-gassed helped convince her that was a good idea. Most of the demonstrations she'd been in before were pretty tame. We both liked artsy black-and-white foreign films, and a number of theaters in Berkeley and San Francisco featured them. So we saw a lot of Ingmar Bergman; Pagnol's trilogy, *Fanny, Marius,* and *Cesar;* a number by Truffaut, including *400 Blows;* and Jean Renoir's film about war, *La Grande Illusion*. Seeing *400 Blows* again reminded me of Frankie. I realized I hadn't thought about her in a long time but, when I did, I still missed her.

Another great thing about Greta was that she loved to travel around California. She introduced me to some of the best parts of the state—Point Reyes, Monterey, Big Sur, the Napa Valley, and Lake Tahoe. Both of us especially loved camping in isolated spots by the ocean.

Greta began appearing in my dreams. In the first one, I was pointing out a shoeless man walking down the street. I told Greta he had a senile psychosis, but she didn't pay attention. Another dream involved two women; one who showed me an old Victorian house in which I was supposed to find a part of myself. She also told me I had to make love to a depressed woman in that house. I found her sitting quietly on the edge of a bed. She had had a mastectomy; I didn't want to make love to her. When police came and took the shoeless man into custody, I was relieved.

"Your new friend, Greta, is already showing up in your dreams."

"Is that important?"

"Well, dreams often use real people or unknown figures to try to bring out parts of a person that are unconscious. In those two dreams, there are three women and the man: Greta, the woman who tells you to make love to the woman who is ill, and the ill woman herself. You say the man is senile and psychotic, and Greta ignores you. What kinds of feelings did you have in the dream?"

"Creepy. Bizarre. Things felt out of control until the man was taken into custody."

"The dream may make more sense if you considered that all the characters in the dream may be parts of yourself."

"Well, maybe the old man, but the women? How could they be parts of me?"

"Jung believed that both men and women have male and female characteristics. Men have an inner feminine part and women an inner masculine. Those parts can be positive or negative depending on the dreamer."

"Really?"

"Yes, but don't be too concerned with the intellectual aspect. What's more important is what kinds of feelings are brought up for you."

Dr. Burns could be frustrating because he rarely used technical terms. I wanted to know everything I could about the theory behind these things. Of course, I started buying Jungian books, such as Jung's *Collected Works* and any other books that would explain these things in more detail. During the week after that appointment, I read everything I could find on a man's inner feminine as well as a woman's inner masculine. That was one hell of a lot of reading.

The next session I felt armed. "I did some research, and I think I understand the ideas in my dream."

"Oh?" Dr. Burns smiled, raising his eyebrows.

"Yes. The women in my dreams are aspects of my *anima*; in my case, the wounded feminine. The part damaged by the dark mother, like the woman who had a mastectomy—deprived of breasts, she can't be a mother. She can't nurture me. The man was also a part of me—something prematurely aged, emotionally deteriorated. What Jung called the *senex,* the archetype of the old man. Like the wounded Fisher King in Parsifal, he was bitter, rigid, dying, uncreative, and longing for renewal. I also had a number of other dreams in which similar older men appeared. He was often dying and would ask me to do things he didn't have time left to do. So I not only have problems with my mother, but also with the father part of me." I spent most of the session talking, explaining what I learned from my reading. Before I realized it, the hour was over. Dr. Burns sat silent, listening, and occasionally nodding, but he wasn't smiling.

"Well, I'm sorry. The time's up. You did an impressive bit of research, but try to stay connected to the feelings the dreams bring up for you."

The next session I told my dream of the night before. "I was trying to solve some problems using high school algebra, but the problems required the use of differential equations."

Dr. Burns smiled. "What feeling did that dream bring up?"

"Frustration. Maybe my unconscious is telling me that solving my problems requires much more complex means than I have."

"Yes, and mathematics is very, er, heady, isn't it? Besides that, your problems are emotional, not intellectual, aren't they?" He smiled gently.

I had begun to understand why I would feel invaded by the analysis. I was excited to learn about myself, but I wasn't too happy about what my unconscious was bringing up—and it certainly wasn't being complimentary. I had always remembered my dreams but, after starting analysis, they flooded me. I think my unconscious was getting my attention and wasn't going to let up.

I finished the first year of graduate school with straight A's. The second year involved only one day of seminars and four days of clinical work in a hospital psychiatry department. I found seeing patients for the first time exciting and rewarding. Psychological problems I had only read about in textbooks were now real people sitting right in front of me. The further clinical training included a deeper review of the various treatment modalities and schools of thought in psychology and psychoanalysis. It was then that I learned of a new treatment approach for psychosomatic problems: biofeedback. What was most interesting to me about biofeedback was that among the problems it purported to treat was migraine headaches. I had less of them during analysis, but I still got them and anything that held the smallest promise of stopping them certainly fascinated me. What particularly intrigued me was that it was the first treatment approach I ever heard of that included relaxation training.

So I bought the basic equipment, learned the treatment procedures, and taught myself to relax. Despite my previously skeptical attitude about meditation, I also learned how to do it. To my surprise, I found relaxation and meditation could produce a wonderful sense of peace and calmness. To my astonishment, by using relaxation, meditation, and biofeedback, I learned I could control physical pain. Eventually, my headaches stopped completely. I was so elated that relaxation and meditation then became a part of my daily life. I also began using biofeedback for chronic headaches and pain problems at the clinic.

I quickly began to get positive feedback for my clinical work and, before long, the clinic chief appointed me director of education. The praise I received at the clinic partly offset the humiliation of the analysis. In fact, it may have been a compensatory role because I rather quickly became the clinic egghead of sorts. This was borne out by another synchronistic dream.

I dreamt I was driving on the freeway from my analysis appointment to the clinic when a spider came down from the visor. When it was exactly at my eye level, the car lurched and died, forcing me to get off the road immediately. I had that dream the morning of an analysis appointment. When I related it to Dr. Burns, he suggested I was "speeding away from analysis too quickly to get to the more emotionally comfortable clinic."

Again, I thought that was a rather far-out interpretation. That is, until I got in my car and sped off to the clinic. Shortly after I got on the freeway, a spider came down from the visor and, when it reached eye level, I said, "Oh shit!" Well, you can guess the rest. While I waited by the side of the road for a tow truck, I opened the hood and looked at the engine. It looked like someone had taken a blowtorch to it. When I got to the clinic, I called Dr. Burns and said, "Guess what?"

"Did your car blow up?"

It was another lesson in synchronicity.

During the same month, some of President Nixon's top aides resigned amid allegations that the White House had obstructed justice by attempting to cover up the Watergate affair. That summer, a Senate investigation of Nixon's secret air war against Cambodia finally ended the bombing.

Around the same time, I started having a series of terrifying death dreams. In one of them, as I came to a clearing in the center of a misty forest, I saw my gray naked lifeless body lying on a cold marble slab, my hands crossed over my chest. Another dream was a death ritual of dumping of rag-wrapped dead bodies into a large pool. Someone there told me I was supposed to dive into this dark putrid pool of dead bodies. I dove in; stiff arms and legs of corpses brushed against me. In yet another, while walking among some smoking, partly destroyed ancient ruins I came across a dead man's hand sticking out of the rubble. Its blackened twisted fingers stretched upwards. Curiously, the hand looked like mine.

I told Dr. Burns that those dreams reminded me of one I had during the time I was doing autopsies. "These aren't more anticipatory dreams, are they?"

"Are you afraid they are?"

"Yeah, I'm afraid they're about dying."

"Well, you can get a medical exam, but I doubt they're about your actual death."

"What do you think they mean?"

"Well, dreams of dying are rarely a sign of approaching death. More often, they are more like harbingers of some deep change in the psyche. The ego often experiences major inner changes as a kind of death of itself."

"You mean like an old part of me is dying off and something new is coming?"

"Exactly."

I laughed. "I'd prefer that to dying."

"But what about dying? Are you afraid to die?"

"Of course I'm afraid to die, aren't you?"

"Not exactly, but what I feel about death isn't important. It's what you feel."

I told him about the first time I thought I was dying—when I was in Catholic school—and about the mask above my head.

"That's very interesting."

"Interesting? It scared the *hell* out of me."

"Did it ever speak to you?"

"No, it was just *there*. It made a kind of scary humming sound."

"Did you ever think of talking to it?"

"Are you kidding?"

"No. It can be a way of learning more about it. We call it 'active imagination.' It's like dreaming the dream onward."

Back at my apartment, I decided to try this nutty procedure, but I didn't want to start with the mask. Although it hadn't appeared for years, I was still scared of it. I didn't want to bring it back quite yet. So I started with the hand sticking up from the ground. In my imagination, I dug it out, found the arm, then the shoulder, and kept digging until I the whole person was uncovered. He was still alive! He opened his eyes, and his eyeballs were bright white compared to the black soot all over his face. Before he opened his eyes, his face looked like the mask.

"Shit, what *happened* to you?" I asked.

He could barely speak, but he mumbled with an accent, "The same thing that's going to happen to you if you're not careful! Where the hell have you been?" His white eyes glared with anger. Then he started coughing and spitting out small pieces of dirt.

I brushed him off, and then helped him sit up. "Who are you?"

"Professor Amnestius. A professor of archeology."

"What happened to you?"

"What's it look like? I got buried in the very thing I was studying."

"And that's going to happen to me?"

"Yes, if you're not careful."

"Can you explain that?"

"Later. Let's get me cleaned up."

I helped the professor clean up and got him some new clothes. I wondered if I was carrying this active imagination thing too far.

"I need to rest now. Can we talk later?" he asked.

"Sure. How will I find you?"

"The same way you just did."

"Dig you up again?"

"No, stupid, you already did that. Just close your eyes and ask for me."

The next week I told Dr. Burns what happened with the active imagination. "Aren't I a little old to be having imaginary friends?"

"Never too old." He smiled.

When I told him I asked the professor if I had to dig him up again, it was the first time I saw Dr. Burns laugh. He laughed so hard he almost cried. I liked that he could laugh so freely.

"Well, that was quite a first active imagination experience!"

"Don't you think it's a little psychotic?"

"No, not at all. If you were psychotic, you wouldn't know it was in your imagination—you'd think it was reality."

"It seemed real."

"Yes, often it does. It was your conscious mind accessing part of your unconscious, like a waking dream."

◆   ◆   ◆

That same week at the clinic, the director of rehabilitation medicine called. He said their annual meeting was coming up and asked me if I would be a panel member to discuss depression and catastrophic injuries. He knew of me because I had done some consulting in his department with severely depressed patients with major spinal cord injuries. I was flattered and, without thinking, I agreed. When I hung up the phone, I felt a twinge of anxiety. I called the director back. "Er, how many people will attend this thing?"

"Oh, maybe 350, maybe 400. Is that OK?"

"Sure." When I hung up the phone, I felt my stomach go into knots with anxiety. What the fuck did I just agree to? I've never given a speech in my life!

My anxiety got worse. I decided to talk to Professor Amnestius again. He was right; I just closed my eyes, asked for him, and poof! There he was.

"Well, you took your time now, didn't you?"

"I'm sorry. I didn't know you wanted to talk again so soon."

"Never mind that I've been waiting years. 'So soon,' humph."

"You've been waiting for years? I don't understand."

"Of course you don't. You've been asleep all your life."

"Asleep? I'm sorry I don't get it."

"There's a lot you don't get. Anyway, what's the problem?"

"How did you know I had a problem?"

"Loren, I know everything. Just describe it in your own words."

I told him about the problem of agreeing to give the speech. "Is there anything you can do to help me with it?"

"Of course I can, but you have to promise to do what I tell you to do, otherwise, as they say in Chicago, 'forget about it.'"

"What should I do?"

"Give the speech, but don't wear a tie. Wear pants and a jacket that don't match and, lastly, confess to the audience."

"What? Confess? That's nuts! What do you mean by confess?"

"You promised, so now you have to do it—all of it. You'll know what to confess when the time comes."

"But why should I? What sense does that make?"

"I can't tell you now. I'll explain it after you do it. Bye."

Now I *really* thought this talking to an imaginary person was nuts, but I didn't feel as if I had a choice. I asked Dr. Burns about it the next week.

"Why not? But really, it's entirely up to you."

"You wouldn't let me do something stupid, would you? I mean, the goal of analysis is to make me *more* sane, right?"

"Of course, but I can't make your decisions for you."

◆ ◆ ◆

I wrote a speech called "The Dark Side of Healing." When the time came, I was still extremely anxious. All the other speakers were experts in the field of Rehabilitation Medicine. I was a green intern with no real expertise in anything. I had visions of passing out at the podium, throwing up, or just freezing on the spot. I dressed the way the professor said to but, until the moment before my turn to speak to the mass of faces in front of me, I still didn't know what to confess. When my turn arrived, I looked down at the trembling paper in my hands. Then I said, "As a member of the psychiatry department I've had the opportunity to work with a number of people with stage fright but, until this very moment, I had no idea what they were really talking about." With that, the otherwise serious audience burst into laughter. The anxiety and tension disappeared—and I gave my speech.

Later that day, my department chief came to my office. "I understand you gave a hell of a speech to the Rehab group."

"I really don't know how it went, but the funny thing is, after weeks of anxiety, I actually enjoyed it."

"Well, Dr. Lever just called me. He not only praised your speech, he wants you to be the psychological consultant to his department."

"But I'm only an intern."

"Well, it hasn't been done before, but if you want to, take it. It'll look great on your résumé."

That night I had to talk to the professor. I told him about how it went. "Now can you explain your crazy conditions?"

"Not so crazy after all, I would say."

"But why those things? And why was I so anxious?"

"Because you were afraid your audience would see things about you before you did."

"Huh?"

"You *wore* the ineptitude you felt and confessed your lack of experience. Their laughter broke that tension and made you one with your audience. Before that, you unconsciously expected them to be hostile and critical. *That* was the cause of your anxiety."

"You're amazing. And for an archeologist, you're a great psychologist."

"No. I'm only you. You amazed yourself. Bye."

The next rime I saw Dr. Burns I explained what happened with the speech and my talk with the professor.

"I wonder what he meant by saying that he was only me. I don't have that kind of wisdom."

"Well, where do you suppose it came from?"

"I want to say him, but I know he's in my mind. It's confusing."

"Maybe it's confusing because you think of your mind as your ego."

"Isn't it?"

"Your ego is only a part of your mind, a small part. All of your ego is in your mind, but your mind is much more than just your ego."

"So he's a deeper part of my mind that my ego isn't aware of?"

"Yes. He comes from the same place as your dreams."

I found it astonishing that there was such wisdom in the psyche, especially mine. I had a lot more questions for Professor Amnestius. I also wanted to tell Greta about him.

24

In the Belly of the Whale

During the first year of analysis I had more than twenty death dreams. Fortunately, they seemed to be on the wane by the time I finished my internship. The "death stage" of analysis and discovering Professor Amnestius gave me immense respect and awe of the unconscious. One afternoon while in session, I was trying to explain to Dr. Burns what those dreams brought up for me.

"Exploring those dreams makes me feel how fragile my ego is."

"How do you mean that?"

"Well, as parts of my ego collapse, I feel how fragile my sense of connection with the people in my life is."

"Yes. Go on."

"I guess I'm not as terrified of death as I am of dying alone—without my family, children, and friends."

"Well, everyone does die alone."

"Yes, but knowing that we all die alone anyway doesn't help. I think my fear of death just expresses how disconnected from others I really am—so much so that, if I died now, it would feel like dying without being loved. I know it sounds stupid, but a loveless death terrifies me."

"It doesn't sound stupid. It's probably a universal fear."

"Well, this is all very pathetic. I mean, what's the point? I don't feel any better now than when I started this. Actually, I feel worse."

"That's not unusual. You feel you're pathetic?"

"Of course I do. What good is this insight if it makes you feel worse about yourself?"

"Not all insights are comforting. Trying to be conscious is hard work—and a burden."

"Great! Well, time's up. See you next session."

◆ ◆ ◆

When I finished my master's degree I believed, as I had after my bachelor's degree, that I knew next to nothing about psychology. So with the same anxiety I had in the past, I applied to a number of doctoral programs. Fortunately, the one that accepted me was in San Francisco.

After my internship, the clinic hired me as a psychological assistant. This was fortunate because they paid me a decent salary, and I would have more to send to my girls as well as pay for my education.

Although I was still keeping up with world news, political events became less and less important as my inner life continued to take on more significance.

Spiro Agnew resigned his vice-presidency after admitting no contest to charges of tax evasion. Then Nixon resigned. "Tricky Dick" finally got his due, *except* a month later the new president, Gerald Ford, pardoned Nixon for all crimes he "committed or may have committed." The following spring, all remaining American forces left Vietnam. The day after the last troops left, the North Vietnamese took Saigon.

The longest American war, one never formally declared and incited by paranoia and false information, was finally over. America dropped nearly eight million tons of bombs on a country no bigger than the state of Wisconsin—three times more than were dropped during all of World War II. In North Vietnam thousands of homes, school buildings, hospitals, and hundreds of churches and temples were destroyed or heavily damaged. If the bombing hadn't been destructive enough, seventy-five million liters of defoliants were sprayed over the farmlands, forests, and villages of Vietnam. By the end, fifty-eight thousand Americans were dead and more than five million Vietnamese. Of those, four million were civilians. The number of Vietnam veterans who committed suicide equaled the number of soldiers killed in the war. Robert McNamara, once the godfather of Vietnam, later said, "We were wrong, terribly wrong. We owe it to future generations to explain why." What a sardonically nice afterthought. Good luck, Bob.

Vietnam was "my war." I was relieved that it was over, but it left me cynical and angry about the inhumanity of the world—and the hypocrisy of my life. Much of my outer life still seemed like a farcical mishmash of illusions and misperceptions gleaned from my parents' pathetically narrow platitudes about life, the fraudulent promises of politics, and especially my exposure to religious dogma. Those colossal deceptions made me hate the world. As far as I was concerned, I knew next to nothing about myself or, for that matter, anything else. There was no truth, no meaning, and no God.

◆ ◆ ◆

The next stage of analysis was heralded by another series of even more humiliating dreams. At the time, I'd wished I never had them.

"I dreamt I was questioning a man. He was tall, with a swarthy complexion, austerely dressed, quiet, and somber. He said he didn't want to answer my questions because the answers weren't worth the energy it would take to speak. I thought of him as 'Schizoid Man.'"

"What's the feeling about him?"

"Scary. He seems exhausted, cold, indifferent, and completely closed off. Alive, but dead."

"Do you think he's a part of yourself?"

"That's not a very comforting thought. I guess he is. I think I'm afraid of answering *your* questions."

"Why is that?"

"Well, I'm afraid of my answers, afraid of revealing myself."

"What don't you want to reveal?"

"Anything. I already feel bad about myself. The death dreams were hard enough to talk about. Maybe, like the guy in the dream, I'm just nothing anyway—the questions not even worth answering."

"Perhaps he's like a defense. You want to protect yourself because you already feel vulnerable. But being Schizoid Man is much more dangerous than being vulnerable."

"Yeah, that's a good word, vulnerable. I feel it in my chest."

"What does your chest feel like?"

"Tight, hard, painful. Like it's hard to breathe. The feeling reminds me of another dream."

"Do you want to talk about it?"

"No." I laughed. "OK, I'll tell it. I was about four or five. My mother was very angry. I don't know why. She's punching my chest. I start to cry and say, 'That hurts.' She says, 'No it doesn't, and if you don't stop crying, I'll give you something to cry about.' I'm afraid she will kill me—that's what she'll give me to cry about. Then she makes me go away."

"Did that actually happen?"

"I don't know. I think so, but I don't remember. It seems like something she would do. That's her way of talking, 'I'll give you something to cry about.' She hated it when I cried. She liked to say, 'I'll kick your ass up between your shoulders.' A favorite expression."

Dr. Burns looked away from me.

"What's the matter?"

"It's…it's just that I'm sorry. Sorry that happened to you."

I didn't know what to say. It surprised me that he looked sad.

"Your mother was very angry," he continued. "Angry at something, but probably not you. That's too much anger for any child. But you must have felt as if it *was* you."

"Yeah, I did. I could never make her happy. I thought she was unhappy because of me. Actually, I thought she hated me." I told him about the time she told me that my father would leave her if she had a third child—me.

On the way home I remembered part of a poem in *Phoenix*, by D. H. Lawrence. "Are you willing to be made nothing?/Dipped into oblivion?/If not, you will never really change." Dr. Burns should have had that above his door.

◆   ◆   ◆

The next session we didn't talk about my mother because I had more dreams I needed to talk about.

"I had several dreams about being back in the old neighborhood. In one, I was with Greta again. I was in a gang, and there were other gangs around. One of them was a gang of black guys. It was dangerous, and I was concerned about Greta. She knew nothing about that side of life."

"You were worried that she might get hurt?"

"Yes, she has no idea about that part of my life."

"Why haven't you told her about it?"

"Shame, I guess. I don't know if she'll understand. I don't feel good about what I did in those days. I also had another break-in dream. I had a large beautiful Victorian house that had been ransacked. The inside was filthy, a shambles. There was a black man hiding somewhere in the background. My brother Dino was there. I was very angry with him, and I was confronting him. 'Why do you hate blacks? You don't even know any.' He replied, 'How many do you *really* know?' Then somehow, I knew Dino was the burglar and that he had let the black man into the house. Now I *am* afraid to go home," I laughed.

"Afraid of another break-in?"

"Not really. This time I'm not going to resist the interpretation."

"You have an interpretation already? What do you think it means?"

"I think that rather than you breaking in, Dino is the burglar this time. He's broke in and let something in that I don't want to look at—either him or the black man, or both."

"That's a good start. What's he bringing up?"

"On the surface it seems like his hatred of black people, but I think it's really my feelings about him. So maybe he's bringing up my hatred."

"Of black people?"

"No. I didn't hate the blacks. He did. My hatred of *him*. Something I still don't like talking about."

"Going to try to be the Schizoid Man? Don't stop, you're doing pretty well so far. So Dino let the black man in. Why is that a problem?"

"I just don't want another break-in." We both laughed.

I told Dr. Burns about Dino, my fight on Lincoln Avenue, and how he had just stood there and watched me nearly beaten to death.

"From that day on, I hated him. That wasn't the only thing, but it was a turning point. It was as if I saw a part of him I never knew existed."

"A part like what?"

"It was beyond coldness, it was sinister, sadistic. As if he enjoyed seeing me beat to shit. After that, my childhood world broke apart."

"Like it is now?"

"Yeah. Another variation on the theme, except I don't have any outer event to relate it to. Well, except for the war."

"Why do you suppose Dino is coming up in your dreams now?"

"Unfinished business, I guess."

"You've never been able to forgive him?"

"I wasn't thinking of forgiving him. It never occurred to me to do that."

"Well, suppose he is a part of you in some way?"

"Does everything in my dreams have to be a part of me?"

"Well, most of them are. But go on about Dino."

"Dino as a part of me? The thought sickens me. There is no way I'm like him. I couldn't be." I resented Dr. Burns even suggesting it.

"I'm not suggesting you're like him in any outer way. You are a very different person. But perhaps he introduces the black man, another part of your own psyche."

I didn't like that much better. "I don't understand what you're trying to say."

"Dino had a devastating impact on your life. You trusted him to care about you, protect you, but he let you down—almost let you be killed. That caused you to hate him. Your parents didn't treat you much better. All of that could have made you hateful."

"Of course it did. Wouldn't it you?"

"Perhaps, but I've never had an experience like that. That's not relevant. What's important is that you must still feel a lot of anger and hatred because of it. You seem defensive about it."

"Maybe. I'm not aware of being angry with anyone—except the fucking politicians. That's not hard to understand is it?" He was irritating the hell out of me.

"No, it's not. But maybe that's not the only place your anger is directed."

"OK, where else is it directed?"

"That's a good question. Can we come back to it next time?"

"Why do we always seem to stop when we get to something important?"

"Are you angry?"

"No. Yes. Well, maybe. I don't know. I'll see you next time."

He had the nicest way of pissing me off.

◆ ◆ ◆

If the other dreams hadn't been bad enough, that night I dreamt that I was a Nazi officer in charge of transporting women and children to a death camp. I hated what I was doing but did it anyway. I had explosives strapped to the front of my body. A gunfight broke out with American soldiers. I worried that the explosives would be hit. The dream made me feel sick. It wasn't the first dream I'd had of being a Nazi, and I didn't tell any of them to Dr. Burns. I thought I was beginning to understand myself, but I obviously wasn't who I thought I was. The picture of myself painted in my dreams was disgusting—like Dr. Jekyll's Mr. Hyde.

The next morning I sat at the kitchen table playing with my stiletto, pushing it at my abdomen, making a tiny hole in my shirt. It was tempting. I wondered if Dr. Burns would be surprised—if he would even care. I was a fucked-up person living in a fucked-up world. What was the point? Analysis seemed like one more way of discovering that I was even more fucked up than I thought. I was beginning to feel like Schizoid Man. He wouldn't be afraid to die. And even though I was afraid of dying, I wasn't sure I wanted to live either.

I decided to take a drive in my car, not knowing or caring where I was going. I drove around for hours and ended up parking across from a small church somewhere in Oakland. I hadn't been inside a church in a long time. For some reason I decided to go in. It was open and empty, so I sat in a pew in front of the altar. After sitting there a few minutes, an unexpected voice came wrenching from my guts—"Oh God, please help me." It was the deepest emotion I'd felt in a long time. Then, to my amazement, the most bizarre thing happened. A thin, horizontal buzzing line that seemed like a current of mild electricity started under my feet and very slowly moved upwards, passing through my whole body. When it went past the top of my head, the sound of the buzzing line stopped and vanished into the air above my head. Suddenly, I felt wonderful, as if I didn't have a problem in the world. I had exactly the same problems as before, except now I knew with absolute, unexplainable certainty that everything was going to turn out fine.

In our next session, I told Dr. Burns about the experience in the church.

"What does that mean? What exactly happened to me?"

"I don't know."

"What do you mean you don't know?"

"I can only say what it isn't, not what it is. What I mean is that it isn't a defense like denial or repression because you know you still have the same problems. If you thought your problems were no longer real, I'd have to say it was a defense."

"Well, if it's not a defense, what could it be? Is it inside me or outside?"

"Loren, some experiences fall outside psychiatry and psychology. They're just not within our scope of knowledge. Jung studied many aspects of religion, but he always tried to remain an empiricist."

"I guess I'm confused again. There has to be an explanation."

"Well, because I can't explain it doesn't diminish its importance. It *was* a very powerful and very special experience. One I suspect is quite rare. It may have saved you from suicide."

"I didn't say anything about suicide."

"No, you didn't. But were you thinking about it?"

"Yes. I didn't think I wanted to live anymore."

"That dream of Dino may have been more significant than you thought. It brought out a part of yourself you don't want to look at—something you've repressed."

"Shit."

"What is it?"

"I had a dream about being a Nazi after our last session. I've also had others I haven't told you about. They're pretty sick."

"You didn't want me to know about them?"

"Of course not. I guess I don't want to lose your respect."

Dr. Burns smiled gently. "I don't think it's me you're worried about. It's very difficult to realize there are parts of yourself you'd rather not acknowledge. All this dark material is unacceptable to your ego. You find it appalling so you feel totally revolted with yourself—like that's all you really are."

"Isn't it?"

"No. They're parts of yourself you've repressed and have never come to accept. That's why they come up in your dreams. Your psyche wants you to be aware of them and, eventually, integrate them. Maybe that's the part you wanted to die."

"Why did I want it to die?"

"Because of your identification with a false self. Loren, you could have died in childhood, so you had to construct a personality and a way of being that would help you survive. You became a fearless warrior of sorts, like Dino. He didn't seem afraid of anything or anyone and looked as if he had the ability to survive. For a while that may have been adaptive, but when you were almost killed and he didn't even try to help you, your repressed vulnerability came to the fore. The vulnerability was always there; you just pushed it into your unconscious. Before that, maybe it was expressed only by the mask."

"My psyche knew all that?"

"Yes, your unconscious knows what you need to learn about yourself. That's why it shows you these things, not to torment you, but to heal you."

"Did my unconscious cause the experience in the church?"

"Perhaps the answer to that lies within religion."

"But religious experience is part of the psyche too, isn't it?"

"Yes, but that doesn't mean we can explain it. At least not at this point in time."

I have to admit I was disappointed. Not that it was Dr. Burns' fault. It just seemed as if he should know more about the church experience. I decided to talk to Professor Amnestius.

When I called for him, he was standing in front of a cross and was dressed in beautiful vestments.

"Why did you change from your clothes into these things?"

He came down from where he was standing. "They're only symbols of what your conscious mind understands."

"What was that experience in the church about?"

"You were pretty desperate and might have killed yourself. You asked God for help—and you got it."

"I wasn't consciously planning on killing myself."

"True. You didn't know it consciously, but you were."

"I didn't think I believed in God anymore."

"It's yourself you don't believe in, not God, or you wouldn't have cried out for him. You were appealing to a power within yourself."

"That's what Dr. Burns sort of said."

"He's right."

"What religion does God come from?"

He laughed. "Some part of God is in all religions. They all teach different things about God. Some religions even condemn other religions. I guess they teach what they think they know about it."

"Why do you say *it*?"

"God isn't a Him or Her. It can't be completely described because it's a potentiality."

"What do you mean *potentiality*?"

"Like you, like everyone, like everything, God is becoming. It hasn't completely arrived yet." He was smiling.

"You mean God isn't perfect?"

"Of course not. Is anything perfect?"

"No, I don't think so."

"Nothing is perfect, not even God. All I know is that the potentiality of God is toward something good."

"Why do you say something good? Why not something bad? The world's not that great a place as far as I'm concerned."

"True. At times it's a terrible place where horrible things happen."

"Why does God allow that?"

"I told you, God is potentiality. The "thing-ness" or personhood of God is an illusion. God doesn't allow or not allow; it participates to the best of its ability. That's the hopeful part, its potential moves in a positive direction."

"How do you know it's positive?"

"Nature, the psyche. If you cut yourself, the wound tries to repair itself rather than stay the same or worsen. If your psyche is damaged, it moves toward healing itself. That's God."

"So God is in us."

"We *are* God, the potentiality of God."

"So when I asked for help from God, I was asking myself?"

"Yes, at that moment you appealed to the God potential in you, and it moved you in a positive direction."

"Why aren't everyone's prayers answered then?"

"They're not always sincere. In Latin, *sincerus* means clean, pure."

"Then individuation is our God potentiality?"

"Absolutely, perhaps the best example. But it can't be accomplished in a single lifetime."

"Why not?"

"Life is just too short for all the potentiality we have. Maybe some day it will be long enough. Your present life is not your beginning, and your death will not be your end—at least not for a long time. Bye."

Next to what happened in the church, that talk was the most extraordinary thing I ever experienced. I hadn't thought about reincarnation since Theosophy School, and I wasn't sure if I could believe it. But the Professor always seemed to know what he was talking about.

If the psyche did have a natural urge toward healing and psychospiritual wholeness that would certainly be a God-like attribute within a person. That type of process might also demonstrate that suffering is not only a necessary and inevitable part of life, but show that it's the way to redemption. Which, if I remembered correctly, is very similar to Buddhist ideas about suffering—we suffer because we are trapped in our ignorance. Maybe my suffering was an initiation into a lifelong journey, not a lifelong cross to bear. If that was true, the stumbling stones that appeared in my dreams, illusions, and problems might be the building blocks of my psychospiritual path, like guideposts in a journey toward personal healing, greater consciousness, and spiritual awareness.

◆   ◆   ◆

It took some time to tell Dr. Burns about my talk with the Professor in the next session.

"So what do you think?"

"It's one of the most astonishing experiences I've ever heard."

"But do you think it's true? Should I believe it?"

"Loren, I have no idea. Maybe that's where faith comes in."

"What do you mean?"

"I mean faith isn't like a belief, it's rather something you trust is right and comes from your heart instead of your head. It's what you *feel* is important and relates to those values you find meaning in."

"Yeah, I get it. That's absolutely right. But did Jung believe in reincarnation?"

"Well, in his biography, *Memories, Dreams, Reflections*, he did say that he felt as if he had lived before. As far as I know, he didn't include that in his theories."

"Maybe he didn't live long enough."

"Maybe. His biography was written at the end of his life. Even then many thought of him as a mystic or a little too far-out. I think he said there wasn't enough empirical evidence for it. So even if he personally believed it, he wouldn't add it to his theories."

After that session I realized how dangerously close I came to doing myself in without even realizing it. It made me aware that there is a very thin line between me dying and what was trying to die in my psyche.

Jung would say the individuation is the goal of life, but what about the goal of individuation itself? I was beginning to think that the ultimate goal of individuation is self-love and the discovery that God is within. The other is that the soul requires more than one lifetime to achieve what it needs to. I think he would say that those conclusions are outside the empirical scope of his method. As a pragmatist, I would say, with enough self-reflection, they seem self-evident. It's difficult to believe that my journey ends after one lifetime, or even began with this one. One life span is not nearly enough time to accomplish all of my soul's work; and it took a long time to plant the seeds for this one.

By extending that personal thought to the collective, it seemed to me that humanity is at a very early stage of its psychospiritual evolution; a stage where our hearts have not kept pace with the enormous strides of our minds. When I thought about the world and its billions of souls—so many still lost, groping for light in the darkness of a world perpetually at war—it seemed obvious that we are still far from being fully grown. War is, by far, the most horrific testament to our lack of emotional and spiritual development. If we were anywhere near our Godlike potential, we would see war like deicide. Why not settle world conflict with a game of chess with all the spectators alive and healthy to applaud the winner?

◆ ◆ ◆

That night I had a dream that felt like a confirmation of what the Professor told me and of what Dr. Burns and I talked about. The following week I told Dr. Burns about the dream.

"There was an infant sitting in the middle of a large tree. A bolt of lightning suddenly struck the base of the tree causing a fire and, at that same moment, the child achieved *satori*. The fire wasn't harmful to the tree or the child. Then people came from all around to hear what the child had to say."

"That's a remarkable dream. What are your feelings about it?"

"I looked up *satori*. It's the Japanese Zen Buddhist term for enlightenment. *Satori* can come from disciplined effort like meditation or just by spontaneous revelation. I thought it was interesting that my unconscious used Zen Buddhism since Buddhists have a disdain for thinking. I often think too much. At first, I thought the child was vulnerable way up in that tree, but he turned out to be quite strong. So am I going to become enlightened?" I laughed.

"Well, the dream has several archetypal symbols: the tree, the divine child, lightning, and fire. It seems like a very condensed dream about individuation. The child is initially vulnerable and in a precarious place, not unlike the barriers life throws in our path that can block growth. The tree is like life itself. The lightning is a powerful natural force that comes from the heavens and lights things up, as in overcoming the darkness of unconsciousness. The fire here isn't dangerous but seems more like a source of energy linked with spiritual power and a symbol of purification and transformation. For Jung, the divine child symbolized the potentiality of becoming psychically whole. He believed the last stage in the development of Christianity would be expressed by the symbol of the divine child."

"Why a divine child?"

"The child represents the symbolic connection or union in consciousness between time and eternity, between the personal and archetypal parts of the psyche, and between the historical and transhistorical dimensions of existence. You can read about it in his *Mysterium Coniunctionis*."

"Is that what achieving *satori* meant?"

"Yes, it's like a synthesis of conscious and unconscious. Jung compared it to the *unio mystica* of the alchemists, or *tao* in Taoism, or *samadhi* in Hinduism, or like in your dream, *satori* of Zen Buddhism. In Zen, *satori* is also often used prospectively, the enlightenment the aspirant desires."

"The dream felt very positive."

"Oh, yes. It's reassuring, as if to tell you that you're on the right path."

That session was the most remarkable of any that I'd had with Dr. Burns. It was then that I decided I wanted to become a psychoanalyst, a path I felt sure of, finally doing the work I knew I was supposed to be doing.

25

Reasons of the Heart

I never expected analysis to last through graduate school, but it did, and well past. I continued to work at the hospital clinic and, when I finished my doctoral internship there, the clinic hired me as a full-time staff member. That was September 1975; the time Lynette "Squeaky" Fromme, a sidekick of convicted cult leader Charles Manson, tried to assassinate Gerald Ford. Ford must have had some strange karma, because a couple of weeks later, another woman tried the same thing. Maybe it was because he pardoned Nixon.

During the next two years I prepared for the psychology boards, took the exam, got my license, and started a small private practice.

I also was making enough money to buy my first house. I found a quiet place not far from the city and set among rolling hills of protected watershed land; a half-acre with a beautiful old rustic house on a gentle slope with a creek at the bottom border. Surrounding the house were live oaks, horse chestnuts, sequoia redwoods, pines, flowering fruit trees, and others I never even heard of. Deer, foxes, and raccoons freely roamed the property. Because I had more than enough space in the house, I used one of the extra rooms as a therapy office, and in another I created a meditation room with a small altar. Living there was like a fantasy or otherworldly dream. For me, an impossible dream.

I thought of Bud and my mother who had both dreamed of owning a home but never did. Thinking of my mother continuing to live through the severe winters of Chicago saddened me. Her arthritis had become so bad she was unable to work and couldn't walk without a walker. One fall on an icy city sidewalk could completely cripple her. I knew Dino and Mickey wouldn't be much help to her. They rarely saw her unless they needed something; Dino used her as a pinch-hit babysitter, and Mickey liked to borrow her credit card.

I called and convinced her to move to California. Knowing she was a compulsive pack rat, I added the caveat that she only bring what was necessary; I would find an apartment for her and anything she needed. I should have known better;

she arrived with two Atlas semis loaded with everything she owned, including old newspapers and every recipe she had ever clipped out of a magazine. Her new apartment was so crammed, she had to clear a path to the sofa and the bathroom. I should have known better; her way of life would never change.

My life finally felt as if it was beginning to take shape, but the events of the years to follow made it feel as if it had been torn apart again, so my personal analysis was far from being over. Revelations about myself continued to pour out of my psyche as from an inexhaustible fount of unconsciousness. I knew I had to continue this work for my own benefit. Becoming a psychologist wasn't just academic; it made the responsibility even greater, since now other psyches were being entrusted to my care. I knew that if I didn't have a deep enough understanding of my life and my own psyche, I couldn't possibly help my patients. I also realized that what I felt and believed about myself would be reflected in the work I did with others. That made my responsibility even more daunting. Jung was fond of saying that if you were going mountain climbing with a guide, he or she had better already have been there.

When I finally decided to apply for training as a psychoanalyst, it was clear that the Jungian school was the one I wanted to pursue. The more I read of Jung, the more I felt his ideas were closest to my own. The Freudian school felt too narrow and restrictive, especially since its views of religion and spirituality seemed outdated and unable to account for the interrelationship between spirituality and psychology. I didn't doubt that Freud's ideas applied to certain individuals, maybe even to some religions, but his overall dismissal of spirituality as a defense seemed shortsighted. His view of reincarnation was as reductive as his view of religion; simply another defense against the anxiety of personal annihilation.

My attitude about applying for training as an analyst seemed to confirm that I had grown some in the course of my analysis. Despite the strong competition with other applicants, it was the first time I did not experience overwhelming anxiety about whether I would be accepted. I wanted the training, but for the first time I didn't feel that my acceptance rested on whether I was a good enough person. It was just something I needed to do as part of my personal and professional journey. As a condition of acceptance, candidates were not only required to have had several years of analysis before applying, but were required to continue analysis as long as they were in training. That was fine with me—analysis was not only part of my path, it had saved my life.

Analysis made me painfully aware of just how much inner work I still needed to do. Despite that, I applied for training and was granted an interview. The first part of it was with a group of analysts, and the second part was a shorter interview with one analyst.

"So, Loren, what will you do if you're not accepted?" he asked.

"I'll read as much Jung as I possibly can and continue in my analysis as long as necessary."

"You won't feel rejected?"

"No. For the first time in my life, I won't."

"Why is that?"

"Well, because I need the training as part of my personal journey, and I believe it will deepen the work I do with patients. I don't want to do it because of my *persona*. If I'm not accepted, I'll have to find other ways to deepen my understanding."

A few weeks later I received a letter of acceptance from the Jung Institute. I felt as if I had come home.

◆ ◆ ◆

Tom and Beth called and told me they had returned from Canada and had found a small apartment in the Mission District of San Francisco. They invited me to dinner. "Just knock on the garage door," Tom said.

When I got to their address I understood what he meant. Their "apartment" was primarily a garage with a makeshift bedroom to the side of it and an even smaller kitchen off the bedroom. Tom answered my knocking by opening the garage door. He looked older and even more disheveled than the last time I saw him.

"We don't have a car so we parked ourselves in here." He had that little elfish smile I loved so much. "C'mon in."

"It's great to see you, Tom."

He looked outside the garage, peering furtively up and down the street. "Hurry up and come inside before someone sees you."

Beth was in the sparsely furnished bedroom that served as the living room as well. She looked as beautiful as ever, her long red curly hair flowing around her face. We all hugged each other.

"We have a surprise for you, Loren," Beth said.

She took me to the corner of the room and in a tiny pink and white crib was a baby about six months old. "Oh, my God. Why didn't you guys tell me?"

"It was a surprise. Besides we didn't want the Feds to know," said Tom.

"She's beautiful. She's got more hair than you do, Tom."

"She's going to have lots of red hair like her mom."

Dinner was weak Ceylon tea and butter cookies.

"It's not much, but it's more than we had in Canada, if you can believe that."

"Really?"

"Yeah, they were after us all the time up there."

"Is that why you were looking outside?"

Beth shot a troubled glance at me as if to say, "Please don't go there."

"So what have you heard from Don?" I asked.

"He writes me."

"And?"

"He just writes."

I knew Beth was uncomfortable. She was glancing at me as she did before. I tried changing the subject. "So what took you so long to come back?"

"They're still after me, Loren."

I looked toward Beth. Her face was down and covered by her hair. "There's been an amnesty, Tom. Carter pardoned the resisters in '77. You're safe now. You know that, right?"

"I heard in Canada, but I don't believe it."

"Did you talk to your draft board, or a lawyer?"

"Fuck no! I don't want them to know where I am."

From behind Tom, Beth was shaking her head at me. I had a feeling that this was futile.

Before I left about ten o'clock, I went out to my car. Its title was in the glove box. I took it out and signed it over to them. It was a shiny, baby blue '69 Volkswagen Beetle, and the spider-cursed engine I had replaced a few years back was almost perfect.

"What's this?" Tom asked in amazement.

"It's a car for you. With the baby you'll need it."

"Jesus, Loren. You can't give us your *car*."

"I just did. Where's the bus stop?"

"At the end of the block."

As I walked off, Tom called to me, "We're going to have to move out of the garage so we can park the car." We all laughed.

On the bus ride back home I wondered about what I had just done. I'm not sure if what I had done was strength or a weakness. It *was* a "me" kind of thing to do. Not that I ever gave someone a car before, but I liked being able to give others whatever I had to give. Besides, I could afford another car, they couldn't. I thought, too, about how wonderful it was to see them again, but something in

Tom had seriously changed. He was more reclusive, paranoid, and refused to see any of his friends but me. I had already heard from Don that Tom wasn't answering his letters.

I didn't hear from them for several months, and then Tom called. He was silent a long time and seemed to be crying. Then he blurted out, "Beth committed suicide, and the Feds took my baby."

I didn't know whether to believe him or not. "Where are you?" He gave me the address of a hotel in the Tenderloin—the worst section of San Francisco. When I got to the hotel, the Volkswagen was parked not far from the front door, grimy, and abandoned. I found Tom in a room on the second floor of the fleabag hotel. The door was ajar. I called out. No answer. I pushed the door aside and looked in. Tom was slumped on the only piece of furniture in the room, a tattered armchair, staring blankly at the torn wallpaper. The solitary window was cracked and so dirty that the sky outside looked gray. Pieces of old newspaper were scattered on the floor. The place was cold, filthy, and smelled of old food. Tom was crying; drool oozed slowly from one corner of his mouth. I stood there a few moments just staring at him. Finally, he spoke, "The Feds took my baby."

"My God, Tom. I'm so sorry. What happened to Beth?"

"Killed herself. Took some pills. I don't know why."

"Tom, you need help. You need some medication. Let me take you to see a psychiatrist I know."

"I don't want help. I just want to die."

I gathered him up from the chair and brought him unannounced to a psychiatrist I knew from the institute. Luckily, he agreed to see Tom on his lunch break.

"You find this guy on the street?"

"No, he's one of my best friends."

"Well, I gave him a prescription for an antipsychotic. He's paranoid schizophrenic. Thinks the Feds took his baby. I called the County Social Services, and they confirmed his wife did commit suicide. It wasn't the Feds who took his baby; it was the county. I don't know where he got that idea, but Protective Services found him unfit to keep his child. I'm referring him to one of the city clinics. They might hospitalize him. You can take him there now if you can."

I took Tom to the clinic and left my name as his only contact. I knew his parents were somewhere in Wisconsin, but I didn't know exactly where, and Tom refused to tell the clinic. He was admitted to the County Hospital and released a few days later. When I tried to see him again, he had already left the hotel. They had no idea where he might have gone. I never heard from Tom again. I doubted he was alive but, if he was, he was probably sleeping somewhere on the streets of

San Francisco. I never did find out where his baby was either. One of my best friends, his wife, and their child vanished into nothingness. All that remained of them was the grimy baby blue Volkswagen sitting somewhere on a street in the Tenderloin. I don't know if his fate was any better out of the war than in it; he and Beth were casualties of it anyway. As I walked away from the hotel I thought of some lyrics of the Simon and Garfunkel song, "He Was My Brother."

◆ ◆ ◆

I got a call from Dino's wife saying that Mickey had been diagnosed with melanoma. When I phoned Mickey's doctor in Chicago, she said it wasn't melanoma, but multiple myeloma, a cancer formed by malignant plasma cells in the bone marrow. She felt his condition was already advanced and, while it was a guess, she suspected he might live for six months. I called Mickey and asked him to come to California to spend some time with me. To my surprise, he agreed—if I would pay for his ticket. I arranged for his ticket and a time to pick him up at the airport. He would stay with my mother.

Mickey was a sad sight as he hobbled against his cane out of the passenger tunnel at the airport. A black pinstriped suit he must have bought on Maxwell Street hung loosely on his once stocky fighter's frame. He looked a few inches shorter and stunted. Beneath his usual black, thin-brimmed Furgora hat, his face was pasty white. Because of his continual wincing, I knew he was in constant pain. Now "Little Mickey," his street name, looked more like Tiny Mickey.

After he settled in at my mother's place, I found an oncologist for him in San Francisco who specialized in multiple myeloma. Mickey restarted the chemotherapy he began in Chicago as well as treatment with other anticancer drugs and analgesics. His doctor said all that could be done was to make him comfortable.

I began spending a lot of my free time with Mickey. Being with him was bittersweet. We had never been close. Brothers or not, we were just too different. Now our closest moment would be facing his death together. Something we *did* have in common was humor, except he didn't realize just how funny he was. He could have been Archie Bunker; like Archie he also named his favorite bar after himself. I had forgotten how amusing his Chicago accent and atrocious grammar was. I hadn't heard "forgetabotit," "proberbly," and "supposably" for a long time. Mickey had been most successful as a cabbie—well, at least he did that the longest. His straight-faced cabbie stories were priceless and uproarious, especially the one about the drunk he was frantically driving around on the almost exitless Edens Expressway looking for a bathroom. He filled the floor of Mickey's cab with urine. Mickey could, with the most expressionless face, ask, "Why does all this shit happen to me?" He was the only guy I ever knew arrested by a prostitute, or what he had thought was a prostitute. If that wasn't bad enough, she had found Bennies in his room and added illegal amphetamine possession to the offense. He singled himself out as a casualty of God's greatest wrath. I would have thought of him as Job, except he didn't even believe in God, much less try to please Him. He was simply the archetypal victim. At least he stopped drinking when he became ill.

Mickey's illness brought back some of the feelings I had had when I was having death dreams. But I finally realized, as Dr. Burns tried to point out, that my death dreams were only superficially about mortality. More importantly, they represented my fear of letting go of an ego identity. An identity fashioned as a defense against feeling unable to control my life and feeling inferior from having been unloved. It became apparent that I had to understand and resolve the deeper meaning of my fear of death to ever fully accept myself. So after four years, I decided to break off my relationship with Greta to face being alone.

Greta broke into tears when I told her what I thought I needed to do.

"We have to break up so you can *find* yourself? You sound like Kierkegaard. Are you going to join a monastery? I hoped we would get married."

"What do you mean? Because he broke off his engagement to Regine?"

"Not because he broke it off, but why. *Cogito ergo doleo*, Loren."

"Meaning?"

"I think, therefore, I'm depressed. Oh, never mind. Do what you want."

Kierkegaard broke off with Regine in order not to expose her to his melancholy. Greta didn't understand why I needed to do this and thought it rather extreme. She always thought I was a bit too "heavy." I guess this proved it.

This confrontation involved several years of relative isolation from my friends. Apart from my patients, I only saw people when I had to. The isolation also provided the time to study the psychological, philosophical, and spiritual aspects of death. In particular, Buddhist views of death impressed me. Unlike Christians, who believe that your birthday is the most important day of your life, the Buddhists think the day of your death is most important, "the crowning and most glorious moment." For them, death is a mirror that reflects the whole of one's life, and the moment of death offers a last possibility to understand the nature of mind itself.

The Buddhist perspective gave my fear of death a different meaning. I began to see that my ego's fear of losing control was the result of my overidentification with it, meaning that if I gave up my ego, *everything* about me would be annihilated. But, more importantly, my dreams seemed to be deliberately prodding me not only to face death, but also to accept it in some positive way. Like in doing that I could then move on to some other experience that lay beyond it. The professor's words crept into my mind: "Your death will not be your end." Now I wasn't sure exactly what that meant, but it felt like another instance of something more I should be doing. Perhaps if I accepted that my ego wasn't the precious thing I thought it was, then I could see that it might even be holding me captive. As though my ego was keeping me from moving toward something beyond it. All this reminded me of a quote by Rilke, "Our deepest fears are like dragons guarding our deepest treasure."

Even after nearly three years of relative isolation, I don't think I completely resolved my fear, but I felt stronger knowing I could finally face death alone and without panic. As I thought about it analytically, isolating myself might have been a defense to keep me out of love relationships. If so, I was still running scared of something. I seriously questioned whether I was capable of really loving anyone.

One thing I knew for sure was that I wanted to be with my girls, so I decided to take Jean to court to get partial custody. I learned that she had remarried. I hoped that her marriage would provide her with a different target, and that the job of getting legal custody would be easier. While I won the right to visit the children every other week, the victory was short-lived. Jean proved herself capable of multiple targets and escalated her tactics. She was determined to make the children's lives miserable if they continued to visit with me and mine as well if I persisted in trying to see them. She wrote a letter, supposedly from them, saying they "didn't want to visit me and if I continued to try and see them, they would resent it." From its language, I knew she wrote it and that she had made them sign it. If that wasn't enough, she repeated her old stories about my being a drug-addicted hippie living in a commune.

I talked with Dr. Burns about this. He thought that perhaps, in the children's best interest, I might stop visiting and wait until they were older when they could decide for themselves to go against Jean.

Almost as Dr. Burns had predicted, when Lynn turned sixteen she decided to come and live with me—a Promethean act on her part because while Jean had already made Lynn's life an emotional wreck, coming to live with me was about the worst thing Lynn could do to her. I was elated to have Lynn with me. From the day she moved in, every evening Lynn would anxiously wait for me to finish seeing patients so we could talk. The hours and hours of talking were making up for the years of silence. The new relationship with Lynn encouraged her sisters to begin visiting—at first ostensibly to see her—but Lynn's presence opened a door for them to visit me despite their mother's fury. The more they visited, the more enraged Jean became. Her slurs grew nastier and crueler. But even the girls began to see her anger as less about them or me than of her need to be in control. Their age allowed them to begin making more choices for themselves, and Jean was increasingly aware that she was losing control.

Then Mickey told me his condition had taken a bad turn. "My doctor said he couldn't give me any more chemo. He said it would only make me sicker because it would be too toxic." He put his head down and started to cry. It was the first time I remembered seeing Mickey break down.

"Jesus. I'm really sorry. It must have been scary as hell to hear that."

"It was. I don't wanna die, Loren. He said the only thing left for me was maybe a bone marrow transplant."

"You know who supplies the bone marrow, don't you?"

"The doctor said the donor should be the closest of kin, like either you or Dino. Or maybe Christie, but she's not as close as you two."

"How do you think Dino would feel about that?"

"I don't know if he would do it. He's so far away."

"Yeah, he's too far away to be practical. I guess it means me then."

"Would you do it?"

"Sure, I would. But would you consider doing some things I know about before we make the decision?"

"Things? Like what things?"

"Well, I've tried some approaches with patients of mine that involve hypnosis, relaxation, and visualization. Like we did for pain control when you first came out, remember?"

"Yeah, that worked pretty well. I remember I forgot my cane in your office after we did that."

"It would at least be worth a try. I know enough about the effects of donating bone marrow to make it worth our while to try a different approach."

Mickey agreed. So we did some hypnosis sessions, and I made him some tapes to teach him to visualize his condition as getting better. To my surprise he listened to the tapes and did what I told him. I guess he was that desperate, since he didn't usually follow through on much of anything. What happened was astonishing; within two weeks Mickey's blood values started improving. Every two weeks thereafter they got even better. In a couple of months his oncologist said he didn't understand why, but Mickey's bone marrow was reproducing itself. When Mickey told him what we had been doing, his doctor said he never heard of anything like it, but he should, by all means, continue with it. Long story short, Mickey went into remission. He started gaining weight, his face turned pink, he had much less pain, and he stopped using his cane altogether. The transformation was remarkable. Mickey suddenly had more energy than he'd had in years and wanted to do something, so we started a small stained glass business together and, because of Mickey's remission, we called it Resurgence Stained Glass.

At the same time, through no effort on my part, my practice grew well past what was considered full-time. I had so many patients I started referring them to other analysts. I was making so much money that poverty seemed permanently sealed in the past. For the first time in my life, I was buying things without even looking at the price tags.

◆ ◆ ◆

The year I graduated from the Institute, shortly after Laurie's 18th birthday, Ann called me from Los Angeles to say that Jean had attempted suicide by taking an overdose of pills. She had gone into cardiac arrest at home and was resuscitated by the paramedics, but it was too late. When Ann called, Jean was in the hospital on life support with no signs of brain function. The girls and I were in shock; devastated by the possibility that she might die. I called my mother.

"Mom, Jean attempted suicide."

"Why do you care? She was nothing but trouble."

"Mom, she's the girls' *mother*."

"All she ever did was to keep you from them."

"Don't you understand? She's going to die."

"Like I said, she never did anything for you."

I didn't want that conversation. "Well, look, I've got to go. I just wanted to let you know. I'll talk to you later." I don't know what I expected or hoped for, but that was Mom at her defended best.

It wasn't long before Jean was gone. Under the advice of her doctor, Jean's husband stopped the life support. No matter how Jean had treated the girls and me, I was still horrified that she chose to end her life. I realized again that I hardly knew her because she never talked about herself in any depth. I didn't know what suffering she had gone through that made her who she was, but I knew her wounds must have been deep and painful.

♦   ♦   ♦

Unfortunately, Mickey's miraculous remission didn't bring any new awareness of himself—he started drinking again. Searching the local haunts, dragging him out of bars, and talking him out of his car keys without fighting in parking lots didn't help. He was arrested four times for drunk driving in the next few months. True to form, Mickey took no responsibility for his drinking; instead, he blamed the police for "following him around town." Staying in California much longer meant he would go to jail soon, and he knew it. So he decided to return to Chicago and, when he did, it didn't take long for him to regress. The first night after he arrived there, he was badly beaten up in a bar fight. Not long after, his cancer recurred and, in a few months, he was dead—seven years later than predicted. He was forty-eight.

Jean's and Beth's suicides, then Mickey's death, along with the other suicides sent me reeling. I needed time and space to sort things out, so I took some time off and went down to a favorite spot by the ocean at Pacific Grove. The crashing of the ocean waves and the salty moist air was soothing. My outer life was going remarkably well, but those losses felt senseless and left me depressed. While sitting on my favorite rock outcropping by the ocean, I decided to talk to the Professor.

"Can you please tell me what the hell is going on? Why all these deaths? Why so many suicides?"

"Death and loss are never easy. You can't control them. You know this in your head, but your head will never understand this—only through your heart. The heart has its reasons. Let your tears cleanse your eyes so you can see."

His simple but profound words wrenched something loose inside me. I began to cry, as I never had before. My whole body shook as if some inner dam of anguish burst. I don't know how long I cried. It seemed like forever. I didn't know tear ducts held so many tears. Maybe I had been saving too many, too long.

The Professor was silent until I stopped. "You learned to think with your head; now learn to think with your heart."

As always, his incisive words were like an arrow striking its target with a breathtaking thwack. I knew precisely what he meant. My head perpetually sought reasons and bypassed my feelings. I began to understand that my feelings did have their own reasons.

Trying to think with my heart allowed more compassion for myself. Beginning with my childhood friend Clay, I had more than my share of suicides. I haven't spoken about others. Those I have described were enough to make the point. I began to see the illusory quality of suicidal thoughts. They are illusions because they express unbearable suffering without the awareness that a deeper truth lay beneath them. Unaware of my own truth, I, too, came dangerously close to that precipice. I finally understand why I might have committed suicide. It wasn't just suffering that brought me so perilously close, but rather my deep confusion about who I really was. Because I couldn't see beyond my false self and its pain, I could have easily done away with myself. If I had, I would never know that the real cause of my suffering was that I had no conscious connection to my soul. Suicide is the illusory anguish of feeling devoid of a soul.

But suicide was something I could never consciously do to my daughters. Those who took their lives left behind a greater devastation among their loved ones than they likely faced themselves in the hereafter. I knew I had to accept that I lost them and forgive them. In their fatal moment, all they could feel was their pain.

◆   ◆   ◆

A few years after Mickey died, Dino was shot seven times, but he survived. I remembered what Mr. Gianni had said to me almost twenty-five years earlier, "Someday somebody's gonna whack him." A few years later he mysteriously died. He was fifty.

When I told my mother Dino was dead, she looked at me with a half-smile, almost a sneer. "Well, you know," she said, "they say these things happen in threes."

Her words nearly knocked me to the ground. Her response to Dino's death revolted me, but her unconscious and thinly veiled hatred of me was even more stunning. I was speechless.

I returned to Chicago briefly for Dino's funeral. Like his second wedding, his funeral could have been a scene in *The Godfather*. I felt badly that I hadn't spent more time with his family—and ashamed that I had been so preoccupied with my own life. I kneeled at his casket, touched the sleeve of his jacket, and said a prayer for him. At that moment, I also felt ashamed that I had never forgiven him. Who was I to judge him? I didn't know why his path in life was so different from mine. For that matter, I hadn't understood how the three of us ended up on the paths we did. Could I have been Dino, and him, me? All of us were deeply wounded and each of us responded to it in his own way. What I knew for sure was that we regarded our dreams differently. Mickey thought they were "weird shit," Dino thought they would give him a winning lottery number, and I thought they were trying to tell me what I was supposed to be doing. Go figure that.

26

The Truth Breeds Hatred

When I returned to California I was offered a consulting job for the staff of two hospice groups. My practice was already too busy, but I thought I could learn something by doing this work. As part of being a consultant, I attended a number of workshops on death, dying, and bereavement. One of them was in Montreal, and the Dalai Lama was the featured guest. I wanted to see him as much as I wanted to learn whatever I could about death and dying. I was deeply impressed with his simplicity, grace, and humor. Sogyal Rinpoche, the author of *The Tibetan Book of Living and Dying*, was also there.

On the last day of the conference, the final panel discussion was a dialogue on love. Before that panel began, the organizers of the conference announced that they wanted to introduce a special guest—a ten-year-old boy who was dying of leukemia and whose last wish was to meet the Dalai Lama. He was brought to the front stage where the Dalai Lama sat and was introduced to him. The Dalai Lama presented him with a long white brocade scarf that he draped around the boy's neck and then kissed his head. The scarf, with its eight embroidered symbols is a Tibetan token of blessing and friendship. Then the Dalai Lama asked the boy to sit with him while the presenters gave their talks on love. As the presenters spoke, the Dalai Lama's attention seemed more on the boy than on the presentations. He was concerned that the boy was comfortable and not too warm from the floodlights. A Cistercian monk gave the last talk; it was rather tedious, academic, and a bit self-aggrandizing. When he finished, the Dalai Lama, whose attention was still on the boy, was asked to comment. He looked up, thought for a moment, and then said, "I'm sorry, but it is all too complicated for me." With that the audience burst into a standing ovation. As I looked around me, tears accompanied much of the applause, like mine.

Sitting next to me was a woman who was also crying. A newspaper reporter, who had been sitting a row back, asked both of us to stay behind so she could interview us. She interviewed the woman first and, as I listened to her, it became apparent that in addition to death and dying, we had many other interests in common. While I was being interviewed, I noticed that she was waiting off to the side, and I hoped she stayed around. At the end of it, she walked over to me. We nervously introduced ourselves at nearly the same time. We both said, "We seem to have a lot in common." Our laughter broke the awkwardness. Her name was Dominique.

"Do you have time to go for a coffee with me?" I asked.

"Well, I'm meeting some friends for dinner at six but, until then, I'd love to."

At a nearby coffee shop, we both chattered on and on about one thing or the other like old friends. I felt mesmerized by her sparkling eyes and the way her curly dark brown hair seemed to dance on her head.

"Are you listening?" she smiled.

"Oh, yes. Sorry. Did you say you lived here?" I faked.

"Québec."

"You say that differently."

"*A la francaise.* We say, 'Kaybec,' not 'Kwubec.' *Au Québec il faut parler français seulement.*"

"Meaning?"

"'In *Québec* one must speak only French.' We are very fanatical about it."

"Yes, I think I heard that Québec is trying to secede from Canada."

"Hey, how about you join me and my friends for dinner? We can show you the sights of Montréal."

"I'd like to, but I have some things I have to do," I lied without knowing why.

"*C'est dommage, monsieur.* 'It's a shame.' Well, we must stay in touch then."

I loved the way she spoke. "Yes, we must. I'd like that." We exchanged addresses and phone numbers and hugged goodbye—then I kicked myself all the way back to the hotel.

After that, we wrote often to each other and sometimes talked on the phone. About a year later, we agreed to meet in Paris while I was there on vacation.

I arrived in Paris a few days before Dominique and rented a studio apartment in the Latin Quarter. The windows looked out over a small private walled garden of flowers and ferns. It was ideally situated, close to the Panthéon on the Montagne St-Genèvieve and, not much farther away, les Jardins du Luxembourg, and the Sorbonne. While waiting for Dominique to arrive, I explored other parts of Paris using the Metro. The station Cardinal Lemoine was close by, and each day I walked to a bakery and café where I had a croissant and espresso before getting on the Metro.

I understood why so many fell in love with Paris. It was easy to do. Being in Paris was a transfusion of enlivening excitement; it gave me butterflies. Its profusion of history, literature, art, and architecture was both exhilarating and overwhelming. In some ways, it reminded me of Madrid but, like falling in love, Paris felt unusually familiar. Like a new lover, I treasured everything about her—her culture, her cuisine, and her language. Even to my ear, its language was melodious. I especially loved hearing children speak. I envied them that they were born to speak with such beautiful and pleasing voices. Wherever Americans got the idea that the French are aloof, indifferent, and cold is lost on me. I found them to be consistently friendly, cordial, and helpful—even patient with my awkward efforts to speak and hear their language. Despite the obvious difficulty it would pose, I was determined to learn this splendid language.

But a few of my experiences in Paris were frankly bizarre. Sometimes, as I was sitting at a sidewalk café having a coffee, I would become aware of the ghostly presence of German soldiers; some sitting at the same cafés, or marching goose step down the streets, especially the Champs-Elysées. At that point, I knew little of French history but certainly was aware that the Germans had occupied Paris during World War II. What was most disconcerting was glancing down the front of myself from time to time and noticing the gray, black, and silver regalia of a German officer's uniform! As soon as I noticed it, it disappeared. These peculiar episodes felt foreboding.

I had another strange experience when I had arrived in the *Gare du Nord* train station from the airport. While I stood there trying to get my bearings, I became uncomfortably mesmerized by the clickety-clack sounds of the arrival and destination signs. Although it was obviously not as loud to me as it would be to a hearing person, I found the clattering distressing, nearly painful. Yet I could find no conscious context for these peculiar happenings. My mind seemed to be playing tricks on me.

When Dominique arrived I decided to keep the things about the Germans to myself, at least until I understood them better. We enjoyed each other's company, and together visited places each of us wanted to see. We were both interested in the "big" Parisian sites and, in a few days, we had seen most of them. I also was curious to see the one-time abodes of American expatriates like Hemingway, Joyce, Gertrude Stein, Rilke, Fitzgerald, and Anais Nin. I particularly wanted to see *Le Dome Café* on boulevard du Montparnasse, a favorite expatriate café during the 1920s and '30s. Luckily, it was still there, much as it was more than fifty years ago.

Our time together seemed to be going smoothly until the third night when, unbeknownst to me and sometime in the middle of the night, Dominique suddenly left. In the morning, all that remained of her was a note: "*Mon cher* Loren, I'm sorry to do this, but I have to get out of Paris *now*. Hopefully, I can explain this at a later time. *Beaucoup de l'amour*, Dominique."

I searched my mind for some reason she might do that but came up with nothing. Maybe I snored too loudly? After two more days in Paris, I decided to spend the rest of my time in the south of France. I drove through Avignon, Aix en Provence, Arles, Marseille, and finally to Nice. From there I returned to Paris by the TGV and then flew home.

While it was a wonderful journey, I never could get Dominique out of my mind. My dreams were puzzling and felt as though they were about Dominique. In one of them, I was a young German officer living in Paris during the occupation. I was myself, yet not myself. The place I lived was the home of a French family, and I was very attracted to their young daughter. She didn't look like Dominique, but for some reason I thought of her. I was apparently in love with her, and we were having an affair. In any event, in another dream, I was again a German officer; the war had ended, and I had to leave Paris. Before I left, the French Resistance killed my lover because she had been intimate with me. I don't know how I knew this, but somehow I knew she tried to escape by taking a train from the *Gare du Nord* station, but the Resistance found her hiding in the baggage department. The dream ended with the clacking sounds of the destination signs—and one single shot. Somehow, I knew she was shot in the head.

When I arrived back in California, a letter from Dominique postmarked in Corsica was waiting for me. I eagerly tore it open. "*Mon cher* Loren, I hope my ridiculous departure didn't spoil the remainder of your trip. It was nothing you did or didn't do—you were a darling companion. I'm in Corsica, and by now you're likely home, or on your way. I'm very sorry I left like that, but something about being in Paris made me panic. I just had this urge to get out of there as soon as possible. I know this sounds silly, but it felt like a matter of life and death. All I can tell you at this point is that while I was looking forward to being with you in Paris, from the moment I got there, I just had a sense that something was terribly wrong. Then the night I left I had a dream (I didn't tell you). It seemed to imply I once lived in Paris and that something terrible had happened to me. I don't know what happened but, whatever it was, it was scary enough that I knew I had to get out of there."

Coupled with my own strange dreams, Dominique's dream and panic attack completely blew me away. I wondered if the Germans had occupied Paris before I was born. The husband of one of my patients had been a member of the French Resistance during World War II, so I asked him about it. He confirmed that the Germans had entered France by May 1940, and Paris quickly fell to them by June 1940. The Americans liberated Paris in 1944. I asked him about French women who collaborated, or became intimately involved with German soldiers during the occupation. He said that after the liberation of Paris, some of these women had their heads shaved and were paraded through the streets, some were tortured, and others were killed.

If these events referred to previous lives, both Dominique and I could have died during those years. Not that it proves anything; it doesn't. It just gave some possible metaphysical context to the apparently synchronistic and uncanny experiences we each had in Paris. I heard from Dominique a few times after I last saw her; the final time to tell me she was going to be married. She disappeared as she did that last night in Paris, but this time I understood why I had met her.

Not long after I returned from France, my mother died. Even though her health wasn't good, her death from congestive heart failure was unexpected. Long before she died, she expressed the wish that she be cremated and that there not be a memorial service. She had said, "I don't want anyone staring at me when I'm dead." Her passing did not leave me in a state of mourning or grief as it might have if we'd had even a reasonably close relationship. The grief I felt was more for her, about the pain she suffered but never revealed and the dismal quality of her life. My sorrow was that nothing she had wished for in her lifetime had been fulfilled. As Christie and I cleaned out her apartment, it reminded me of Blackhawk Street and every other place she ever lived, teeming with bric-a-brac, untried recipes, and unread newspapers. Poignant reminders of how few genuine mementoes she possessed. Even with her uncountable collection of things, her life had remained empty.

I realized then how much my relationships with women had been distorted by that anachronous childhood promise to my mother. For years, the illusion that all women were wounded and needed to be taken care of was sealed in my unconscious, impairing my capacity to either give or accept genuine love. I could open my arms but not my heart. It was ironic that my attempts to look after my mother didn't satisfy her. At the end of her life, she reminded me that I was the "biggest disappointment" of any of her children. For the first time, I didn't take her criticism personally; it was her final defense against a lifetime of vulnerability. I was perplexed but pleased by the unusual images of her that came to me after she was gone. She was very happy, almost jubilant, kicking her heels and singing "Zippity doo dah, zippity ay," as if death finally brought her happiness.

My mother's death also marked my tenth anniversary as a psychoanalyst. By then I had achieved more than I ever dreamed possible. Most importantly, my daughters and I were finally reunited. I had a comfortable, beautifully furnished and safe home in a peaceful setting, more money than I ever imagined, and was respected in my profession. It seemed there was nothing I couldn't buy for my girls or myself. I even bought the car of my dreams, a Porsche 911. There was little more in the outer world I could wish for.

Despite what I had, one of the looming effects of having lived in poverty was that I always worried that a day might come when I could simply lose it all and end up back where I started. Then there was the nagging delusion that I never deserved to get out of it in the first place.

◆   ◆   ◆

The next year, I awoke one morning to find myself spinning in a world of complete silence. I tried watching things like the movement of tree branches outside my window, the shower spraying, and water pouring in my sink, but I couldn't hear them. It was hard to stand up without holding onto things, as though I was inside the vortex of a soundless hurricane. Maybe I had the flu. I hoped I had the flu. I remembered being told as a child that I could wake up one day completely deaf. I canceled my appointments for the day and went to the local emergency room. After a short examination, the doctor said I had Ménière's—a disease many already hearing-impaired people dreaded. He gave me a referral to an ear doctor. Instead, I found the best ear doctor in California and went to see him. After testing my hearing, pouring cold water in my ears, and poking around, he confirmed the diagnosis.

I watched his lips move without sound. "I'm afraid you have Ménière's, endolymphatic hydrops. You have no hearing in your right ear, and your left is almost deaf as well."

"What's the prognosis?"

"It's hard to tell, sometimes the hearing returns, sometimes not. The fluid in the inner ear can damage your hearing permanently. It's mostly a waiting game."

"Can it be treated?"

"I can give you a diuretic to possibly drain off the fluid buildup, and Meclizine for the dizziness."

The Meclizine made me feel as if I was thinking through cheese cloth, and the diuretic made my hands and legs go into spasm apparently from potassium depletion. My condition was not very conducive to doing psychotherapy. In the past I had always been able to manage, but now I had to get headphones and a boom box to hear. As awkward and embarrassing as that was, I was surprised that my patients didn't seem to mind as long as I could understand them. If a deaf psychologist wasn't an oxymoron, I don't know what was. It reminded me of being told that I should never pick a profession in which I had to hear. I consulted several university ear doctors but mainly got the same information. The only positive thing was the recommendation of an FM hearing system, which was much stronger than using hearing aids and less cumbersome than a boom box. Getting an amplified telephone that would rupture most people's eardrums also helped.

I tried treating myself with vitamins. Never, ever ask ear doctors about vitamins. I also used a machine I had in my office to treat the inflammation. Although there was no professional literature indicating it could be used for the condition, it worked remarkably well to diminish the vertigo. It was a crazy idea that worked. After several hearing tests over a few months, my doctor said that there was a small recovery of some hearing in my left ear, but the right was gone forever. All told, I had about seventeen percent hearing left in the speech range. I could still hear airplanes and motorcycles, not much help unless you work in the street or walk on runways. The initial Ménière's attacks that came every few weeks and lasted several days lessened considerably, and I slowly adjusted to using the FM system.

I also consulted a counselor for the deaf recommended by a dear friend. We talked about what my options were, and she suggested the intriguing possibility of brushing up on my sign language and perhaps being a therapist for the deaf and hearing impaired. Then she asked me what my grief was like. My grief? I was surprised because the question released a lot of hidden sadness and despair. Despite having worked with many handicapped patients, I hadn't even thought about my own grief.

It nearly amused me that I could be a psychologist and psychoanalyst and still be so out of touch with my feelings. Fortunately, I was able to work pretty much at the same capacity as I had before, but I kept her suggestion in mind.

If the hearing problem weren't bad enough, my practice began to feel the effects of the newly arrived managed care system. Most patient referrals started going through HMOs and managed care companies, neither of which I wanted any part of. I could see that managed care would likely harm patients by compromising their confidentiality, bureaucratizing treatment, and severely restricting access to it. Several of my psychologist and physician patients, who also hadn't joined managed care panels, began to lose their practices. Some of them left the field altogether. I got the feeling that the decline of my practice was right around the corner. And it was. Within the next five years, my patient load shrunk to half, making it impossible to maintain my expenses. I tried desperately to keep the practice afloat by selling my stocks and spending my savings but, despite that, five years later I was bankrupt. It seemed especially ironic that having three academic degrees and being one of the most highly trained psychoanalysts, my referrals virtually dried up. I was angry with many of my colleagues for greedily jumping on the "mangled care" bandwagon and virtually handing over the power of our profession to pencil pushers.

The additional loss of hearing, the changes in my field, and being dangerously close to losing my home left me depressed and anxious. It seemed like some cruel cosmic gag. Everything I had worked so hard and long for was on the verge of collapse. My fantasy that I could lose everything seemed to be coming true.

It was difficult to imagine what I would do if my practice failed. At the same time, I couldn't help wondering if these changes weren't something more than quirks of fate—as if, once again, there was a deeper message I was supposed to be getting from all this. I wondered again if something more remained of what I was supposed to be doing with my life. Maybe I needed to give it all up and become a monk. Although it had been a long time since I talked to the Professor, I decided to talk to him again.

His opening words surprised me. "Ask all your questions now. This is the last time I will talk to you."

"But why? You can't leave me now. What will I do without you?"

"Ask your questions. I'll tell you at the end."

"OK. Why was I born nearly deaf and now this?"

"So you could learn to hear."

"What? That doesn't make any sense."

"It does if you think about it with your heart. Why did you choose a profession in which you *had* to hear? Your teachers always told you never to pick a profession where you had to hear, didn't they?"

"Yeah, they did. I thought I was just stubborn."

"They were trying to make it easier for you, but they didn't understand you needed to learn to hear. What you possess naturally, you take for granted and don't need to learn from. What makes you suffer makes you learn."

"Why did I need to learn how to hear?"

"In the past you didn't want to hear the suffering of others. It was too painful. But since then, you have spent time a great deal of time hearing their suffering. You learned the truth of their suffering. Now you need to hear yourself and know your own truth."

"What is the truth?"

"There is no truth, only approximations of it. Seek what is true but hope you don't find *the* truth. *Veritas odium parit*. Truth breeds hatred. When you find *the* truth, you hate what's not *your* truth. Your ignorance makes you hate."

I had so many more questions and, for the first time, I was afraid the Professor would leave me with them unanswered. "What is my truth then?"

"This is what you have to ask yourself. But like everyone, you are becoming God. That is one of your truths."

"Why haven't I been told these things?"

"Your unconscious is always telling you, you just don't always listen. They have all been said before—many times. 'The kingdom of God is within you.' 'You are Buddha.'"

"Why haven't I believed that?"

"Fear mostly. It's safer to find God outside yourself than inside. If God is inside it means you are sacred; not only you, but everyone is sacred, life is sacred, the universe is sacred. Then you have to treat everything in the universe as sacred. Becoming God is an awesome responsibility."

"Why haven't I wanted to be responsible?"

"Because being responsible means that you must turn inward for answers to your fortune and misfortune. In becoming God, you are completely free to make your own choices about what you think, feel, about your body, and about your spirit. When you are told what to do, you don't have to be responsible, so you are less afraid. To truly know yourself and what you are capable of, you must *consciously* decide to be good or evil, to love or to hate. Then what you choose and accept is true for you is true for everyone, not just yourself."

"In trying to be responsible, how do I know my actions are right?"

"It is not the act in an action that matters but its intention. An act serves the intention behind it. Any act is helpful when its intention is to increase love, understanding, and personal growth. So you ask yourself, 'Does this action bring benefit?' And if it involves another, 'Is the benefit agreeable to both?'"

"How do I know my intention is what I think it is?"

"You think too much with your head. Responsibility for your actions comes from your heartfelt intentions not the accuracy of your thinking. Consciousness is a burden. If you want a rule book, you don't want to be conscious. You are not perfect and, at least in this life and place, you never will be. You are always becoming and only as conscious as you are at the moment. You take a pill because you believe it is for your benefit and then discover you took the wrong pill, one that could cause you harm. You take responsibility for the action and learn from it, but the intention is still right."

"Why do so many religions teach that God is outside?"

"To project God outside is a stage in the evolution of spirituality. One day we will realize that we are the drops of water in the ocean of divinity that is God; and there will be only one religion, one church."

"Which one will that be?"

"The church of love."

"Who will be its members?"

"It has no outer membership. Those who know they belong, belong. Its members know each other by their deeds, understanding, and love. It has no rivals or barriers, no hierarchy or structure—for no one is greater than another. It has no ambition, only the practice of the truth of love seeking only to serve all beings through love."

"Who are its teachers?"

"It acknowledges and praises the great teachers of all the ages who have paved the path and have paid the price; those who have shown the truth of love. You are its teacher—your own teacher. But you teach with humility, without conceit or dogma. Dogma is only for those who are afraid and can't yet think for themselves. Dogma codifies and predetermines beliefs and values and robs you of the choices and mistakes needed to find your individual truth. The teacher is a very careful and cautious guide who does not preach, make judgments, or tell you what is right or wrong. The teacher's task is only to help you find *your own answers*. Without your own answers, you become a hollow, misguided puppet, mimicking borrowed ideas and values. The teacher instructs by example, by love, not by words alone."

"But...aren't you my teacher?"

"I told you, I am *you*."

"OK, OK. Yes, you have."

"How do I know if I'm individuated when I've completed my journey?"

"Try to imagine the most despicable and misguided person you can think of, then, with all the honesty you can muster in your mind and heart, ask yourself if you can say, 'There but for the grace of God, go I.' If you can say that, you have individuated. To do that is your path. The world will change only if you change yourself first. I have to leave you now so that you will listen to yourself and answer your own questions. Like so much in your life, I am only an illusion. That is all. Goodbye."

Our last conversation left me with the deepest sense of being loved for the first time in my life. At first, I thought it was the Professor who had loved me, but then I realized that, like Dr. Burns, he was only helping me to love myself.

After that last conversation with the Professor, I studied religion and eastern philosophies even more than I had before. I concluded just what the Professor had said—all of them contain some truth, yet, no one system contained "*The Truth.*"

I began to think that the problem with most traditional religions was their reliance on the belief that God was wholly external. The old saying, "If God didn't exist, we would invent Him," seemed true, but for different reasons than most people thought. Like other projections, what I originally saw in God stemmed not only from what I needed to see, but also from what I eventually became capable of seeing through my experience.

Religions that exclude others from grace, whatever truth they contain, have little to do with God. The view that in God's eyes some people are "better" than others is a twisted idea made up by men who haven't yet done their psychological homework. Were that idea not so cruel, it would amuse even God. That archaic dichotomy between people and God only stultifies spirituality and creates naïve and unanswerable questions like "Why is there evil?" Evil exists because we haven't grown up yet.

What I came to understand of my dreams, fantasies, and illusions eventually led to my own psychospiritual truth, a view that more closely matched my experience, my views of the psyche, and my values. The cornerstone of my truth is that neither God nor we are static, fixed entities; rather, we are inseparable and always growing. We are becoming what we are capable of, rather than just what we are now. Neither is holier, more advanced, nor better than the other is. Most importantly, there is a luminous, godlike, loving being within me that is my psychological self and spiritual soul. That discovery further led to another radical and, to some I'm sure, outrageous idea—that an external God was a projection of my psyche's potentiality.

However unorthodox or profane that idea was, the essence of the spiritual teachings of Buddhism, Hinduism, Christianity, and particularly the once suppressed Gnostic gospels, seemed to support it. The Christian message says, "The kingdom of God is within you." Buddha also taught: "He who experiences the unity of life sees his own Self in all beings, and all beings in his own Self, and looks on everything with an impartial eye." Both *gnosis* of Christianity and *bodhi* of Buddhism refer to a knowledge that transcends empirical reasoning or rational thought. Both of them mean intuitive knowledge derived from internal sources.

To the Gnostic, this knowledge was necessary for salvation. "I say, You are Gods!" (John 10:34).

The psychological significance of Jesus saying, "Amen, I say to you, whatever you did for one of these least brothers of mine, you did for me," means not just what I do to or for less fortunate others but, just as importantly, how I regard the undeveloped parts of my personality, the "least in myself." It was no accident that my dreams often symbolize my undeveloped personality as if it was an inner stranger, like the schizoid man. In the Torah, there are at least thirty-six references imploring the reader to "love the stranger." The Koran also urges its faithful to love lesser others, strangers, captives, and orphans.

The major source of my problems was a disconnection from the unconscious and that inner stranger. Without that association, I couldn't understand my inability to love, depression, anxiety, and poor self-worth. As a young person, to protect my vulnerability I followed a path that nearly destroyed me. I gave up on those who loved me and pursued those who couldn't.

My personal problems were not arbitrary punishments, but rather what the Buddhists call *karma*, the natural consequences of my experiences, as well as the seeds of my future growth. This understanding led to a helpful relationship to the unconscious and to the awareness of the psyche's autonomous, prospective function—of the *potentiality* to be well. It also provided the strength to understand and accept suffering, learn from it, transcend it, in short, to find God in it.

It seemed more and more clear to me that like psychological knowledge, the real goal of spiritual knowledge was not intellectual, but rather of coming to an emotional realization of God within.

If God is in me, I can't hide behind or disown my projections and illusions; but take responsibility for them in order to discover what they are trying to teach me. That awareness changed how I viewed my life, my experiences, and what I will do from day to day. I see now that self-understanding and self-love are my most important work, and my life's outer events have merely been directing me to do that.

While many of my experiences have been beyond my control, my path hasn't been completely hard-wired, since some were not. Many of them were painful and the source of suffering. I couldn't control them, but I learned that I could make choices about them. My particular experiences, in and of themselves, don't really matter, but the way I chose to respond to them matters. By my choices, the worst of my personal sufferings have become the best tools for psychospiritual growth. That was what I learned in my personal analysis: I couldn't really love others until I learned to love myself.

27

My Truth

> Then it was as if I suddenly saw the secret beauty of their hearts, the depth of their hearts, where neither sin nor desire can reach, the core of their reality, the person that each one is in God's eyes. If only they could see themselves as they really are. If only we could see each other that way all the time, there would be no war, no more hatred, no more cruelty, no more greed....
>
> I suppose the big problem would be that we would fall down and worship each other.
>
> —*Thomas Merton*

As I walked backwards for a final look at the empty lot, I nearly bumped into an older black man with silver, curly hair. It seemed as if he had stopped just before I turned around. He silently looked me up and down; his gaze stopped at my shoes.

"I'm sorry," I said. For just a second, I thought of old Joshua.

I could see him saying, "Watch yer sore leg, Jessie."

Instead, the man smiled and said, "Mighty nice shoes, son." Then he slowly turned and went on down the empty street.

It saddened me to think that old Joshua was certainly long since gone.

◆   ◆   ◆

So 555 Blackhawk Street wasn't there any more. Maybe it was only the kick-start for my life's inner journey. Not the kind I would recommend, but, obviously, what my particular soul needed. Perhaps, like the Professor, it, too, was an illusion. And maybe my outer life was mostly a stage on which to battle the adversity of my past and reconcile its painful dichotomies. In reexamining my life, it became obvious that physical realities are much less important.

My lifelong question has always been, "What is my psyche asking me to do with my life?" The circumstances of my later years made me wonder whether I should just give up all I had worked for, become a monk, and spend the remainder of my life in a monastery. The question that led me back to 555 Blackhawk Street.

When I returned to California, I found this wasn't necessary. I decided that I couldn't give up relationships and living in the world to find myself, I had to find myself within them. Nor could I give up my body by becoming ascetic and self-denying. Its ability to bring me peace, relaxation, pleasure, and sensuality were as spiritually important as my mind. Asceticism runs dangerously close to repression, and anything I ever managed to repress only returned to haunt me. Repression is the converse of consciousness.

So my psyche's forceful answer was: "Stop trying to control your life, follow your heart, learn to love yourself, and learn to love others—then exactly what you do won't matter." Sometimes I'm successful but only through the difficult and often humiliating process of self-reflection. A lot of foolishness is the price of a little wisdom.

Apart from self-knowledge, another benefit of self-reflection has been compassion—for myself as well as others. Compassion allowed me to forgive myself for my mistakes, and to forgive those who unconsciously hurt me. I haven't learned compassion once and for all; I doubt that ever ends. It can only be deepened by greater empathy, altruism, and open-mindedness. All so easily said yet so embarrassingly difficult to accomplish.

Once I could see the truth that God is in me, I knew I had to transform that knowledge into action—of embracing my love for myself and deepening my love for others. That meant not only taking good care of myself, but also extending that care and love to others. Only after much inner work have I realized how my anger, fear, and ignorance deprived me of others' love. I let go of many people who loved me only because I didn't love myself.

I've decided what really matters is that my life be one of service—that seems the best way to love. And because I finally learned to love myself, I can be of service without expecting something in return, except the simple joy of just being and loving.

◆　◆　◆

After I had practiced many years, someone asked me if I thought there was any particular truth about the psyche. Based on thousands of dreams I had analyzed, the psychoanalysis of many patients and my own analysis, I said there did seem to be one certainty. The psyche has an innate wisdom and capacity to heal itself. That power is an inborn trait, like an instinct. Not surprisingly, Jung offered the same conclusion many years before. I know he would also agree that access to the wisdom of the unconscious and self-knowledge is necessary for healing. But we come to it only by intensive self-reflection. I also learned that regardless of the reasons people give for seeking help, all their problems began in a dark place in their hearts crying out to be loved.

The practice of psychoanalysis also has been an integral part of my journey. I saw many processes in my patients like my own but not always occurring at the same stage of life. They have been among my best teachers, and their dreams and experiences thoroughly support the prospective wisdom of the psyche. Working with them made understanding myself and my relationships immensely clearer.

All my life, the persistence of my dreams and illusions led me to appreciate the extraordinary wisdom of the unconscious; wisdom not separate from consciousness but as a continuum of the mind. What I learned was that my outer and inner life, psychology and spirituality, are inseparable. While appearing to be opposites, they are simply different dimensions of the same reality. To have any understanding of my spiritual self, I first had to know my psychological self. Those who try to do the opposite, or omit deep psychological work, often make a mess of themselves—and those in their care, as so often happens with misguided spiritual leaders. When we put our trust in religious or political leaders who are intellectual giants but emotional infants, our faith in them has disastrous consequences.

Most of my life I struggled with the illusions of guilt and shame; powerful childish fears of punishment by someone outside myself. Even without a clear adversary, I became their perpetrator. Those emotions were physically toxic, emotionally crippling, and spiritually useless—byproducts of paying deference to parents or an external God whose rules I broke. By taking responsibility for my life instead of blaming others or an external God, I could transform those negative emotions into psychological and spiritual growth. If God is in me, I have no use for fear, shame, guilt, or self-judgments. Now, in place of guilt, I use conscience and my values as a guide. When I make mistakes and feel regretful, I try to learn from them and make amends to those I have hurt. Doing that helps me love rather than condemn myself.

At the beginning of my life, religion was a source of anguish. Whenever I accepted dogmatic ideas without a truly open heart and mind, I caused others and myself great suffering. I neglected personal choices in favor of those that were either premature for where I was on my path—or simply wrong. Later, I discovered that most of my problems and personal suffering came from thinking with my head instead of listening with my heart—another dichotomy I had to learn to bridge.

I finally realized that the mask that floated above my head in childhood was also an illusion. I believe it was the Professor's first attempt to speak to me, even if with an urgency of frightful silence—to alert my wayward ego to the ill-fated course it was embarking on. Although I almost succeeded in forgetting the mask, the Professor fortunately got through in a dream to continue my initiation. Dreams are illusions, too, but often contain remarkable wisdom. I don't know enough yet to say that my entire life is an illusion, just enough to know that its events were rarely only what they appeared to be yet indispensable enough to lead to the truth of my soul.

Perhaps one day in the course of our psychospiritual evolution we will realize that God is in us and that self-love and love for others will replace the projection of an external impersonal God. Maybe then, we will understand ignorance, prejudice, poverty, greed, violence, and war for what they are—humanity's resistance to know its God-like potential.

◆　　◆　　◆

Nowadays my dreams have become quite ordinary. Instead of terrifying me, they are a source of creativity and inspiration so I wake up happier and laugh more. I also find that I cry more easily, not just in moments of sadness, but especially for the success and happiness of others. The tears cleanse my eyes, and the laughter warms my heart. Most importantly, learning to love myself has allowed me to love others.

This is what I've learned so far. I don't know if what is true for me is true for you. But I do know that we all struggle in our own ways, hoping to discover our own truth and find happiness in our lives. If it seems to suit you, I wish you to know that God is in you, too. Really.

Loren E. Pedersen, Ph.D.
890 Holly Hill Dr
Walnut Creek, CA 94596
(925) 932–0294
lorenpedersen@astound.net

www.ingramcontent.com/pod-product-compliance
Lightning Source LLC
Chambersburg PA
CBHW071859290426
44110CB00013B/1213